THE COST OF UNITY

MERCER
UNIVERSITY PRESS

Endowed by
TOM WATSON BROWN
and
THE WATSON-BROWN FOUNDATION, INC.

THE COST OF UNITY

AFRICAN-AMERICAN AGENCY AND EDUCATION IN THE CHRISTIAN CHURCH, 1865-1914

Lawrence A. Q. Burnley

To Terry,
You are my brother on this journey of education and liberation to the glory of God! May we realize reconciliation not only with Him but with one another as His people!
Shalom
Larry Burnley
12/10/14

MERCER UNIVERSITY PRESS
MACON, GEORGIA

MUP/H775

First Edition.

Voices of the African Diaspora

Books published by Mercer University Press are printed on acid free paper that meets the requirements of American National Standard for Information Sciences—Permanence of Paper for Printed Library Materials.

Mercer University Press is a member of Green Press initiative (greenpressinitiative.org), a nonprofit organization working to help publishers and printers increase their use of recycled paper and decrease their use of fiber derived from endangered forests. This book is printed on recycled paper.

Burnley, Lawrence A. Q.
The cost of unity : African American agency and education in the Christian Church, 1865-1914 / by Lawrence A.Q. Burnley. -- 1st ed.
p. cm.
Includes bibliographical references and index.
ISBN-13: 978-0-88146-134-3 (hbk. : alk. paper)
ISBN-10: 0-88146-134-2 (hbk. : alk. paper)
1. Disciples of Christ—History--19th century. 2. Disciples of Christ—History—20th century. 3. Concord—Religious aspects—Christianity—Case studies. 4. African Americans—Missions.
5.African Americans—Religion. 6. African Americans—Social conditions—To 1964. 7. African Americans—Education. 8. Educational change—United States—History. 9. United States—Race relations—History--19th century.
10. United States—Race relations—History—20th century. I. Title.
BX7318.5.N4B87 2009
286.6'3--dc22
2008040025

To my parents, Ms. Frances Mary Kelley Burnley and Mr. Halo Burnley, Jr., for demanding the best effort from your children and for the great sacrifices you made so we could get the best education within your reach. To all of the Ancestors whose suffering, sacrifices, creativity, resiliency, and collective genius represent the shoulders upon which I stand. It was all of you who made this project possible. Thank you.

CONTENTS

ACKNOWLEDGMENTS

There are so many people who have contributed in so many different ways to the development and completion of this book. First, however, I must give thanks to the One who made this possible—*all* honor and *all* praise belong to God! In naming individuals, one always runs the risk of inadvertently omitting someone; however, this is a risk I must take. Paying no real attention to order, but only offering appreciation and thanksgiving, I acknowledge the following persons for their role in my development as a historian. I will begin with Dr. Eleanor Smith, my first professor in African American history (Afro-American history at the time), whose introduction to revisionist historiography changed my life forever. Thank you for introducing me to the scholarship of my esteemed fraternity brother and historian, Dr. Carter G. Woodson, and Dr. Cheikh Anta Diop. The extraordinary scholarship and dedication of these and many other men and women to the reconstruction of African and African American history has helped me learn to love and embrace my Blackness. I thank my friend and academic mentor, Dr. Rufus Burrow, Jr.—a prophetic scholar in his own right—for seeing in me what I did not see, or was afraid to see, in myself. It was you, Rufus, who read my dissertation and thought it worthy of publication. You continued to push, raise questions, and provide critical feedback on additional chapters for this book that enhanced its overall strength. I will thank you the way you want to be thanked—I'll continue to write. Thank you for never stopping to believe that I could do this. Rev. Dr. William W. Hannah, Rev. Leon Riley, and the members of Faith United and University Park Christian churches (one predominantly Black the other White housed in the same building), thank you for giving me an incredible environment to develop as student and to hone my gifts in the ministry of racial justice and reconciliation. Many saw your arrangement in the building as a glass half empty, but I clearly saw it not only half full, but perhaps fuller than anywhere else in the Christian Church. Thanks, Dr. Hannah, for mentoring me in ministry and providing me with a model of the prophetic tradition of the church; there are so few. Thanks to Dr. James M. Washington, an exemplary church historian who challenged me to become "a doctor of the church." The faculty and staff of the Graduate School of Education at the University of Pennsylvania have extended gracious patience and support as I have experienced deep valleys of life during this process. From my heart I say thank you.

Over the years, I've heard many stories about nightmarish dissertation committees. I'm one who has been blessed with a committee who has shown extraordinary patience and great interest in my topic while setting standards of excellence. Dr. Marybeth Gasman came on later in the process to serve as my chair. You have been my cheerleader and held me accountable. Your vision and belief gave me the encouragement I needed to see it through. To you, Dr. Gasman, and to Drs. John Puckett, Howard Stevenson, Jr., Vivian Gadsden, and Marvin Lazerson, thank you so much! To my uncle Charles E. Kelley, a Renaissance man, who was really my first teacher of "Black History"; and my sister and soul mate Dr. Margaret Burnley Spearmon, who is an angel on earth. Thanks for showing me the way, and for coming home and telling the fearful little boy he is good enough to play in the big leagues. To my other siblings Halo III (taken to his eternal home at birth), David, Carolyn, and Connie for encouraging me not to quit and for just being the incredibly loving brothers and sisters that you have always been to me; George and Barbara Quarles, and Nia Quarles-Martin, you are my "in-loves" and prayed me through this; Rev. Drs. Susan Street-Beavers, Jack Sullivan, Jr., and William Edwards—together we make up the Four Musketeers; Rev. Oliver Porter, Robert Washington, Dr. Marcine Pickron-Davis, Jacy Hobson, Rev. Jeff (Mac) Bates, Rev. Dr. Beverly Dale, Rev. Dr. Mary Alice Mulligan, and a host of others for praying, challenging, loving, laughing, questioning, reading, and believing. Thank you, Kim Sadler, for being a God-sent editor and friend. Thanks for hanging in there with me until the end. Thanks to Rev. Dr. William Fox, Sr., for being an encouragement and being excited about the project early on; Rev. Dr. Timothy James, for being willing to be used by God to start me on my way in this Disciples of Christ journey. Thanks to brothers and sisters throughout the Christian Church (Disciples of Christ) and the United Church of Christ who have been prayer warriors throughout this process; Rev. Dr. William Land, a warrior, prophet, mentor, and friend; Rev. Sala Nolan, Dr. Peter Makari, and Angela

Balfour-Franklin, for believing and encouraging; Dr. Julia Speller whom God brought back into my life for the final push; Dr. Randall Bailey for believing, encouraging, and posing a tough question about why Blacks stayed in the Christian Church (Disciples of Christ). Thank you to the administration, faculty, staff, and students of Messiah College who gave me the love and support I needed to "finish the race"; and to Seleena Lindsey and the Faculty Support staff at Messiah College for helping me embellish the manuscript. I give a special acknowledgment of appreciation to the staff of the Office of Multicultural Programs at Messiah College for towing the line in my absence while I completed my dissertation. Thank you! I have experienced the preeminence of Christ in your unwavering support.

No research project of this magnitude is possible without the dedication and assistance of librarians, archivists, and research assistants who dig, search, and dig some more because they enjoy it. First and foremost I want to acknowledge the extraordinary staff of the Disciples of Christ Historical Society in Nashville, Tennessee, for their dedication and attention to detail in responding to the numerous e-mails I sent and the tons of questions I posed during my visits. Thank you for sticking with me on this rather long journey. I also acknowledge with heartfelt appreciation the staffs of the following libraries and archival repositories for their assistance in this project: Van Pelt Library of the University of Pennsylvania; Archives and Special Collections, Hiram College Library, Hiram, Ohio; Christian Theological Seminary Library, Indianapolis, Indiana; Olin Library and Communications Center, Jarvis Christian College, Hawkins, Texas; American Baptist Historical Society, Valley Forge, Pennsylvania; American Baptist—Samuel Colgate Historical Society Library at the American Baptist Historical Society, Rochester, New York; American Missionary Association Archives at the Amistad Research Center, Tulane University, New Orleans, Louisiana; Library of Congress, Washington, D.C.; Kelvin Smith Library at Case Western Reserve University, Cleveland, Ohio; Grasselli Library and Breen Learning Center, John Carroll University, University Heights, Ohio; the Milbank Memorial Library at Teachers College, Columbia University, New York, New York; and the Murray Library at Messiah College, Grantham, Pennsylvania.

To Dr. Chester Fontenot and the editors and staff of Mercer University Press, I offer my heartfelt appreciation for not only seeing the value and import of my book, but for backing it up with the needed resources and expertise to publish it. Thank you for your patience, encouragement, and demonstrated commitment to excellence. Thanks also to Dr. D. Newell Williams for reading the dissertation and offering valuable commentary that strengthened this book.

Finally, thank you to those who have paid the heaviest price associated with this process. I simply could not have completed it without the unwavering love and support of my wife and "souljourner" in life, Naima. You carried the load at home, and you have loved me in spite of me. Thank you, Sweet Tee! I love you! My son Thulani, you've had to be without Daddy when I was away writing, writing, and writing some more. You always receive me back with a smile and a hug. You are a gift and vessel of God's light. Thank you, son! Thank you to my eldest son Rashad, gone to his eternal home much too soon, but God had other plans calling you to "a higher place of praise." Your presence is so powerfully felt as God continues to use you to point me toward the light.

ABBREVIATIONS

AACC	All Africa Conference of Churches
ABHMS	American Baptist Home Missionary Society
ACBM	American Christian Board of Missions
ACEEA	American Christian Evangelizing and Education Association
ACI	Alabama Christian Institute
ACMS	American Christian Missionary Society
BNEE	Board of Negro Education and Evangelism
CWMB	Christian Women's Board of Missions
CBC	Christian Bible College
CCC	Central City College
FCMS	Foreign Christian Missionary Society
FMS	Freedmen's Missionary Society
FWP	Federal Writers Project of the Works Project Administration
GCI	Goldsboro Christian Institute
GCMC	General Christian Missionary Convention
HBCUs	Historically Black Colleges and Universities
JCI	Jarvis Christian Institute
LBS	Louisville Bible School
LCBS	Louisville Christian Bible School
NAACP	National Association for the Advancement of Colored People
NBEC	National Baptist Educational Convention
NCCC	National Convention of the Churches of Christ
NCCC (DC)	National Convocation of the Christian Church (Disciples of Christ)
NFEA	Narratives of Formerly Enslaved Africans
NCMC	National Christian Missionary Convention
PSI	Piedmont School of Industry
SCI	Southern Christian Institute
SPGAH	Society for the Propagation of the Gospel at Home
TCI	Tennessee Christian Institute
TMLU	Tennessee Manual Labor University
UCMS	United Christian Missionary Society

AUTHOR'S NOTE

This is a brief note regarding References to Black People in the United States of America. Given that free and enslaved people of African descent in the United States were denied basic human rights and legal protection under the Constitution during the antebellum period, I will refer to this group as "Africans" as opposed to "African Americans." Pushing this thought further, it can be argued that Africans did not become "American" until the enactment of the Thirteenth (1865), Fourteenth (1868), and Fifteenth (1870) amendments of the Constitution of the United States, with the latter giving limited franchise for black men only. Some would argue further that people of African decent have never enjoyed "full protection" under the Constitution. For the purpose of this study, I will use the term "African American" in reference to black people in this country from the time the Emancipation Proclamation was fully ratified on 18 December 1865. It is well documented that some Africans continued to be enslaved up to that point—and possibly beyond.

In addition, the term "enslaved Africans" or "formerly enslaved Africans" will be used in place of "slave" or "slaves" as an attempt by the writer to restore a sense of humanity, dignity, integrity, and cultural identity in how we view the millions of people who were victimized by the perpetrators of chattel enslavement in the United States and other parts of the world. Chattel enslavement in the United States was a dehumanizing condition in which African people were held; it was not who they were. Black men, women, and children who were held as chattel were not "slaves." They were human beings who were "enslaved." Conversely, whites—and others who held blacks as chattel—are not referred to as "frees," but as persons who "owned" and enslaved other people.

Finally, throughout the book, the term "Freedpeople" will be used in place of the more commonly used term "Freedmen" when making reference to manumitted black people. The use of this term is done for the purpose of being gender-inclusive and in response to destructive forms of literary patriarchy. The term "Freedpeople" will always be capitalized as small way to counter the myriad of policies and practices throughout the history of the United States that tended to—intentionally or unintentionally—dehumanize the nearly 5 million African-American men, women, and children who endured the holocaust of chattel enslavement.

1

INTRODUCTION

Now the Great Fear has been variously named and designated—it has been called in the past, Mob-Rule, Sans-Cullotism, the Yellow Peril, the Negro Problem, and Social Equality. Whatever it is called, the foundation of the Great Fear is this: when a human being becomes suddenly conscious of the tremendous powers lying latent within him, when from the puzzled contemplation of a half-known self, he rises to the powerful assertion of a self, conscious of its might, then there is loosed upon the world possibilities of good or of evil that make men pause. And when this happens in the case of a class or nation or a race, the world fears or rejoices according to the way in which it has been trained to contemplate a change in the conditions of the class or race in question....[1]

On 22 September 1862, President Abraham Lincoln read a second draft of a proclamation to his cabinet. This proclamation was aimed at dismantling the system of chattel enslavement in all states that were in rebellion against the United States of America. The executive order, called the *Emancipation Proclamation*, would go into full effect 1 January 1863.[2] For some enslaved Africans, the news of their seemingly endless struggle for manumission was delayed because their owners withheld it. Those enslaved in Texas did not receive news of their

---

[1] William E. B. Du Bois, "The Hampton Idea," speech delivered at Hampton Institute, 1906, quoted in Herbert Aptheker, ed., *The Education of Black People: Ten Critiques, 1906–1960* (New York: Monthly Review Press, 1973) 8.
[2] Steven Hahn, *A Nation Under Our Feet: Black Political Struggles in the Rural South from Slavery to the Great Migration* (Cambridge: Harvard University Press, 2003) 91.

freedom until 19 June 1865, nearly two and a half years later. Nevertheless, by the time General Robert E. Lee's Confederate forces surrendered to General Ulysses S. Grant's Union Army at Appomattox, 9 July 1865, five million black men, women, and children were no longer bound by the restrictions of nearly three centuries of legalized bondage. During that same year the Thirteenth Amendment, which legislated the abolishment of slavery in the U.S., was adopted by Congress.

In the North and the South, a great majority of newly Freedpeople were finally exercising their freedom to learn how to read and write. Freedom offered millions of black people the opportunity to acquire knowledge without fear of reprisal. Freedpeople literally viewed this opportunity as the key to securing a future that had far-reaching spiritual, economic, and political implications for themselves and their progeny. Black response to this newly secured opportunity was swift, decisive, and often overwhelming. This point is illustrated by Jacqueline Jones who quotes a missionary in Georgia writing in 1870. Jones writes, "A freed person who could read and write would be able to understand a labor contract, correspond with friends and relatives, keep informed of political affairs in the state, and study the Bible. Education was a means of breaking out of the confines of ignorance that served the masters' interest so well, a means of thinking and acting on one's own...."[3]

Another example of African Americans' intense desire for education is expressed by a missionary sent by the American Missionary Association in 1870 who wrote, "Wherever teachers went there were greatly enthusiastic students. In the flush of freedom grandparents and grandchildren surged to the crude schoolhouse to secure the magic of reading and writing. Their demand for training crowded almost every available facility. Families pinched with hunger asked more eagerly for learning than for food."[4]

---

[3] Anthony Wilson to E. P. Smith, 3 August 1870, in Jacqueline Jones, *Soldiers of Light and Love: Northern Teachers and Georgia Blacks, 1865–1873* (Chapel Hill: University of North Carolina Press, 1980) 59.

[4] Joe Richardson, *Christian Reconstruction: The American Missionary Association and Southern Blacks, 1861–1890* (Tuscaloosa: University of Alabama Press, 1980) 37.

To understand the intensity of black agency regarding schooling and literacy development is to understand the relationship between literacy and spirituality among black people during this period. In general, Blacks in U.S. came to accept the evangelical belief that reading the Bible for one's self was an essential part of the process of achieving a "right" relationship with God. The Bible and the Christian religion represented the promise of a better world for many enslaved and free Africans alike. For some, primary attention given to this "better world" reflected the acceptance of an "otherworldly" theology—a theology preached to them by Whites. This theology emphasized redemption and blessing in heaven. It was used as a method to deflect attention from Blacks who wanted to secure a positive socioeconomic and political transformation of their condition in "this world." Others believed that literacy paved the way to improve radically their condition in both "this world" and the "next world" after death.

The dialectic relationship between literacy and religion for Blacks reflects neither a wholesale acceptance of Eurocentric theological perspectives nor a complete retention of African spirituality and cosmological perspectives in the New World. The synergistic relationship between literacy and spirituality among Blacks in general, and among black Christians in particular, reflects the formulation of unique expressions of human spirituality born of cultural syncretism within black communities. In addressing the religious experience of Blacks under chattel enslavement, James Washington argues that the "very disorientation of their slavery provided the opportunity—indeed the necessity—of a new religious synthesis."[5] Albert Raboteau agrees

---

[5] James M. Washington, *Frustrated Fellowship: The Black Quest for Social Power* (Macon GA: Mercer University Press, 1986) ix; For further discussion on African spirituality and black spiritual formation in response to chattel enslavement, see Sterling Stuckey, *Slave Culture: Nationalist Theory and the Foundations of Black America* (New York: Oxford University Press, 1987) 10–17; Gayraud Wilmore, *Black Religion and Black Radicalism: An Interpretation of the Religious History of African Americans* (Maryknoll NY: Orbis Books, 1998); C. Eric Lincoln and Lawrence H. Mamiya, *The Black Church in the African American Experience* (Durham: Duke University Press, 1990) 2–7; John W. Blassingame, *The Slave Community: Plantation Life in the Antebellum South* (Oxford: Oxford University Press, 1979 [1972]) 3–45; Margaret Washington Creel, *"A Peculiar People": Slave Community-Culture Among the*

that the spiritual formation of Blacks is linked to cultural syncretism. He writes,

> African beliefs and customs were transmitted by slaves to their descendents shaped and modified by a new environment; elements of African folklore, music, language, and religion were transplanted in the New World by the African diaspora. Influenced by colonial English and indigenous Native American cultures, aspects of the African Heritage have contributed, in greater or lesser degree, to the formation of various Afro-American cultures in the New World. One of the most durable and adaptable constituents of the slave's culture linking African past with American present was his religion.[6]

Not long after their arrival in the Western hemisphere, the quest to develop literacy soon became a primary element in black people's search for a better life. The religious and spiritual formation of Africans and African Americans would play a profound role in both the acceptance and rejection of the form and function of European-centered schooling. The interconnectedness of literacy and religion was profound for African Americans during the period examined in this study; it can be argued that the two are inseparable.

The opportunity to learn, exercise the privileges of citizenship, earn wages, establish families without fear of having them torn apart, and determine one's own destiny was for African Americans the long-awaited answer to a ubiquitous prayer that transcended time and space.

Gullahs (New York: New York University Press, 1988) 29–66; Machel Sobel, *Trablin' On: The Slave Journey to an Afro-Baptist Faith* (Princeton: Princeton University Press, 1988 [1977]) 1–77; John Hope Franklin, *From Slavery to Freedom: A History of Negroes in America* (New York: Alfred A. Knopf, 1974 [1947]) 3–29. For further discussion on theological and sermonic presentations in direct or indirect support of American slavery see David B. Chesebrough, ed., *"God Ordained this War": Sermons on the Sectional Crisis, 1830–1865* (Columbia: University of South Carolina Press, 1991); and Joseph R. Washington, Jr., *Race and Religion in Mid-Nineteenth Century America, 1800–1850: Constitution, Conscience, and Calvinist Compromise* (Lewiston NY: E. Mellon Press, 1988).

[6] Albert Raboteau, *Slave Religion: The "Invisible Institution" in the Antebellum South* (Oxford: Oxford University Press, 1978) 4.

Freedom and access to an education was the realization of the hopes and dreams of untold millions of black people—and some Whites—who struggled, suffered, and died in the centuries-long movement of resistance to the black holocaust of chattel enslavement. But for many Northern and Southern white Americans, black access to the world of letters produced the "Great Fear" that was eloquently articulated in the opening quote by the brilliant scholar and social activist William Edward Burghardt Du Bois. This Great Fear was informed by racist and paternalistic ideology and a myriad of socioeconomic and political concerns held by both Northerners and Southerners (discussed below). This Great Fear was made manifest in numerous and often violent ways. Its main intent was to undermine the efforts of Blacks and some well-intentioned, albeit comparatively few, Whites who attempted to secure black empowerment, self-determination, and equality. As we shall see, this Great Fear would play a profound role in the shaping of schooling, and would prove to have far-reaching implications for the quality of social, economic, and political life for African Americans.

In the most widely read books of the Christian Church (Disciples of Christ) historiography (hereafter referred to as Disciples, Disciples of Christ, or the Christian Church), scholars' treatment of African-American agency in the establishment of Disciples-related schools for Blacks from 1865–1914 are consistently distorted.[7] As we shall later see, the character of black participation in the establishment of these institutions is either significantly diminished or totally omitted, leaving the reader with the impression that African Americans were merely passive recipients of white benevolence and largesse during the radical education reform period following the Civil War.

The problem of neglect regarding black agency within the historiography of the Christian Church in general, and its educational mission in particular, is one that has long been recognized. In November 1954, Claude E. Spencer, curator of the Disciples of Christ

---

[7] The official name of this Protestant denomination is The Christian Church (Disciples of Christ). The parenthetical designation is of great import to the membership of this Protestant movement as it provides some indication of the amalgamation of two distinct Protestant movements.

Historical Society, wrote to Elmer Lewis saying, "There have been no theses, so far as I know, written concerning Negro education among Disciples of Christ. In fact, the whole problem of our Negro work is a much neglected field and one in which much work could be done profitably."[8] Two years later, Lewis made this observation after examining the Disciples' literature: "Notwithstanding the facts that Negroes were placed in positions of responsibility in many cases, the literature concerned with Negro education among the Disciples of Christ seems to leave the impression that for the most part, the program was made by the white leaders and 'handed down' to the Negro."[9] In 1986, the issue of historians' failure to shed light on the extent of African-American involvement in the founding of schools for Blacks within the Christian Church was addressed by Kenneth Henry, Disciples of Christ historian and Professor of Church History Emeritus at the Interdenominational Theological Center in Atlanta. Henry wrote,

> It is not often clarified, however, that [the establishment of schools for Blacks] was an effort by black and white churches. In many instances, initiative was taken by Blacks to begin schools which were subsequently supported by white churches and individuals.... Between 1865–1917, Black Disciple Ministers were unknown prophets because their powers of self-determination generally were not recognized, and resources they deserved were often withheld.[10]

These men and women—"unknown prophets"—not only made great sacrifices to provide formal schooling for their communities in hopes of securing a better future, but their efforts also paved the way for the establishment of state-funded, universal, and compulsory common school systems throughout the South. My task is not to determine why

---

[8] Claude E. Spencer (curator, Disciples of Christ Historical Society, Nashville) to Elmer Lewis, 17 November 1954, quoted in Elmer C. Lewis, "A History of Secondary and Higher Education in Negro Schools Related to the Disciples of Christ," Ph.D. diss., University of Pittsburgh, 1957, 15.

[9] Lewis, "A History of Secondary and Higher Education in Negro Schools," 40.

[10] Kenneth Henry, "Unknown Prophets: Black Disciples Ministry in Historical Perspective," *Discipliana* 46/1 (Spring 1986): 3–5.

these key players remained unknown and outside of the discourse of "mainstream" intellectual inquiry of the evolution of American schooling. My task is to contribute to the growing body of literature that provides a critical examination and analysis of these extraordinary events. Further, this study conveys a small segment of the contributions of black pioneers who established schools under hostile conditions in the Southern United States.

Over the past thirty years, historians of American education have increasingly given attention to the previously much neglected area of African-American education history. Among the myriad of topics that beckon the attention of professional historians under the umbrella of African-American education history is African-American participation in the development of Protestant church-related educational institutions. The full scope of African-American agency within the context of Protestant church-related education reform is much too broad to address in any monograph. This study examines the agency of African Americans in the founding of educational institutions for Blacks associated with the Christian Church. The philosophical discourse within the Christian Church concerning the purpose, type, and control of these schools is under examination, as well as the racial assumptions and attitudes that informed each of these areas.

Contrary to how historians have traditionally treated the focus of this study, I will argue that African Americans within the Christian Church played an active role, both in cooperating with Disciples' mission agencies and acting independently of these agencies, in the conceptualization and founding of schools for their communities. In addition, Disciples reformers claimed to be motivated by their desire to "elevate the Negro race." However, the nearly exclusive application of the industrial education model in schools established by the Disciples of Christ mission agencies reflects an intentional effort by Whites within the denomination to encumber African-American socioeconomic and political advancement, autonomy, and self-determination. Finally, the conservative approach to schooling for African Americans was largely the result of Northern Disciples' acquiescence to the demands of Southern members of the church for the sake of maintaining unity within the national church.

Other than a few noted exceptions, agency on the part of African Americans in education reform movements in the postbellum period of United States history was largely ignored or inadequately examined by professional historians during the first three quarters of the twentieth century.[11] It would not be until the publication of James D. Anderson's seminal book, *The Education of Blacks in the South: 1860–1935* in 1988 that students of the history of American education would be provided with an in-depth and extended inquiry into educational initiatives for black people generated by black people during the Reconstruction and post-Reconstruction eras.[12] Numerous scholars have acknowledged various aspects of African-American agency in the provision of formal and informal education for their communities, but none have offered an extensive treatment of this critical and neglected aspect of American education history.

Over the years, there have been scholars of church and American education history who have examined the efforts of Northern sectarian organizations to establish institutions of learning for Blacks throughout the South before, during, and after the Civil War. Such scholarship, more often than not, affords limited attention to the views, experiences, and perspectives of Blacks, and gives primary attention to the perspectives of church executives and officers, missionaries/ teachers, school administrators, and field secretaries.[13]

---

[11] Even among the noted exceptions such as Carter G. Woodson, *The Education of the Negro Prior to 1861* (New York: A&B Books, 1989 [1919]); Henry A. Bullock, *A History of Negro Education in the South from 1619 to the Present* (Cambridge: Harvard University Press, 1967); Horace Mann Bond, *The Education of the Negro in the American Social Order* (New York: Ogden Press, 1970); and Thomas L. Webber, *Deep Like the River: Education in the Slave Quarter Community, 1831–1865* (New York: W. W. Norton & Co., 1978), African-American agency is not treated as a central focus of their theses. Other scholarly works examined the founding of Historically Black Colleges and Universities (HBCU), but again, none provide careful examination of the role of African Americans in the process.

[12] James D. Anderson, *The Education of Blacks in the South, 1860–1935* (Chapel Hill: University of North Carolina Press, 1988) 30.

[13] Scholarship falling into this category include Jones, *Soldiers of Light and Love*; Elizabeth Jacoway, *Yankee Missionaries in the South: The Penn School Experiment* (Baton Rouge: Louisiana State University Press, 1980); Ronald Butchart, *Northern Schools, Southern Blacks, and Reconstruction: Freedmen's Education, 1862–1875* (New

Without question, this "top-down" approach of examining the education of African Americans provides historians of education as well as scholars in other disciplines with a critical, albeit incomplete, body of information. What the contemporary historian—with few exceptions—has failed to provide is a more in-depth and critical analysis of the extraordinary efforts and resourcefulness of African-American men and women to establish schools for themselves and their children. There are a few exceptions that give extensive attention to black agency in responding to their own needs for schooling during this period.[14]

As the title suggests, Clara DeBoer's monograph, *His Truth Is Marching On: African Americans who Taught the Freedmen for the*

York: Greenwood Press, 1980); Robert Morris, *Reading, Riting, and Reconstruction: The Education of Freedmen in the South, 1861–1870* (Chicago: University of Chicago Press, 1981 [1971]); Henry L Swint, *The Northern Teacher in the South, 1862–1870* (Nashville: Vanderbilt University Press, 1941); Sandra E. Small, "The Yankee Schoolmarm in Freedmen's Schools: An Analysis of Attitudes," *The Journal of Southern History* 45/3 (August 1979).

[14] Scholarship whose primary focus is the examination of African-American agency in the establishment of schools for Blacks includes Clara DeBoer, *His Truth Is Marching On: African Americans who Taught the Freedmen for the American Missionary Association, 1861–1877* (New York: Garland, 1995); Josie R. Johnson, "An Historical Review of the Role Black Parents and the Black Community Played in Providing Schooling for Black Children in the South, 1865–1954 (Autobiographies, Involvement, Support)," Ed.D. diss., University of Massachusetts, 1986; Angel D. Nieves, "We Gave Our Heart and Lives to It: African-American Women Reformers, Industrial Education, and the Monuments of Nation-Building in the Post-Reconstruction South, 1877–1938," Ph.D diss., Cornell University, 2001; Heather A. D. Williams, "Self-Taught: The Role of African Americans in Educating the Freedpeople, 1861–1871," Ph.D. diss., Yale University, 2002. There is a body of scholarship that examines the founding of church-related colleges for Blacks; however, these too tend to examine source material that provides top-down perspectives of these efforts. Some of the more noted publications in this category include Martha E. Dawson, *Hampton University: A National Treasure: A Documentary from 1878 to 1992* (Silver Spring: Beckham House Publishers, 1994); Joe M. Richardson, *A History of Fisk University, 1865–1946* (Tuscaloosa: University of Alabama Press, 1980); Maxine D. Jones and Joe M. Richardson, *Talladega College: The First Century* (Tuscaloosa: University of Alabama Press, 1990); Rayford W. Logan, *Howard University: The First One Hundred Years, 1867–1967* (New York: New York University Press, 1969); Edward Jones, *A Candle in the Dark: A History of Morehouse College* (Valley Forge: Judson Press, 1967); and Florence M. Read, *The Story of Spelman College* (Atlanta: Atlanta University Press, 1961).

American Missionary Association, 1861–1877, is a salutation of African Americans who, in the face of great danger and who could have made more money elsewhere, remained in the South to teach other Blacks attending schools related to the American Missionary Association. Utilizing fifty-one biographies as primary sources, Josie R. Johnson's dissertation, "An Historical Review of the Role Black Parents and the Black Community Played in Providing Schooling for Black Children in the South, 1865–1954," examines the contributions of black people in the education of black children and the priority Blacks have placed on the education of their children. Noting the lack of knowledge of this aspect of history, Johnson states, "Ignorance of this history affects how Black children are viewed, treated, taught, encouraged, or discouraged in the process of acquiring an education in this society."[15] Angel D. Nieves's dissertation, "We Gave Our Heart and Lives to It: African-American Women Reformers, Industrial Education, and the Monuments of Nation-Building in the Post-Reconstruction South, 1877–1938," examines the role of black women who embraced the industrial model of education as a primary method of uplifting Freedpeople. Noting the neglect of black women by scholars in the area of "Black educational history," Nieves argues that "race-based" schools established and operated by black women represent intentional efforts "to help establish the mechanisms necessary for the creation of a Black nation through the difficult transition from emancipation to political self-determination."[16] In her dissertation, "Self-Taught: The

---

[15] Johnson, "An Historical Review of the Role Black Parents and the Black Community Played," ix. For expanded discussions on distortions, omissions, stereotyping of black people in American historiography and its impact on children, see Donnarae MacCann and Gloria Woodward, eds., *The Black American in Books for Children: Readings in Racism* (Metuchen NJ: Scarecrow Press, Inc., 1972) and *The First R: How Children Learn Race and Racism* (New York: Rowman & Littlefield Publishers, 2001). For a discussion on content analysis of U.S. history textbooks, see the Council on Interracial Books for Children Racism and Sexism Resource Center for Educators' *Stereotypes, Distortions and Omissions in U.S. History Textbooks* (New York: Council on Interracial Books for Children, 1977); and James W. Loewen, *Lies My Teacher Told Me: Everything Your American History Textbook Got Wrong* (New York: Simon Schuster, 2007 [1995]).

[16] Nieves, "We Gave Our Heart and Lives to It," 4.

Role of African Americans in Educating the Freedpeople, 1861–1871," Heather A. D. Williams reexamines the autobiographies, memoirs, letters, and minutes from political organizations of Freedpeople who engaged in revolutionary education reform in the South and who have traditionally been viewed as non-actors and objects of white largesse. She argues that these sources "tell a story of African American determination and agency in launching a transformative educational movement for the American South."[17]

The most widely read scholarly study that examines the founding of colleges and universities established by the Christian Church is D. Duane Cummins's *Disciples Colleges*. In addition, each of the most widely read published scholarly works on the history of the Christian Church give some attention to both the establishment of colleges and universities by the Disciples and, to some extent, the presence and involvement of African Americans within this Protestant movement. These books include David E. Harrell's *Quest for a Christian America: The Disciples of Christ and American Society to 1866* and *The Social Sources of Division in the Disciples of Christ, 1865–1900*; Lester G. McAllister and William E. Tucker's *Journey of Faith: A History of the Christian Church (Disciples of Christ)*; Mark G. Toulouse's *Joined in Discipleship: The Maturing of an American Religious Movement*; Frances Craddock's *In the Fullness of Time: A History of Women in the Christian Church (Disciples of Christ)*; and Winfred E. Garrison and Alfred T. DeGroot's *The Disciples of Christ: A History*.

There are a number of books that provide either a general overview of African-American presence and involvement in the Christian Church or examine the education mission among Blacks by Disciples, but these are not widely read. They include published works such as Brenda M. Caldwell and William K. Fox, Sr.'s *Journey Towards Wholeness: A History of Black Disciples of Christ* (vol. 1); Robert Jordan's *Two Races in One Fellowship*; and William J. Barber's *Disciples Assemblies of Eastern North Carolina*. Unpublished dissertations include John C.

---

[17] Williams, "Self-Taught," 2. Williams's dissertation was recently published: Heather A. Williams, *Self Taught: African American Education in Slavery and Freedom* (Chapel Hill: University of North Carolina Press, 2005).

Long's "The Disciples of Christ and Negro Education"; Elmer C. Lewis's "A History of Secondary and Higher Education in Negro Schools Related to the Disciples of Christ"; and Hap Lyda's "A History of Black Christian Churches (Disciples of Christ) in the United States Through 1899." [18] Long's study focuses on the cultural climate that shaped and informed Disciples' interest in establishing schools for Blacks. Lewis's study focuses on the development of schools for Blacks examined in the current study. Both Long's and Lewis's studies offer some insight into African-American agency relative to the establishment of schools for themselves; however, both studies have as their primary concern the role of mission agencies of the Christian Church in the formation of schools for Blacks.

---

[18] D. Duane Cummins, *Disciples Colleges* (St. Louis: Christian Board of Publications, 1976); David E. Harrell, Jr., *Quest for a Christian America: The Disciples of Christ and American Society to 1866* (Disciples of Christ Historical Society, 1966; repr., Tuscaloosa: University of Alabama Press, 2003); and Harrell, *The Social Sources of Division in the Disciples of Christ, 1865–1900* (Atlanta: Publishing Systems, Inc. 1973); Lester G McAllister and William E. Tucker, *Journey of Faith: A History of the Christian Church (Disciples of Christ)* (St. Louis: Chalice Press, 1995 [1975]); Mark G. Toulouse, *Joined in Discipleship: The Maturing of an American Religious Movement* (St. Louis: Chalice Press, 1992); Frances Craddock, *In the Fullness of Time: A History of Women in the Christian Church (Disciples of Christ)* (St. Louis: Chalice Press, 1999); Winfred E. Garrison and Alfred T. DeGroot, *The Disciples of Christ: A History* (St. Louis: Christian Board of Publications, 1948); Brenda M. Caldwell and William K. Fox, Sr., *Journey Towards Wholeness: A History of Black Disciples of Christ in the Mission of the Christian Church*, vol. 1 (Indianapolis: National Convocation of the Christian Church [Disciples of Christ], 1990 [1988]); Robert Jordan, *Two Races in One Fellowship* (Detroit: United Christian Church, 1944); William J. Barber, *Disciples Assemblies of Eastern North Carolina* (St. Louis: Bethany Press, 1966); Hap Lyda, "A History of Black Christian Churches (Disciples of Christ) in the United States Through 1899," Ph.D. diss., Vanderbilt University, 1972; John C. Long, "The Disciples of Christ and Negro Education," Ph.D. diss., University of Southern California, 1960; and Lewis's Ph.D. dissertation, "A History of Secondary and Higher Education in Negro Schools Related to the Disciples of Christ." The assertion that certain books are "most widely read" is not a conclusion made based on data from quantitative research, but from my lived experience as an ordained clergy of the Christian Church (Disciples of Christ) whose earned Master of Divinity was conferred by a Disciples of Christ institution, Christian Theological Seminary, in 1990. McAllister and Tucker continue to be viewed as the preeminent authoritative source of Disciples history and their work a required text for students of Disciples history and polity.

With the exception of Harrell, in each of the more contemporary studies, the role of African Americans in the founding of schools for Blacks associated with the Christian Church is either dramatically diminished or totally omitted. Blacks are depicted as either passive recipients of white benevolence, or they are relegated to virtual invisibility in the provision of education for Blacks. The following examples demonstrate the diminished and/or nonexistent role of African Americans in the establishment of schools specifically for them.

Writing about schools established for Blacks by the Disciples of Christ, McAllister and Tucker state, "Disciples established several other schools for Negroes in the South. Among these were Lum Graded School in Alabama, the Martinsville, Virginia Christian Institute (subsequently known as Piedmont Christian Institute), and Warner Institute in Jonesboro, Tennessee."[19] McAllister and Tucker's comments are misleading and give the reader the impression that the establishment of Lum, Martinsville, and Warner was the result of the denominational mission agency. Each of these schools was conceived and founded by African Americans, a point that I will clearly document in chapter 7.

The founding of Jarvis Christian Institute in Hawkins, Texas, is consistently presented as an effort that was credited to either its primary benefactor who donated the land or to the efforts of the Christian Women's Board of Missions (CWBM). In 1900, the CWBM took over responsibility for the homeland mission among the Freedpeople for the Christian Church. Writing about the founding of Jarvis Christian Institute (later called Jarvis Christian College) in Hawkins, Texas, Garrison and DeGroot state, "It was also through the influence of the Christian Women's Board of Missions that Jarvis Christian College was founded in 1912, at Hawkins, Texas. For it was the state secretary of the women's work, Miss Virginia Hearne, who induced Ms. Ida Van Zandt Jarvis and her husband to donate land for the college."[20]

---

[19] McAllister and Tucker, *Journey of Faith*, 324.
[20] Garrison and DeGroot, *Diciples of Christ*, 480.

It cannot be denied that the gift of 456 acres by the Jarvis family as well as the institutional support of the CWBM played a crucial role in establishing Jarvis Christian Institute in 1913. What's missing from these presentations of Jarvis's founding, however, is the story of the incredible vision, unwavering hope, resolute commitment, and steadfast sacrifice of black men and women in East Texas over several years that would function precipitously relative to the ensuing actions by the Jarvis family and the CWBM.

Writing about the founding of Jarvis, Cummins states,

> Jarvis Christian College is the only black higher education institution in covenant with the Christian Church (Disciples of Christ) in our own day. It was founded as Jarvis Christian Institute through the encouragement of the Christian Women's Board of Missions (CWBM) and with a donation of 465 acres of land near Hawkins, Texas, by Mrs. Ida V. Jarvis in 1900. Thomas B. Frost [black], a graduate of Southern Christian Institute, was appointed by the CWBM in 1911 to develop the school. With the help of Charles A. Berry, Sr. [black], he cleared and fenced the land, built a dormitory—dining hall—classroom building, and designed the course of study by patterning the new institute along the same format as J. B. Lehman's Southern Christian Institute and Booker T. Washington's Tuskegee Institute.[21]

In his book that chronicles the founding of Disciples colleges and universities, Cummins gives well-deserved, and, as we shall see later, understated, credit to Charles A. Berry, Sr., and Thomas Frost for the extraordinary job they did in clearing the land for the initial phase of the Jarvis campus. African-American Disciples, according to this depiction, don't appear on the scene of the Jarvis story until *after* the land is donated and a commitment for supporting the school is secured. Here again, the crucial role of black Disciples in the conceptualization and development of this vision for a school for black Disciples in East Texas is completely omitted. To acknowledge the CWBM's role of

---

[21] Cummins, *Disciples Colleges*, 90–91.

"encouragement" and what the Jarvises "donated" is both correct and appropriate, but the relegation of black agency to virtual invisibility in the establishment of Jarvis is a gross disservice to black Disciples. This omission serves to perpetuate the myth that Blacks primarily, if not exclusively, functioned as objects of white largesse and benevolence.

Noting that only one school for Blacks was in operation at the time, in 1890, the Christian Church formed the Board of Negro Education and Evangelism (BNEE). Elmer Lewis writes, "Within the ten years immediately following the organization of this Negro Board, three new schools for Negroes were started: the Louisville Christian Bible School, Louisville, Kentucky, in 1892; The Lum Graded School at Lum, Alabama, in 1894; and Piedmont School of Industry (Piedmont Christian Institute) at Martinsville, Virginia, in 1900."[22] Here Lewis leads the reader to believe that each school that was established during the ten years following the organization of the BNEE was a direct result of their vision, mission, and/or initiative. While the BNEE did establish the Louisville school through its own initiative, I will demonstrate how this was not the case, as stated above, with the Lum and Piedmont schools.

Craddock's version of the founding of Jarvis provides some visibility for black Disciples' agency long before the school would open its doors. Craddock writes, "Bertha Mason received a promise in 1903 of several hundred acres of land from Ida Jarvis if the women of Texas would assume responsibility for raising the necessary funds to establish a school for Blacks. It was at this point that Sarah Lue Bostick [black] agreed to help, and during the next ten years, these two women were deeply engrossed in efforts to convince women of the necessity of establishing such a school."[23] More will be said later about Sarah Lue Bostick, a leader of national renown and the first African-American woman to be ordained in the Christian Church. Her role in helping to raise funds for a school in East Texas for Blacks was crucial. Craddock rightly acknowledges this example of black agency, but Bostick's efforts were by no means an anomaly among black Disciples. The story of

---

[22] Lewis, "A History of Secondary and Higher Education in Negro Schools," 51.
[23] Craddock, *In the Fullness of Time*, 51.

unstinting agency on the part of the black Disciples of East Texas has not been adequately told by the scholars of the most widely read books on Disciples of Christ history.

Among the mainstream Disciples of Christ historians, David Harrell stands alone as one who attempts to give visibility to the agency of African-American Disciples in the founding of schools. In a reference to the founding of Southern Christian Institute, the first school for Blacks founded by white Disciples in 1875, Harrell correctly states that "Southern Blacks played little role in the organizing of the school."[24] Harrell, however, goes further in shedding light on black agency in establishing other schools. Writing about Christian Bible College founded in 1884 in New Castle, Kentucky, Harrell points out that "[t]his new Kentucky school received strong support from the General Christian Missionary Convention [black] and the Negro organization selected T. Augustus Reed as principal. Negro leadership in the effort was stronger than in any other Disciple educational project. Preston Taylor was the primary agent in raising funds and apparently a major part of the support of the school came from Negro congregations."[25] In reference to the founding of the Lum school in Alabama, Harrell writes,

> A third Negro school, the Lum Grade School, was opened under the management of the board in 1894 in Lum, Alabama. Robert Brooks [black], a graduate of Southern Christian Institute, was the first principal, and the school made slow but steady progress.... The school was under a Negro board of directors, and, although it received sporadic aid from the Board of Negro Education and Evangelization, it was less dependent on the board than other black schools.[26]

Harrell's acknowledgment of black agency in the Disciples of Christ educational mission with and among the Freedpeople in the South represents a movement toward a more thorough and inclusive

---

[24] Harrell, *Sources of Division*, 187.

[25] Ibid., 194.

[26] Ibid., 195. The actual name of this school was the Lum Graded School.

examination of available source material relative to black participation in this movement. Two points, however, must be made here. First, when writing about the New Castle school, Harrell states, "Negro leadership in the effort was stronger than in any other Disciple educational project." What defines a legitimate "Disciple" educational project needs to be clarified. For Harrell, it seems that a "Disciple" educational project is one sanctioned by a mission agency recognized by the church's General Convention. This is accurate to the extent that, as we shall demonstrate later, up to that point, the New Castle School represented the strongest black leadership for a Disciple educational project initiated by the BNEE. It, however, did not represent the strongest black effort of a school established by persons affiliated with the Disciples of Christ. The polity and organizational structure of the Christian Church is based on local church autonomy. In this nonhierarchical polity, unlike an Episcopal polity, no organized manifestation of the church has authority over another. All relations, theoretically, are based on covenant and cooperation. The significance of this polity and the biblical and theological perspectives that informed it had far-reaching implications on the evolution of this Protestant movement. Moreover, it had implications on its response to the critical socioeconomic and political issues facing the country during the nineteenth century. More will be said about the theology and biblical interpretative foundations and their influence on how the church responded to the conditions of Freedpeople in chapter 4. For now, it is important to point out that a "Disciple educational effort" is one that is not limited to one sanctioning national body. The very polity of the church and its affirmation of the liberty of each individual affirms that an authentic "Disciple educational effort" can be one that is initiated by a local congregation, state convention or assembly, or national body. I will demonstrate that there were other strong examples of black agency and Disciples educational efforts that predate the New Castle School, which Harrell does not acknowledge.

The current study is a social history that contributes to a growing body of revisionist scholarship in the areas of Reconstruction and post-Reconstruction history, American education history, and American church history. This study will shed new light on African-American agency in education reform within the Christian Church during a time that marks the genesis of state-supported, universal, compulsory common schooling for Blacks, and Whites, in the Southern states. Further, under examination is the manner in which white and black education reformers within the Christian Church, from the end of the Civil War to the Progressive Era, responded to attempts by Southern Whites to revive antebellum ideological, economic, and political social patterns.

Critical analysis of the topics raised in this study will center on responses to several questions that include the following: For African Americans in the antebellum South, what was the nature of their experience relative to literacy development, schooling, and other modes of education prior to 1865, and how did this experience shape and inform their response following the Civil War? What were the conditions that characterized the Southern landscape following the Civil War? How did these conditions influence efforts to secure literacy development and schooling in the years following the Civil War? How did the socioeconomic and political conditions in the United States—North and South—shape and inform the discourse of the educational mission for African Americans among Whites and within the Christian Church? What were the arguments brought forward by those within the Christian Church who were both proponents and opponents of developing church-related schools for Freedpeople? What theological, sociological, and anthropological assumptions about the nature and/or intellectual and civic capacity of African Americans were held by white Disciples? How did these assumptions or beliefs shape and inform their educational mission among Blacks? Sally McMillen reminds us that "[a] study of any institution engaged in benevolent work also raises important questions about the motivations of its leaders and volunteer workers."[27] Often operating in the face of violent reprisal or being ridiculed or ostracized by friends and family, what were the motivating factors that moved white members of the Christian Church to engage in an educational mission among and with African Americans? And finally, what are concrete examples of African-

---

[27] Sally G. McMillen, *To Raise Up the South: Sunday Schools in Black and White Churches, 1865–1915* (Baton Rouge: Louisiana State University Press, 2001) xiv.

American agency regarding the conceptualization and establishment of schools associated with the Christian Church? This would include schools receiving formal support by the Disciples of Christ's mission boards as well as schools founded by Disciples independent of Disciples' mission board assistance.

Individual and corporate acts of resistance relative to the provision of schools by and for African Americans associated with the Christian Church are central themes of this study. Thus, acts of resistance both in support of and in opposition to schooling for Blacks are examined. Blacks and well-intentioned Whites made efforts to establish schools and made innumerable sacrifices to secure education for Freedpeople. These were considered acts of resistance against the forces that sought to suppress or deny Blacks significant socioeconomic and political gain, and other benefits of the franchise. Conversely, the various methods employed by Whites within and outside of the Christian Church that were aimed at suppressing literacy development among Blacks will be examined. Such methods include anti-literacy legislation; misappropriation of revenue from taxation ostensibly intended for the provision for schools for landowners; physical and psychological violence; theological treatises designed to justify oppressive educational philosophies aimed at preventing Blacks from either having access to schooling or from becoming literate through more informal methods, and limiting Blacks from accessing particular forms of schooling in an effort to maintain a social order characterized by white male socioeconomic, cultural, and political hegemony.

There are two primary reasons for my selection of the period for this study. First, the Reconstruction and post-Reconstruction eras in U.S. history stand as the most active periods for establishing both secular and church-related schools for and by African Americans. During this period, as aforementioned, examination by scholars of church-related schools and the role of African Americans in this process is a relatively recent development in education historiography.

Second, the period selected for this study represents the most active period in establishing schools for Blacks by the Christian Church and its members. The founding of Jarvis Christian Institute in 1913 serves as one of the most vivid examples of African American agency in education as well as struggles of resistance and control by Blacks and Whites within the Disciples of Christ. The story of Jarvis will be discussed in chapter 7.

In order to arrive at an analysis that will contribute to a broader historical discourse, this study cannot and should not focus on the actions of members within the Christian Church as if they functioned within a vacuum unaffected by the myriad of socioeconomic and political conditions of their immediate environment and those of the broader social landscape. Accordingly, I will give special attention to schooling by drawing primarily from secondary sources. Further, an examination and analysis of the broader socioeconomic and political conditions of the North American landscape from the colonial period to 1865 will be provided. Chapters 2 and 3 give attention to this aspect of the contextual framework.

Using primary and secondary sources, chapter 4 introduces the reader to the religious landscape of the early Republic from which the Christian Church (Disciples of Christ) emerged. The biblical, theological, ideological, and philosophical perspectives of its founders that shaped the foundation upon which the church was established is also examined. Needless to say, these foundations will play a critical role in shaping the views of Disciples' leadership and how the church as a whole responded to the major challenges faced by the Republic. Special attention will be placed on chattel enslavement, Blacks in the church, challenges presented by the secession of the Southern states, and the ensuing war that resulted in the manumission of more than five million Blacks.

Chapter 5 examines how the Christian Church responded to the challenges outlined in chapter 4 with special emphasis on schooling for African Americans. I will examine the predominant attitudes and assumptions concerning race among white Disciples leaders and how such attitudes and assumptions influenced the form and function of schooling for Blacks supported by the church. Special attention is given to the philosophical and theological discourse within the church that shaped their responses, in support of and in opposition to the educational concerns and needs of the Freedpeople. Attention is also given to specific individual and institutional ways in which the church responded to the educational needs of Blacks. I will also provide a critical analysis of the motivation behind these responses.

In order for the reader to have an informed appreciation for how broader contextual realities impacted the development of schooling for Blacks supported by the Christian Church, chapter 6 introduces the reader to the socioeconomic and political landscape in the U.S. between 1865 and 1914. This will provide the reader with a framework to understand better how and why various constituencies responded to the educational needs of African Americans as they did. In addition, I will provide an example of intra-church dynamics centered on church-related schooling for Blacks within the Baptist church. This is done to demonstrate how racially motivated interventions made by the Disciples of Christ are located within and connected to a broader philosophical and ideological framework of how Protestant movements in the U.S. responded to the issue of schooling for Blacks in the South.

Chapter 7 will examine examples of African-American agency in the Christian Church concerning the provision of schooling for themselves as well as the philosophy that shaped this agency. This chapter also examines how Blacks responded to the type of schooling and methods of governance and control by the mission agencies of the Christian Church.

In chapters 8 and 9, I move beyond the time that is the primary focus of this book. In these chapters, I examine the evolution of race relations within the Disciples of Christ and note significant developments that demonstrate how black Disciples responded to their educational needs and quest to secure justice within the church and society. I also briefly examine and critique the manner in which black Disciples leadership has responded, in terms of a national effort, to contemporary challenges in the African-American community with special emphasis on the response to the educational crisis now facing black youth in general, and the support of Jarvis Christian College in particular.

As previously mentioned, this study is a social history. Use of this term, "social history," presents somewhat of a dilemma because it doesn't provide the reader with a clear and concise understanding of the employed methodological approach. Christopher Lloyd articulates this problem when he writes:

> The concept of "social history" is a problematical one and the range of work done under its rubric is now very wide indeed. It ranges from microscopic "people's history," such as that carried out under the auspices of the British *History Workshop* and *Oral History* movements, and…imaginative reconstructions of historical episodes (all based upon detailed personal testimony); through the studies of class consciousness and class interaction of writers…to "macroscopic" long-run structural enquiries…. Faced with such an array of focal lengths it may seem at first glance an impossible task to find a sufficiently comprehensive viewpoint from which to criticize all the explanatory modes adopted by social historians.[28]

If a definitive category is necessary, by using Lloyd's typology, the current work can be considered a "people's history." This history offers a critical analysis of sociohistorical phenomena as they relate to education reform by and for Blacks associated with the Christian Church. Such phenomena occurred within the broader socioeconomic and political contextual framework of the emerging Republic. This broader framework influenced the responses of members within the Disciples of Christ to the needs of Freedpeople in general, but more specifically, to their need, desire, and demand for schooling.

Protestant mission-related initiatives to establish schools for African Americans during the period addressed in this study were quite diverse in terms of ecclesial representation. Numerous denominations such as the Methodist Episcopal Church (white and Northern), Congregationalists, the Presbyterian Church USA, Episcopal Church, Quakers, African Methodist Episcopal Church, African Methodist Episcopal Zion, Colored Methodist Episcopal Church,[29] and the American Baptist Church (white Northern and independent Southern

---

[28] Christopher Lloyd, *Explanation in Social History* (New York: Basil Blackwell, Inc., 1986) 2.

[29] Later renamed "Christian" Methodist Episcopal Church.

Blacks), to name the more active groups, all made significant contributions to the establishment of schools for African Americans. The current study concludes that the efforts of the Disciples of Christ in this particular area of domestic missionary activity was anywhere from moderate to conservative compared to other so-called "mainline" Protestant denominations. In order to place data on the Christian Church's educational mission efforts with and among Blacks in perspective, the study will also present data that reflects efforts of Northern white and black Southern Baptists in this area of education reform during this period.

There are several reasons why the Baptists provide an excellent model for institutional comparison. First, the Baptists were among the most active and aggressive Protestant denominations involved in the provision of Southern schools for the Freedpeople during the time of our present concern. Secondly, the Baptists and the various Methodist movements attracted the largest number of black people. The human dynamics of race within the denomination relative to educating Blacks provides an excellent comparative model to examine similar dynamics within the Christian Church. Finally, the Baptist structure of governance is based on a polity of local church autonomy that is similar to the Christian Church. Power relations and authority within this type of polity are dramatically different from those found in Methodist or Episcopal structures. These denominations govern themselves by a hierarchical polity of ecclesial governance. Therefore, the Baptists provide a more comparable institutional model when examining the sociopolitical dynamics concerning the educational needs of Freedpeople.

To contextualize, explicate, and support the claim of significant African-American agency in the establishment of Disciples of Christ schools, the study will draw on a range of primary and secondary sources, both written and oral. Primary archival sources include institutional records, letters of missionaries, minutes of the proceedings of mission boards' local, state, regional, and national gatherings, field reports of their agents, unpublished letters and speeches, and published speeches and articles of various denominational periodicals. In the section that provides an overview of black agency in the attainment of literacy, schooling, and other forms of education in the antebellum South, oral historical sources are employed as primary sources. A word needs to be said about the use of oral sources. While the oral sources are invaluable tools for the historian to reconstruct historical phenomena, they are not without problems.

In an effort to gain a view of the educational experience of enslaved Africans in and among their communities, the current study uses the Narratives of Formerly Enslaved Africans (NFEAs). The NFEAs, traditionally referred to as "slave narratives," were collected by interviewers of the Federal Writers Project of the Works Project Administration (hereafter FWP) during the 1930s. These oral sources contain both strengths and weaknesses as primary historical source material.

If the NFEAs were the only sources available to the contemporary reader who wanted to learn about how Africans responded to chattel slavery in the U.S., an uncritical reader could formulate an argument supporting the idea that enslaved Africans were content with their condition. It is imperative, however, that the user of this rich source take into consideration how people responded to FWP questions in the 1930s. Readers must be mindful of the age of the interviewee, the race of the interviewer, the socioeconomic conditions caused by the Great Depression, and how nostalgia influenced the ways in which formerly enslaved African Americans responded. Belinda Hurmence makes the following point:

> [A]ll of the speakers were old. Old and poor. They made it into the 1930s, but a lot of them suffered the declining health that stalks old age and poverty. They also suffered the hopelessness of the Great Depression then blanketing the world. Through the screen of the seventy intervening years, it was easy for them to view their past lives in bondage as a time of plenty, a time when pleasures were simple and their youthful energies

high, a time when plantation life meant shelter, food, and medical care.[30]

Regarding the age of the interviewee, C. Vann Woodward reminds the researcher that the majority of the interviewees were in their childhood years during slavery, "a period before the full rigors and worst aspects of the slave discipline were typically felt, and a period more likely to be favorably colored in the memory of the aged."[31] It is therefore plausible that for many interviewees, memories of enslavement could have been of play and lack of want. On the other hand, as Hurmence points out, conditions following the war were not much better for a large number of emancipated Africans. In their adolescent and early adult years, many formerly enslaved Africans were powerless, uneducated, and mistreated by their Northern liberators and the failed promises of Reconstruction.[32] These conditions could also influence the development of fond memories of a childhood in slavery.

The race of the interviewer must be considered when using NFEAs as a primary source. The FWP interviewers were over-whelmingly Southern Whites. Their interviewing methods and procedures as well as their biases were often consistent with the "Jim Crow etiquette and white supremacy" that dominated the sociopolitical climate of that period. This was also a period of lynching and other forms of violence toward African Americans. One must take into

---

[30] Belinda Hurmence, ed., *Before Freedom, When I Just Can Remember: Twenty-Seven Oral Histories of Former South Carolina Slaves* (Winston-Salem: John F. Blair Publishers, 1989) xii. By identifying several concerns associated with the NFEAs, I do not in any way want to question the validity or value of oral sources as authentic literary forms. Over the past fifteen years there has been a growing discussion among African scholars who view oral sources or "orality" as literature. For a closer examination of this discussion see Okumba Miruka, *Encounter with Oral Literature* (Nairobi: East African Educational Publishers, 1994); Ngugi Wa Thiong'o, *Penpoints, Gunpoints, and Dreams: Towards a Critical Theory of the Arts and the State in Africa* (Oxford: Clarendon Press, 1998) 105–20; Duncan Brown, ed., *Oral Literature & Performance in Southern Africa* (Athens: Ohio University Press, 1999); Toyin Falola and Steven J. Salm, *Culture and Customs of Ghana* (Westport: Greenwood Press, 2002) 59–65.

[31] C. Vann Woodward, "History from Slave Sources," *American Historical Review* 79 (April 1974): 473.

[32] Hurmence, *Before Freedom*, xii.

account how these racial dynamics may have influenced the interviewee's responses to questioning by Southern white interviewers. It is reasonable to believe that an insensitive interviewer may have invoked anger, fear, suspicion, distrust, and a host of other feelings that could influence the answers to questions in a variety of ways. [33]

The fact that states are disproportionately represented in the narratives collected by the FWP is another problem according to Woodward. He points out that "Arkansas, which never had more than 3.5 percent of the slave population, furnished about 33 percent of the ex-slaves interviewed, while Mississippi, which in 1860 contained more than 10 percent of the slaves, is represented by little more than 1 percent of those interviewed."[34]

Related to the issue of geographically disproportionate representation is the concern for over- and under-representation of those interviewed. Woodward writes, "Among categories of the population represented by larger than their proportional number are urban residents, males and former house servants, with a consequent under-representation of rural population, females and former field hands."[35] It has been well documented that the experience of the field hand and house servant were dramatically different. It would not be surprising if the average life span of the field worker were less than that of the house servant. This could account for the over- and under-representation in the 1930s.

Charles Perdue alerts the researcher to other possible problems when using the NFEAs. These include factual errors such as attributing material to the wrong source; giving the incorrect antebellum location for the residence of the formerly enslaved African interviewee; and censorship of data in the form of distortions (bowdlerization) and/or omissions (expurgation).[36]

---

[33] Woodward, "History from Slave Sources," 473.

[34] Ibid., 472.

[35] Ibid.

[36] Charles Perdue, Jr., T. E. Brandon, and R. K. Phillips, eds., *Weevils in the Wheat: Interviews with Virginia Ex-Slaves* (Bloomington: Indiana University Press, 1976) xxiv-vi.

Needless to say, the NFEAs must be read with a great deal of skepticism. This, of course, is the approach historians must take with any primary or secondary historical source document. As with other traditional sources, the NFEAs have drawbacks, but also have much to contribute to historical inquiry. The narratives give voice to those who have been voiceless in traditional historiography. It was not until the 1970s when historians began to utilize the NFEAs with some consistency as primary source material. The NFEAs provide the researcher with evidence of virtually every aspect of life under slavery from the perspective of Freedpeople. Finally, the NFEAs provide us with a view of white Southern society that is not from a white perspective. In addition, they also provide us with some insight into the nature of African and Native American relations during the antebellum period.

Many within the academy argue that the challenge to any historian engaged in the reconstruction of sociohistorical phenomena is to minimize subjectivity in his/her analysis. Those who hold this view go on to argue that the optimal, albeit impossible, result of historical inquiry would be a completely objective interpretation of the subject under investigation. David Tyack is correct in his assertion that any historical analysis is influenced by the lens through which one does his/her analysis. He realizes that one person's understanding of reality "may appear quite different to diverse groups of individuals. That fact alone destroys the possibility of a single objective account of the meaning of events to various peoples."[37]

I am a middle-class, African American, heterosexual male who is an ordained minister in the Christian Church (Disciples of Christ); therefore, the lens through which I examine source material for this study is shaped by these and many other socioeconomic and political factors that have informed my interpretation of reality. I relate very much to the struggle voiced by one of the preeminent historians of African American resistance, Vincent Harding, in being concerned with how our personal identity with the struggles of those for whom we seek to give voice could be used by critics and detractors. Some could,

---

[37] David B. Tyack, *The One Best System: A History of American Urban Education*, (Cambridge: Harvard University Press, 1974), 4.

and indeed have, argued that the scholarship of revisionist historians—and those from other disciplines—is diminished for having
failed the test of achieving "scholarly objectivity." I recognize and
affirm the need for the scholar to be as objective as possible when
examining and interpreting historical phenomena. At the same time, I
acknowledge and embrace the subjective nature of the examination
undertaken here. Like Harding, I am clear that my first commitment
"was not to the ambiguous abstractions of 'objectivity' or 'scholarship,'
but to the lively hope and faith of a people in struggle for a new chance
to be whole."[38]

Finally, I offer a word about the role of black women and the
interpretive methodology of this study. The role of African and
African-American women in the liberation struggle of black people in
this country has only recently been afforded the attention it deserves
by scholars. The role of black women in the formation and
advancement of the black church in general, and their role within the
church in the provision of schooling in particular, takes on a level of
invisibility in Disciples historiography; a level that surpasses the
manner in which black men have been treated. The reality of this
oppressive form of patriarchy is made manifest in both secondary and
primary source material. In the former, scholars give preferential
attention to male leadership, especially that of preachers, field
secretaries, principals, and so on. In the latter, male dominance at local,
state-wide and national gatherings; the manner in which minutes
reflect the presence, or lack thereof, of women attending these
gatherings; and the near total exclusion of women's voices in
periodicals are just some of the ways black women are made invisible
and marginalized in the historical discourse.

I am careful not to engage in anachronistic interpretation by
placing women in situations or giving credit without sufficient data to
support it. Special attention, however, is given to examining the role of
black women. In other words, I attempt to be conscious of how the role
of women can take on invisibility due to the maleness of my own lens.

---

[38] Vincent Harding, *There Is a River: The Black Struggle for Freedom in America*
(New York: Harcourt Brace Jovanovich, 1992 [1982]) xix.

Concerning the involvement of women, inference or comments suggesting probability may be offered when empirical data are lacking. Such inferences or comments will only be made when evidence on the role of women acquired from other scholars allows for an informed deduction or conclusion concerning their explicit or implicit contribution.

It is my hope that the current study makes some small contribution to what Evelyn Brooks Higginbotham refers to as her attempt "to rescue women from invisibility as historical actors in the drama of black empowerment." The story of African-American agency in the establishment of schools related to the Christian Church is "not the exclusive product of a male ministry but...the product and process of male and female interaction."[39] Had it not been for the black women who suffered under the tripartite oppressive reality of classism, racism, and sexism, it can safely be said that the social phenomena commonly referred to as the "black church" simply would not be as we have come to know it. Concerning the debt that the black church owes black women, Du Bois said it best when he wrote, "As I look about me today in this veiled world of mine, despite the noisier and more spectacular advance of my brothers, I instinctively feel and know that it is the five million women of my race who really count. Black women (and women whose grandmothers were black) are...the main pillars of those social settlements which we call churches; and they have with small doubt raised three-fourths of our church property."[40]

---

[39] Evelyn Brooks Higginbotham, *Righteous Discontent: The Women's Movement in the Black Baptist Church, 1880–1920* (Cambridge: Harvard Press, 1993) 2.

[40] W. E. B. Du Bois, *Darkwater* (1918), quoted in Higginbotham, *Righteous Discontent* (inner flap of cover). For a powerful examination of black women clergy see Bettye Collier-Thomas, *Daughters of Thunder: Black Women Preachers and Their Sermons, 1850–1979* (San Francisco: Jossey-Bass Publishers, 1998).

2

CRITICAL PERSPECTIVES ON
EDUCATION AND SCHOOL REFORM

The role of African Americans in the development of schools established for them by members and agencies of the Christian Church (Disciples of Christ) from 1865 to 1914 cannot be understood apart from an informed appreciation of the educational experience of Blacks generally in the United States from the arrival of their enslaved African descendents in 1619 to 1865. Thus, it becomes necessary to discuss the developments within the broader sociopolitical context of the burgeoning new Republic, particularly as it relates to the genesis of common schooling, religion, and the emergence of a republican ideology.

Republicanism and Schooling

The American Revolution gave birth to a new nation that would be built upon a foundation of republicanism. The primary challenge for the "founding fathers" of the new republic was to develop a method of education that reconciled order and freedom. There was also a need for a system of education to galvanize a young republic consisting of an increasingly ethnically diverse population—and one that lacked a national identity, a cultural heritage, and mature national institutions. According to Andy Green, "Education was caught between the twin poles of liberty and control. Its function, in a sense, was precisely to reconcile freedom and order; to make sure that the liberties of a democratic state did not conflict with the basic structure of the capitalist system."[1] Education was clearly a political tool to solidify the republic

---

[1] Andy Green, *Education and State Formation: The Rise of Education Systems in England, France and the USA* (New York: St. Martin's Press, 1990) 177. For further

and to inculcate particular values and beliefs among the citizenry of the new nation. To Benjamin Rush, a signer on the Declaration of Independence, "it was both possible and desirable that education should nurture certain political ideas; indeed, it should endeavor to convert men into republican machines."[2]

The primary ideological thrust that shaped and informed the thinking of the founding fathers in general, and the "fathers of common schools" in particular, was that of *Protestant republicanism* and *capitalism*. Carl Kaestle identifies ten characteristics of what he refers to as "native Protestant ideology."

> The ideology centered on republicanism, Protestantism, and capitalism, three sources of social belief that were intertwined and mutually supporting. Native Protestant ideology can best be summarized by enumerating ten strands or major propositions: the sacredness and fragility of the republican polity (including ideas about individualism, liberty, and virtue); the importance of individual character in fostering social morality; the central role of personal industry in defining rectitude and merit; the delineation of a highly respected but limited domestic role of women; the importance for character building of familial and social environment (within certain racial and ethnic limitations); the sanctity and social virtues of property; the equality and abundance of economic opportunity in the United States; the superiority of American Protestant culture; the grandeur of

---

discussion on the genesis and foundations of philosophical issues associated Republicanism in the early period in the U.S., see A Kristen Foster, *Moral Vision and Material Ambitions: Philadelphia Struggles to Define the Republic* (Landham MD: Lexington Books, 2004); Douglas Adair, *The Intellectual Origins of Jeffersonian Democracy: Republicanism, the Class Struggle, and the Virtuous Farmer* (Landam MD: Lexington Books, 2000); and Bill Brugger, *Republican Theory in Political Thought: Virtuous or Virtual?* (New York: MacMillan Press, 1999).

[2] Green, *Education and State Formation*, 178; Carl Kaestle, *Pillars of the Republic: Common Schools and American Society, 1780–1860* (New York: Hill and Wang, 1983) 79; Lawrence Cremin, *American Education: The National Experience, 1783–1876* (New York: Harper & Row, 1980) 180.

America's destiny; and the necessity of a determined effort to unify America's polyglot population, chiefly through education.[3]

It needs to be stated explicitly that native Protestant republican ideology is racist, patriarchal, and xenophobic. As its theorists presuppose, it is based on distorted interpretations of the Bible, the superiority of the white race, especially white Anglo-Saxon Protestant males, and antithetically, the inferiority of those outside this group. In the context of the early Republic, this presupposition positioned all people of color in a subordinate position to that of Western Europeans, with people of African descent relegated to the bottom of this social spectrum.

In the above quotation, Kaestle only implies this point when he parenthetically says "within certain racial and ethnic limitations." Kaestle acknowledges that the version of native Protestant ideology in the new nation was assimilationist, centralist, and moralistic, but it was clearly one that was racist. The racist nature of republican Protestant ideology and those who espoused it will be demonstrated more fully later. William Watkins's critique of Benjamin Rush, however, serves as an ample example of this point. Watkins writes, "Architects of colonial, racial, and ethnic ideology, such as the respected Dr. Benjamin Rush, declared American Indians as unclean and 'strangers to the obligations both of morality and decency.' Further, Indians were not only 'too lazy to work but even to think.' As for Blacks, Rush associated their skin color with leprosy, and wrote of their 'morbid insensitivity of nerves' and repeatedly proclaimed them diseased."[4]

In fairness to Rush, it must be stated that he also held views of Blacks that would place him in the minority among his peers. Ronald Takaki reminds us that "Rush was a critic of Slavery and believed Blacks had the potential of Republican virtue.... Rush insisted that Blacks were not inferior to Whites in their intellectual ability and capacity for virtue." In an address on slavery delivered in 1773, Rush said, "Slavery is so foreign to the human mind that the moral faculties as well as those

---

[3] Kaestle, *Pillars of the Republic*, 76–77.

[4] William H. Watkins, *The White Architects of Black Education: Ideology and Power in America, 1865–1954* (New York: Teachers College Press, 2001) 11–12.

of understanding are debased, and rendered torpid by it. All the vices which are charged upon the negroes in the Southern colonies...such as Idleness, Treachery, Theft, and the like, are the genuine offspring of slavery...."[5] A critical understanding of the role racism played in the evolution of native Protestant republican ideology is of great import. I will examine the central role this ideological perspective has played in the educational experience of Blacks in the U.S. in general, and within the Christian Church in particular during the period under examination in this study.

A common belief among the architects of the new nation was that the survival of the American Republic depended on the morality of virtuous, propertied, industrious, and intelligent yeomen. Yeomen and citizens were seen as the embodiment of virtue among republican thinkers. Republicanism was deemed to be among the highest moral social systems. To survive, it needed a system of education to foster the moral qualities of individuals. John Pierce, who served as Michigan's superintendent of schools between 1836 and 1841, underscored the critical relationship between education, virtue, and republicanism. In 1837 Pierce wrote, "Generally speaking, the child undereducated in knowledge and virtue is educated in the school of depravity. And what is true of the individual is true of the community."[6] Virtue was understood to mean a citizen of the new nation who exercised self-control, self-sacrifice, and restraint, and was industrious and moral. American education had as its central purpose to produce such citizens.

The purpose of education in this new nation would be to secure both freedom and order in the new democratic and republican government. According to Lawrence Cremin, the aim of the founding fathers concerning American education was (1) relative to the form of government; (2) a truly American form; (3) useful and aimed at improving human condition; and (4) exemplary because it would teach the world liberty and learning. The founding fathers believed that the

---

[5] Ronald T. Takaki, *Iron Cages: Race and Culture in Nineteenth Century America* (London: Athlone Press, 1980) 29; Benjamin Rush, "Address to the Inhabitants of the British Settlements in American upon Slave-Keeping," in Takaki, *Iron Cages*, 29.

[6] Quoted in Cremin, *American Education*, 141; Kaestle, *Pillars of the Republic*, 79–81.

republican experiment would be emulated by the world, and in the words of Thomas Jefferson, would "meliorate the condition of the human race." An American education meant it would be purged of monarchial forms and would raise an empire that would have redemptive implications for the world.[7]

Religion and Schooling

Scottish philosophy rooted in realism had a tremendous impact on American education in the nineteenth century. As we shall see in chapter 4, given the Scottish heritage of two of the primary founders of the Disciples of Christ, this philosophical tradition would prove to be influential in shaping and informing their educational mission among African Americans.

A dominant text used by the early reformers was William Paley's *The Principles of Moral and Political Philosophy*, which was published in 1785. According to Cremin, Paley's manuscript was a "bland utilitarian view in the context of nonsectarian New Testament Christianity." In 1835, Paley's book was replaced, in terms of influence, by *The Elements of Morals and Science* written by the Baptist minister Francis Wayland. This book was also rooted in the Scottish tradition. Scottish philosophy was more liberating than constraining. It provided a brand of Enlightenment thinking that was more acceptable to many Christian thinkers.[8] Understanding the relationship between native Protestant ideology and republicanism, and its impact on the purpose and function of schooling, is critical and deserves further delineation.

During the first quarter of the nineteenth century, Unitarianism gained substantial influence among the colonies in the Northeast. William Channing, an influential American thinker and a Unitarian pastor, provided a theological and philosophical bridge between faith and reason. Rightly comparing Channing's approach to Christianity with that of John Locke's, Cremin writes, "In formulations reminiscent of Locke's *Essay Concerning Human Understanding* and *The Reasonableness of Christianity*, Channing told Americans that they could

---

[7] Cremin, *American Education*, 1–3.
[8] Ibid., 27–28.

determine the essentials of Christianity from an attentive and unbiased search of Scripture and that they would find nothing essential to Christianity contrary to reason."[9]

This understanding of the relationship between God and humankind had a profound impact on the concept of education and its purpose. For Channing, God is benevolent and humankind at its core is just and would facilitate human progress toward improvement. As a Unitarian, Channing believed in the "goodness of God and the dignity of every human being"—a belief that informed the Unitarian belief in universal salvation. The education of the child was not only the responsibility of the parents; all of creation would play a role in this process. Cremin articulates the role and purpose of education from Channing's perspective this way:

> The purpose of that education was to energize the child, to set in motion a lifelong effort toward self-culture, or the harmonious growth and cultivation of all the human faculties in the direction of their divine manifestations. Insofar as the teacher had responsibility for assisting and encouraging such effort and the knowledge and ability to do so, he was entitled to the highest possible respect from society—his office being "the noblest on earth," more important even than the minister's or the statesman's.[10]

A Calvinist brand of Protestantism dominated the Northern colonies.[11] They stressed reading of the Bible and education as being paramount for salvation. Lyman Beecher, a prominent Congre-

---

[9] Ibid., 31.

[10] Ibid., 32.

[11] "Calvinism," named after John Calvin, is a Protestant theological doctrine that emphasizes the sovereignty of God and is characterized most notably for tenants such as predestination or election, absolute depravity, limited atonement, the irresistible power of God's grace, and the perseverance of the saints. For an expanded examination of Calvinism, especially its expression in North America, see Aliki Barnstone, Michael T. Manson, and Carol J. Singley, eds., *Calvinist Roots of the Modern Era* (Hanover: University Press of New England, 1997); and Victor B. Howard, *Conscience and Slavery: The Evangelistic Calvinist Domestic Missions, 1837–1861* (Kent: Kent State University Press, 1990).

gationalist preacher and president of Lane College, declared war on Unitarianism. As a Calvinist, Beecher believed God was just and humankind was corrupt at its core. God was sovereign, and God would accomplish human progress in and through the new Republic. Beecher published two rather controversial sermons in 1832 that reflect the millennialist attitudes of his time and that would have some influence on education reform for the new Republic.[12] In the first sermon, *A Plea for the West*, Beecher asserted that the millennium would commence in America. By divine providence, the U.S. would lead the world to moral and political emancipation. The primary battlefield would be in the West and the focus of the battle would be whether or not the "sons" of the West would be educated "for the purposes of superstition, or evangelical light; of despotism, or liberty." Beecher would argue that the education of the nation was the most important work of all.[13]

In the second sermon, *A Plea for the Colleges*, Beecher argued for the need to develop literary colleges to prepare Americans to fulfill their role in ushering in the millennium. The purpose of educating institutions was to move an "unsubdued spirit of republican independence." The unsubdued spirit could overthrow law and authority. For Beecher, there was a need to reverse this tendency by training a new generation to subordinate this spirit to the rule of law; only then would freedom flourish.

Beecher's concern about the sociopolitical consequences of an "unsubdued spirit" reflects the broader concerns of Northern and Southern Whites. This concern was elevated during the years following the Civil War because the movement of Blacks was no longer

---

[12] "Millennialism" in the Protestant context has to do with a belief that prophecy, as written in the book of Revelation in the Bible, will be fulfilled with an earthly 1,000-year period of universal peace and the triumph of those who are righteous before God. "Pre-Millennialist" Christians believe this period will occur prior to the second coming of Christ, while "Post-Millennialist" Christians believe that the second coming of Christ will be followed by this period. For an expanded elucidation of this doctrine see F. L. Cross and E. A. Livingstone, eds., *The Oxford Dictionary of the Christian Church* (Oxford: Oxford University Press, 1985) 916; and Van A. Harvey, *A Handbook of Theological Terms* (New York: Collier Books, 1964) 150–51.

[13] Cremin, *American Education*, 37.

controlled by chattel enslavement. This concern would prove to be a significant, if not the primary, motivating factor in the provision of schooling for Blacks by Whites in the Christian Church. I will expand upon this point in chapter 5.

Other religious or theological perspectives that were influential during the early national period include Charles Finney's emphasis on human agency, Thomas Paine's deism as articulated in his *Common Sense*, and Horace Bushnell's *Discourse on Christian Nurture*. Bushnell's manuscript had a profound impact on Christian education pedagogy. It was reissued twice, once in 1847, and again in 1861 (under the title *Christian Nurture*), after its initial publication in 1845. Bushnell viewed the household as central in the education of the child. It was critical to see and understand the relationship between the individual child and those who nurtured the child. For Bushnell, a person is not innately good or depraved (sinful), rather, "virtue and depravity is tied to the relation of parent and child." He warned against barbarism as a major threat to republicanism, and education was seen as the best defense against this threat.[14] Technology, such as railroads and the telegraph, and ministerial leadership were deemed as critical in facilitating education through schools and colleges. According to Bushnell, it was loyalty that would be the saving point for the new nation. Likewise, education would play an indispensable role in fostering such loyalty in its citizens.

Samuel Stanhope Smith recognized the efficacy of a common system of schooling in shaping the new Republic. Smith, who was more centrist in his thinking, served as president of the College of New Jersey (Princeton) from 1795 to 1812. He argued that "an enlightened people cannot easily be enslaved." He also argued for "common education for the entire citizenry." Further, he argued for the "cultivation for sublime sciences," especially physics and chemistry, and for liberal arts. Smith, according to Cremin, was convinced of the significance of education. He saw it "as the enterprise par excellence for the formation of human personality and the shaping of national character." As an educator and former college president, Smith's

---

[14] Ibid., 33–35.

influence was apparently broad as some of his former students would go
on to lead institutions such as the University of Pennsylvania and the
University of North Carolina.[15]

Clearly, within the context of the early national period, Protestant
expressions of Christianity and republicanism were practically
synonymous and were associated with economic growth, material
accumulation (each buttressed by a system of enslaved labor), and
western expansionism. Throughout his career, Benjamin Rush asserted
that republicanism and Christianity were interwoven. In his proposed
design for a unified system of education in Pennsylvania, nurturing
students in the doctrine of the New Testament would be a central
component of the curriculum in the lower levels. Addressing this issue
in 1806, Rush argued that without republicanism and Christianity as
core values of education, "there can be no virtue, and without virtue
there can be no liberty, and liberty is the object and life of all
republican governments."[16] In 1841, Catherine Beecher, eldest
daughter of Lyman Beecher who authored several textbooks on
domestic economy, would express a similar belief that was common
among her contemporaries when she wrote, "The principles of
democracy are identical with the principles of Christianity."[17]

In the minds of the Republic's founding fathers and early
reformers, God's salvific plan was being ushered in through Protestant
Christianity and American expansionism. This thinking was tied to the
Protestant doctrinal belief in the second coming of Christ. America saw
itself playing the lead supporting actor, if not the lead itself, on the
stage of the millennial event. An example of this millennial attitude and
thinking is provided again by Benjamin Rush who stated, "I was
animated constantly by a belief that I was acting for the benefit of the

---

[15] Ibid., 24–26.
[16] Benjamin Rush, *Essays, Literary, Moral and Philosophical*, 2nd ed. (Philadelphia:
Thomas and William Bradford, 1806) 8, quoted in Cremin, *American Education*,
118–19.
[17] Catherine Beecher, *A Treatise of Domestic Economy* (New York: Harper and
Brothers, 1841) 25, quoted in Kaestle, *Pillars of the Republic*, 93.

whole world, and of future ages by assisting in the formation of new means of political order and general happiness."[18]

In order fully to play its role in the building of a kingdom on earth, America needed to educate her citizens. Her churches played a role that went far beyond offering theological treatises of the importance of education. By the first quarter of the nineteenth century, Presbyterians developed a parochial school system that grew to 100 schools in 26 states. Some church-related schools began to attract advanced students and became academies or colleges. The Evangelical Lutheran Synod in Ohio, Missouri, and in other states were also successful in establishing schools. In part, their success was because of their predominantly German-American constituency. They had to provide continuity of language and culture between the home and the school. Generally speaking, common schools did not meet this need—although there were exceptions. The language and culture of Presbyterians were more consistent with that of the common schools; therefore, this was not an issue.[19]

Concerning the role of the church in the evolution of formal schooling in the early national period, Andy Green writes, "Quakers, Presbyterians, Baptists, Mennonites, Lutherans, and Moravians set up schools in abundance. It was not until the mid-eighteenth century that this educational sectarianism began to break down because of the lack of financial resources. Schooling gradually became more secular." [20] The Catholic Church is perhaps the most successful sectarian movement in terms of the survivability of a complete system of primary, secondary, and higher educational institutions. Ironically, the cause of their rise is related to the decline of Protestant schools. The evolution of the

---

[18] Cremin, *American Education*, 114.

[19] Ibid., 55–56.

[20] Green, *Education and State Formation*, 177. For further examination on the evolution of Catholic schooling in the U.S. see John L. Elias, *A History of Christian Education: Protestant, Catholic, and Orthodox Perspectives* (Malabar FL.: Krieger Publishing Co., 2002) 191–222; Edward J. Power, *Religion and the Public Schools in 19th Century America: The Contribution of Orestes A. Brownson* (New York: Paulist Press, 1996) 126–52; and Neil G. McCluskey, *Catholic Education in America: A Documentary History* (New York: Bureau of Publications Teachers College, Columbia University, 1964).

Catholic system is in large part due to its response to the rise of public, state-supported, universal, common school systems that espoused Protestant ideology. Protestant ideology encouraged reading of the Bible and was anti-Catholic in many ways. Unable to secure state support that was ostensibly funding only non-sectarian schooling, the Catholic Church began a massive effort to develop a separate system of education.

As we shall see in chapter 4, the Christian Church, through its founders, traces its ecclesiastical antecedents to the Presbyterian and Separate Baptist traditions. The philosophical and theological influence these traditions have on the Disciples' educational mission is significant and will be examined.

Schooling and the Reproduction of Social Class

From its inception, stratification based on social and economic class existed in the U.S. and was pervasive throughout the new Republic. Not only was formal schooling directly influenced by social stratification; it also served to perpetuate and sustain it. In the early Republic, the quality of education attained by children was partly affected by which of the relatively diverse options their parents could afford or by their racial and/or gender classification.

Thomas Jefferson, a strong advocate for state-sponsored education, did not advocate for the same type of education for all people, and for some he didn't advocate for education at all. In a letter to his nephew Peter Carr, Jefferson cited two class distinctions, the *laboring* and the *learned*. The former would be provided with general education that was accessible to all Whites, and the latter would be provided "professional schools" or academies of higher learning. The learned were those who were deemed to be "headed towards positions of political, social, and intellectual leadership."[21]

As we have already stated, the founding fathers believed that for republicanism to survive, an intelligent yeomanry was needed. Daniel Webster, Benjamin Rush, Jefferson, and others believed an organized

---

[21] Ibid., 48; Cremin, *American Education*, 109.

and state-financed system of education was needed to create and reproduce the virtuous citizenry needed to build, sustain, and expand the Republic. The purpose of education, though not explicitly articulated by the early reformers, was to establish, sustain, protect, and expand the domination of white Anglo-Saxon Protestant male socioeconomic and political hegemony. This was an ostensibly republican and Christian form of capitalism. Virtue was to be understood and accepted only to the extent that it did not threaten to disturb the dominant class and racial stratification of society. Neither was it to disturb the existent power relations within the social framework of the new Republic.

Despite the egalitarian and humanistic rhetoric of the founding fathers and early education reformers, there existed an enormous gap between the ideas of native Protestant republican ideology and the extent to which formal schooling benefited, or failed to benefit, the constituents it purported to serve. To make this point, Samuel Bowles and Herbert Gintis argue, "The popular objectives, slogans, and perspectives of reform movements have often imparted to the education system an enduring veneer of egalitarian and humanitarian ideology, while the highly selective implementation of reforms has tended to preserve the role of schooling in the perpetuation of economic order."[22]

Supposedly, one of the primary attributes of a republican democratic form of education was that its function would be antithetical to a monarchial form that fixed "each class of citizenry to its proper place in the social order." Like a monarchial-influenced system, the emerging system of education in the early national period would in fact "fix" certain classes or groups within the society to a particular place in the social order. When examining the relationships between landowners and business elites and poor Whites, between men and women, Whites and Blacks, and other racial/ethnic groups, it becomes clear that education and access to quality and diverse forms of schooling were never created to challenge structures that perpetuate oppressive power relations. Bowles and Gintis make this point when they write,

---

[22] Samuel Bowles and Herbert Gintis, *Schooling in Capitalist America: Educational Reform and the Contradictions of Economic Life* (New York: Basic Books, 1977) 152.

The educational system serves—through the correspondence of its social relation with those of economic life—to reproduce economic inequality and to distort personal development. Thus under corporate capitalism, the objectives of liberal educational reform are contradictory: It is precisely because of its role as producer of an alienated and stratified labor force that the educational system has developed its repressive and unequal structure. In the history of U.S. education, it is the integrative function which has dominated the purpose of schooling, to the detriment of the other liberal objectives.[23]

In chapter 5, I will address the almost exclusive use of industrial and vocational forms of education for African Americans by Whites within the Christian Church. I will also address their staunch opposition toward the provision of other forms of schooling such as classical and higher learning for Blacks. Examination of the theology and philosophy that informed particular approaches to schooling for Blacks will provide an excellent example of how education is intentionally used as a method of social stratification.

Gender and Schooling

Prior to the Civil War, the role of white women in schooling as teacher and student, and to a much lesser extent, free black women, evolved quite considerably.[24] In large part, this was the result of a response to the evolving needs of the new Republic. Like free and enslaved Africans, girls and women benefited from the Protestant belief that salvation was dependent, in part, on one's ability to read the Bible. One of the consequences of this belief was access to literacy training for girls and women who otherwise may have remained illiterate during

---

[23] Ibid., 48.

[24] A note of clarification may be helpful concerning the use of the terms "men" and "women." Unless otherwise noted, use of the terms "men" and "women" throughout text are in reference to white men and white women. The massive socioeconomic and political disparities between black men and women and their white counterparts during the period under examination resulted in radically different existential realties for these groups, thus making this clarification necessary.

this period. According to Elisabeth Hansot and David Tyack, early public schools were almost exclusively for men. Men were taught to read and write while women were taught only to read. During the colonial period, the father was considered the "governor" of the household. He had the primary responsibility for literacy development and the teaching of Christian virtues for all family members. Hansot and Tyack point out that the father "was not only the head of the family but also usually more literate than the mother." They also postulate that the shift from male to female responsibility for literacy and moral development may have been caused by a decline in male church membership. As church membership became more "feminized," pastors began to emphasize women's role in the moral development of children because they were the ones in church.[25]

Girls were not allowed to attend Latin grammar schools that were for those preparing for university study. They were also not allowed to attend the legally mandated district schools in certain parts of the Northeast. Women did attend what was known as "dame" schools. According to Hansot and Tyack, one of the primary functions of these schools was "to prepare boys for entry into the district grammar school. They started boys on their ABC's and gave girls the basic literacy they would need to fulfill their religious and family duties." Some of the more affluent families sent their girls to private "venture" schools.[26] Still other families, those who could afford it, sent their daughters to Europe as a means to overcome the educational barriers for women in the early Republic. According to Maxine Schwartz Seller, women with means often took great risks in an effort to attain formal schooling. "Women crossed borders," writes Seller, "for educational reasons even when travel was uncomfortable and dangerous. Wealthy colonial families sent daughters to Europe to receive education not available at home."[27]

---

[25] Elisabeth Hansot and David Tyack, *Learning Together: A History of Coeducation in American Schools* (New Haven: Yale University Press, 1990) 15–16.

[26] Ibid., 19.

[27] Maxine Schwartz Seller, "Boundaries, Bridges, and the History of Education," *History of Education Quarterly*, 31/2 (Summer 1991): 197. For an examination of the experience of white women in the colonial period, and how this topic has been

Kaestle puts forth two arguments to explain why support for educating women occurred during the early national period: (1) during that period, even though men assumed they were intellectually superior to women, it was generally believed women were just as capable as men to receive a common school education; and (2) women needed a good education in order to be effective as wives and mothers. Benjamin Rush argued for the importance of educating women in his monograph *Thoughts Upon Female Education* published in 1787. Rush argued that "The equal share that every citizen has in the liberty and the possible share they have in the government of our country makes it necessary that our ladies should be qualified to a certain degree, by a particular and suitable education, to concur in instructing their sons in the principles of liberty and government."[28]

Thomas Jefferson wanted his daughters to be educated. According to Cremin, in 1818, Jefferson wrote to Nathaniel Burwell, acknowledging "that he never thought systematically about the education of females, although he did comment on the advantages of teaching them dancing, drawing, music, household economy, French literature, and alerting them to the danger of novels." Acting on the desire for his daughters to receive an education, Jefferson sent Marie and Martha Jefferson to attend a convent school in France.[29] Cremin is more than appreciative of Jefferson's contribution to common schooling in the U.S., but writes, "Granted [Jefferson's] abiding concern with the education of people, he defined the people in political terms—as free white males."[30]

As we have stated, women were educated to fulfill effectively their roles as wives, mothers, and homemakers. Given the broader republican concern in the development of virtuous and moral individuals (white men), the role of women in the nurture of "a virtuous generation" took on increased significance. Describing the

---

treated by historians, see Mary Beth Norton, "The Evolution of White Women's Experience in Early America," *The American Historical Review* 89/3 (June 1984): 593–619.

[28] Benjamin Rush quoted in Kaestle, *Pillars of the Republic*, 27–28.

[29] Seller, "Boundaries, Bridges, and the History of Education," 197–98.

[30] Cremin, *American Education*, 113–14.

paternalistic view of the evolving role of women in shaping the new Republic during the national period, Kaestle writes,

> As wives they were to create an evening sanctuary from the busy, corrupt, daytime world their husband inhabited. As homemakers they were to manage a frugal and healthy household, according to the latest knowledge of domestic science. As mothers they were to nurture and instruct children to make a virtuous new generation for the perilous society. The concepts of the home as sanctuary and the wife as domestic scientist were substantially new, and the emphasis placed on childrearing became more emphatic after 1830, with the role assigned more strictly and consistently to women.[31]

This growing emphasis on the role of women contributed significantly in opening new opportunities for them to become teachers, which paved the way to increased access to schooling.

According to Kaestle, school curriculum for girls emphasized the development of domestic skills. Such limited curricular options for women existed not because of a presupposition of intellectual inferiority, but because of a male-dominated society. Some education reformers such as Horace Mann argued for women to receive every educational opportunity afforded to men. Others, including women, significantly contributed to the entrenchment of the domestic function of women and the influence this role had on their education and opportunities for schooling. One such influential writer was the aforementioned Catherine Beecher. Commenting on Beecher's influence, Cremin writes, "[Catherine Beecher] wrote a whole series of textbooks and manuals designed to instruct the new American woman in her responsibilities. The pious mother, she believed, could do good will only as the instructed mother, steeped in wisdom about health, cookery, clothing, the economy of time, the care of the sick, and the management of the household—in short, in the wisdom of domestic economy."[32]

---

[31] Kaestle, *Pillars of the Republic*, 84.
[32] Cremin, *American Education*, 65.

During the early national period, there was significant opposition at the idea of using public funds for the education of girls. This did not have anything to do with a fundamental opposition to female education. Rather, it had more to do with issues of class and economics. According to Hansot and Tyack, this opposition had to do with the fact that "elite families could prepare their sons for college at public expense in the Latin grammar schools, while only those families who could afford to pay both private tuition and the local poll tax could send their daughters to private schools."[33]

Over time teaching opportunities became more and more available for women. Michael Katz believes this shift is directly related to shifts in the economy and demography of urban areas. Increased population in urban areas caused increased demand for teachers. This resulted in a financial crunch on local communities. Schools began hiring women in greater numbers "because towns paid them half as much as men, who, in an era of expanding commercial and industrial opportunity, increasingly had before them job prospects more attractive than teaching. By feminizing its teaching force, a town could double its school places or extend the length of the school year and hold its salary roughly constant." In addition to these causes for the "feminization of teaching," Katz adds, "As the ideology of domesticity implied, the moral and spiritual role assigned to women not only justified but also mandated their entrance into classrooms as surrogate mothers." Many believed the schools should be an extension of the home, and presided over by "wise and loving mothers."[34]

It's important to note here that an increased opportunity for women to teach during this period does not translate into increased power. On the contrary, increased teaching opportunities were joined by a decline in power by women in the enterprise of formal schooling. This a point made by Sally Schwager.

A decline in the status of women educators is, however, equally widespread in the larger context of women's educational

---

[33] Hansot and Tyack, *Learning Together*, 22–23.
[34] Michael Katz, *Restructuring American Education* (Cambridge: Harvard University Press, 1987) 12.

history.... The movement of women teachers from colonial dame and subscription schools and from the early academies into public school teaching by the mid-nineteenth century represented a decline in women's authority over the profession even though women's opportunities increased numerically. This pattern was repeated across regions as urban school systems came to dominate the American landscape, and it appeared again as women moved into the university.[35]

The increased access women had to schooling, and their evolving role as transmitters of native Protestant republican ideology, had its first impact at home. This access was not for their personal benefit of liberty, freedom and/or equality, but for their utility with regard to the reproduction of the dominant ideology within young boys and men.

As I have illustrated above, for free or enslaved Africans in the antebellum South, gender differentiation was of little consequence relative to having access to schooling. While there were exceptions, access to formal schooling below the Mason-Dixon Line, whether one was male or female, enslaved or free, was for all practical intent and purposes nonexistent. It is imperative, however, that I mention another form of education in which black women played a most crucial role. Within communities of enslaved Africans an informal system of education existed that must not be overlooked or undervalued. African women transmitted values, beliefs, and norms of enslaved Africans in their struggle to survive the horrors of chattel enslavement. This transmission of knowledge occurred primarily within the family—both nuclear and extended. The extended family often included people who were not biologically related.

More often than not, as it was with her counterpart in the white community, it was the mother who played the principal role in this educational process because she had the primary responsibility of rearing children. According to Thomas Webber, the mother facilitated the "transmission of religious beliefs, a longing for freedom, a desire to learn, a way of viewing and dealing with white people, and a sense of

---

[35] Sally S. Chwager, "Educating Women in America," *Reconstructing the Academy* 12/2 (Winter 1987): 336.

identification and solidarity with the other members of the quarter community [the living quarters or community of enslaved Africans]."[36] Stories also played an important role in the education of the children. The mother would gather the children to tell them "the stories of Africa, and the folklore and songs of the quarter community which she had learned from her own parents or grandparents."[37] Unlike her counterpart in the white community, black women carried out their role as "educator" of children within the quarter community while dealing with the unimaginable and often brutally violent demands—including rape—that were placed upon them under slavery. Peter Wood attempts to give us a glimpse of the complexity of black women's reality on the plantation. He writes,

> Black women often worked in the fields, as many of them had done in Africa, but they also assumed primary responsibility for a great deal of domestic labor. House servants were forced to cook and clean, wash and press, sew and mend, to suit the demands of their colonial mistress. With varying degrees of oversight, a plantation cook handled all aspects of food preparation, from tending the garden or visiting the town market to washing the dishes and throwing leftovers to the pigs. Indeed, when it came time to slaughter the hogs and cure their meat, she supervised that complex process as well. Day after day, year after year, she was obliged to balance the endless demands of the white household and the ongoing needs of her own family. Nothing illustrates this conflict more dramatically than the fact that the mother of a black infant was sometimes required to stop suckling her own baby and to serve instead as the wet nurse to a newborn child in the family of the master.[38]

The curricular and ideological patterns that shaped and informed schooling for women prior to the Civil War outlined here would be

---

[36] Webber, *Deep Like the River*, 160–61.

[37] Ibid., 163.

[38] Peter H. Wood, "Strange New Land: 1619–1776," in Robin D. G. Kelley and Earl Lewis, eds., *To Make Our World Anew: A History of African Americans* (London: Oxford University Press, 2000) 80.

replicated for black women attending schools established by the Christian Church. As we shall see in chapters 5 and 6, with the exception of schools whose purpose was to train male clergy, black women had access to the same institutions as men, but were often limited to taking specific courses that prepared them as homemakers, domestic servants, or teachers. Unlike Whites, at schools whose curriculum reflected the Christian Church's opposition to higher learning for Blacks, black men had few other options women could not access.

Consolidation, Bureaucratization, and Opposition

In response to changes in the market economy that were partly ignited by technological advances in the modes of production, major shifts in the overt purpose, organization, and administration of education took place.[39] The purpose of education shifted from an emphasis on the function of education being moral formation, to an education that developed a labor force to support capitalist production. According to Bowles and Gintis, this shift occurred between 1820 and 1860. In terms of organization and administration, schools moved from local, decentralized institutions often run by non-professionals to centrally controlled, highly bureaucratized systems of education that were increasingly being run by professionals and becoming more and more disconnected from the communities they served.

During the late eighteenth and early nineteenth centuries, dramatic socioeconomic developments would impact schooling and school reform in a fairly profound manner. According to Bowles and Gintis, during this period,

> Commerce expanded dramatically.... The value of foreign trade increased four-fold. Larger commercial interest profited from the expansion of trade, amassed substantial concentrations of capital, and sought new arenas for profitable investment.

---

[39] I refer to the "overt purpose" of education because it is not clear that the purpose of education in the new Republic from the beginning did not have as one of its primary functions the maintenance and expansion of a capitalist market economy, which is a key component of native Protestant republican ideology.

Increasingly capital was used for the direct employment of labor in production rather than remaining confined to the buying and selling of commodities and related commercial activities. The expansion of capitalist production, particularly the factory system as well as the continuing concentration of commercial capital, undermined the role of the family as the major unit of both child-rearing and production.[40]

These changes in production had a major impact on social relations in rural and urban settings, and, of course, on the direction of school reform. Commenting on the impact of industrialization on family and village life, Tyack writes,

As village patterns merged into urbanism as a way of life, factories and counting houses split the place of work from the home; impersonal and codified roles structured relationships in organizations, replacing diffuse and personal role relationships familiar in the village; the jack-of-all-trades of the rural community came to perform specialized tasks in the city; the older reliance on tradition and folkways as guides to belief and conduct shifted as mass media provided new sources of information and norms of behavior and as science became a pervasive source of authority; people increasingly defined themselves as members of occupational groups—teachers, salesmen, engineers—as they became aware of common interest that transcended allegiance to particular communities, thus constituting what Robert Wiebe calls "the new middle-class."[41]

Most contemporary historians of American education agree that industrialization and urbanization of the mid-nineteenth century served as a primary catalyst to speed up the process of consolidating the organization and administration of common schools. Cities, responding to rapid increases in population, led the way in developing a more organized society. The influx of ethnically diverse populations in urban areas necessitated the need to organize services such as public health,

---

[40] Bowles and Gintis, *Schooling in Capitalist America*, 157.
[41] Tyack, *The One Best System*, 5–6.

education, and law enforcement in a more systematic manner. The maintenance of order, the ongoing development of a national consciousness, and the development of a common culture in the midst of increasing diversity presented major challenges for reformers. Green states the problem this way: "The great problem for modern societies lay in the creation of a collective morality under new social conditions. With the historical dissolution of segmented, communal societies, where social solidarity had depended on the immediacy of community and rigid subordination to tradition and collective consciousness, new forms of integration had to be located."[42] Such was the challenge brought on by industrialization and urbanization—both in terms of how the reformers responded, and how those in rural areas and homogeneous villages in large cities were impacted by the attempts of reformers.

In response to new technologies and modes of production, the function of schooling to influence moral formation began to decline and focused more on meeting the needs of industry. The bureaucratization of schooling became necessary in order to keep up with and support socioeconomic changes caused by industrialization and urbanization. "Schooling was essential," writes Tyack, "because it adapted people to new disciplines and incentives of urban-industrial order and supplied the 'directive intelligence' and specialist required in complex society."[43]

Tyack states that reformers were seeking to create "the one best system" that would effectively respond to the challenges of the nation toward the end of the nineteenth century. This system should reflect the organization and efficiency evident in the industrial urban settings, i.e., operate like a well-run factory. This system should have a clear chain of command, division of labor, use of technology, punctuality, a regularized set of procedures, clearly established lines of communication, set standards for teachers' training, pedagogy, use of texts, curriculum, and admission and performance standards for everyone involved in the system, including administrators, teachers, and students. Tyack writes that "efficiency, rationality, continuity,

---

[42] Green, *Education and State Formation*, 36
[43] Tyack, *The One Best System*, 29.

precision, and impartiality became watchwords of the consolidators. In short, they tried to create a more bureaucratic system."[44] In addition to the conditions caused by industrialization, Kaestle states that reformers were also responding to a lack of uniformity in schooling, penurious district control, poor facilities, irregular attendance, short school terms, poorly trained teachers, insufficient supervision, and indifferent parental support.[45]

The centralization of schools was led by a coalition of "urban elites" such as business and professional men, university presidents and professors, and progressive school superintendents. One of the key points that helped the reformers succeed in consolidating control over schools was the broad consensus and cohesiveness of this group from early on in the reform process. "Although the reformers' specific proposals," writes Kaestle, "about centralized supervision, tax support, teacher training, and consolidated school districts met considerable resistance, the educational reform cause benefited in general from widespread consensus about the importance of common schooling."[46] Bowles and Gintis argue that reformers' success in realizing consolidation was due in part to the interests of larger property-owning elites who were served by the "teachers, lawyers, doctors, and other professionals" who made up the primary force of the consolidation movement.[47]

Opposition to consolidation and centralization came from several directions; they were a heterogeneous group but failed to achieve the kind of cohesiveness and ideological consensus that existed among the reformers. According to Green, those opposing consolidation "included German Lutherans and Mennonites who wished to maintain their cultural identity and favored separate schooling; Catholics who objected to Protestant hegemony and anti-Irish prejudice in public schools; and some free Blacks who argued that separate schooling was preferable to racism and low teacher expectations of black pupils in public schools."

---

[44] Ibid., 28–29.
[45] Kaestle, *Pillars of the Republic*, 107.
[46] Ibid.
[47] Bowles and Gintis, *Schooling in Capitalist America*, 162.

Other groups opposing reform included "private school proprietors, and groups suspicious of reform and opposed to increased taxation."[48]

Catholic and Jewish immigrants led the attack on religion in public schools. This was primarily because of the predominance of Protestant ideology in public schools, and the inculcation of these values that tended to be anti-Semitic and anti-Catholic. These groups opposed consolidation in an effort to maintain control of their children's school experience. This would provide children with congruency between the culture of the home and that of the classroom. For them it was a struggle for the survival of their languages and longstanding values and traditions.

Consolidation meant loss of power for those who wielded it within local decentralized schools. Laymen who occupied leadership positions in decentralized systems presented some of the most stringent challenges for reformers. According to Tyack, "Laymen often retained the very powers that schoolmen sought." Superintendents were seen as meddling politicians by localized laymen, often resulting in undermining the extent of the superintendent's authority or realm of influence in hiring or shaping curriculum.[49]

Prior to 1865, the form and function of schooling that emerged largely in the Northeast, and to a much lesser extent in the South, would have a profound influence on the form and function of schools associated with the Christian Church for Freedpeople. The primary function of schooling was to advance capitalist production and the reproduction of native Protestant republican ideology. By extension, this function enabled the maintenance of the position of power and dominance enjoyed by white males, and to a lesser extent certain privileges enjoyed by white women. The methods engaged to organize and administer schools and set educational standards for teachers and administrators would all prove to be highly influential in the establishment and functioning of schools for Blacks affiliated with the Christian Church. Schools established and controlled by white Disciples or those established by Blacks and eventually controlled by

---

[48] Green, *Education and State Formation*, 191.
[49] Tyack, *The One Best System*, 78–79.

Whites, however, would not espouse curricula and pedagogical methodologies designed to facilitate self-determination for black people and the realization of their greatest potential. I will demonstrate in chapters 6 and 7 how white-controlled schools for Blacks associated with the Disciples of Christ were designed to keep black people in a subordinated and controlled socioeconomic and political station in the US. Indeed, black and white Disciples education reformers held very different views on the form and function of schooling for Blacks. These differences lay at the center of a growing conflict and tension within this Protestant movement known as the Christian Church (Disciples of Christ).

3

SCHOOLING, RACE, AND THE EDUCATION OF BLACKS IN THE UNITED STATES PRIOR TO 1865

Black people continually attempted unorthodox forms of resistance, and were rewarded with even more unorthodox punishment.... According to black tradition, it was not unusual for rural Blacks to have fingers or hands cut off, if they were caught in defiance of anti-literacy laws.... Unorthodox though it may have been, this was an unmistakable form of resistance: at its simplest level, a challenge to white laws and white men; at its best, a forceful personal movement toward self-determination and independence of mind. Collectively, this secret learning represented a people's thrust toward new self-definitions, toward the creative transformation of culture.[1]

In addition to the broader philosophical and ideological thinking that shaped education prior to 1865 as addressed in chapter 2, any discussion or analysis of this subject must be accompanied by an understanding of how the concept of *race* shaped and informed the development of schooling in the U.S. It is equally necessary for the reader to understand the broader educational experience of black people, enslaved and free, prior to 1865.

The above quote by Vincent Harding crystallizes the dualistic nature of the resistance that surrounded the struggle of enslaved and free Africans to attain literacy and schooling. On one hand was the "unorthodox" resistance toward chattel enslavement and anti-literacy

---

[1] Vincent Harding, *There Is a River: The Black Struggle for Freedom in America* (New York: Harcourt Brace Jovanovich, 1992 [1982]) 163.

laws. This took the form of black men and women struggling to secure the secrets of letters they believed to be the key to a more fruitful and abundant life both on earth and after death. On the other hand was the equally unorthodox resistance of Whites who acted out their vehement opposition to literacy development among Blacks. Many Whites, especially those among the planter elite of the South, were convinced that literacy development among enslaved Africans presented a direct threat to their ability to maintain an established system of power relations. This system was characterized by white male domination and an agrarian system of production whose profit margin and expansion depended upon a system of enslaved labor.

In the years following the Civil War, Blacks viewed literacy and schooling as indispensable and essential tools of resistance in their struggle for liberation. Heather Williams makes this point when she writes,

> In slavery, the very act of learning to read had been a secret form of resistance, but in its aftermath, Freedpeople transformed the act of becoming literate from a clandestine occurrence into one of life's necessities. Secret readings of news papers had kept enslaved people informed of political debates whose outcomes could determine their fates. Writing a pass had allowed slaves to move about without owner's knowledge.... Literacy became central to the project of freedom and citizenship because African Americans realized as literate people, they would be better able to negotiate in a world dominated by educated Whites.[2]

In order to achieve any level of appreciation of the intense zeal with which black people longed for schooling in the years following the Civil War, their experience regarding schooling prior to 1865 must first be examined.

---

[2] Heather A. D. Williams, "Self-Taught: The Role of African Americans in Educating the Freedpeople, 1861–1871," Ph.D. diss., Yale University, 2002, 12, 15.

The Northern Experience

Ideological formations that shaped educational philosophy in the North and the South were laden with ontological presuppositions of the innate inferiority of people of color in general, and people of African descent in particular. Such thinking was reinforced by Protestant theological perspectives that were informed by an approach to biblical interpretation aimed at appropriating its message in a way that protected and advanced the socioeconomic and political interests of the dominant group—as defined by this group. Whites interpreted the Bible to benefit themselves. They believed they were *the* inheritors of God's blessing, and conversely, Blacks were inheritors of God's curse, which for some explained and justified their state of involuntary servitude. A quote from Philip Schaff, an influential Reformed preacher and professor of Church History at Union Theological Seminary in New York, is representative of the type of thinking that thrived in nineteenth-century America. Writing in 1861, Schaff states that

> Ham, the father or Canaan, represents the idolatrous and servile race; Shem, the Israelites who worshipped Jehovah, the only true and living God; Japheth, those gentiles, who by their contact with Shem were brought to a knowledge of the true religion.... *Whether we connect with it or not, it is simply a fact which no one can deny, that the Negro to this day is a servant of servants in our midst.* Japheth, on the other hand, the progenitor of half the human race, who possesses a part of Asia and the whole of Europe, is still extending his posterity and territory in the westward course of empire, and holds Ham in bondage far away from his original home and final destination.[3]

---

[3] Philip Schaff, *Slavery and the Bible: A Tract for the Times* (Chambersbury PA: M. Kieffer and Co.'s Caloric Printing Press, 1861) 5–6, quoted in Sylvester A. Johnson, *The Myth of Ham in Nineteenth-Century American Christianity: Race, Heathens, and the People of God* (New York: Palgrave MacMillan, 2004) 39–41. The emphasis is Schaff's. For further examination of attempts at theological and biblical justification of chattel enslavement by Christians, see Joseph R. Washington, Jr., *Anti-Blackness in English Religion, 1500–1800* (New York: Edwin Mellen Press, 1985) 231–72.

Distorted anthropological designations by white males, of
themselves and others, supported by equally distorted biblical
interpretation, sought to solidify their position of power, justify chattel
enslavement, and preserve the subordinate sociopolitical position of
women. Theologically based racial and gender designations and
hierarchical categorizations of humanity, which would soon be
reinforced by "scientific formulations," were used to advance the
Western doctrines of "Manifest Destiny" and millennialism. The
rhetoric used by apologists for African colonization, and later the
foreign missionary enterprise, was replete with symbolism and the
language of "saving the savage and heathen" and Christianizing the
"cannibals of the savage dark continent of Africa." Countless black
Christians would embrace such thinking, which resulted in a self-
defeating paradox. Sylvester Johnson describes the paradoxical dilemma
this way:

> The same black Christians who spoke so heartily of Africa as
> "the fatherland" deplored native African religious forms and
> sought to stamp out "idolatrous" African worship. American
> Negroes who were Christian also believed, as did their white
> counterparts, that Africa was lost in spiritual darkness and that
> Africans had become uncivilized and backward because they did
> not worship the God of Christianity. Black American sentiment
> toward Africans, therefore, was ambivalent at best.... And
> although white religionists instigated the ideas of missionary
> conquest and Christian superiority, the rhetoric of Christiani-
> zation and spiritual uplift were quickly taken over by Negro
> Christians themselves.[4]

---

[4] Johnson, *Myth of Ham*, 74; also, for an excellent discussion on the origins of
racist biblical interpretation see Shawn Kelley, *Racializing Jesus: Race, Ideology and the
Formation of Modern Biblical Scholarship* (New York: Routledge, 2002). For a
discussion on the treatment of race in science see John P. Jackson, Jr., and Nadine M.
Weidman, *Race, Racism, and Science: Social Impact and Interaction* (Santa Barbara:
ABC-CLIO Publishers, 2004). Perhaps one of the most thorough examinations of
the evolution, use, and function of the concept of "race" is Scott L. Malcomson, *One
Drop of Blood: The American Misadventure of Race* (New York: Farrar, Straus and
Giroux, 2000).

Needless to say, biblical interpretation that attempted to support black bondage enjoyed popularity in the Southern church longer than it did in the North; Northerners, however, continued with their own formulations of racist biblical interpretation that shaped their philosophy for black education. Illustrating this point, Cremin writes,

> Whites in the North at every level of education did in fact repeat the litanies of savage origins, Biblical stigma, and biological inferiority. By contrast, however, some elements of the white community taught otherwise. Often the instruction was at best conflicting: The same teacher or preacher would assert the equality of all persons before God in one paragraph and the inferiority of the Negro before his fellow human being in another; or the teacher or preacher would assert the principle of equality and practice the behavior of inequality—even the Quakers maintained segregated schools in their meetings.[5]

As we shall see, the discourse among Whites within the Christian Church who were most active in shaping schooling for Blacks reflects both conservative and liberal perspectives. These perspectives reveal both theological and ontological views of Blacks. The discourse also includes their views on the type of schooling that should be provided for African Americans. In the case of the Disciples of Christ, I will demonstrate how conservative perspectives were influential in shaping the type of schooling provided for Blacks. There were some Whites, albeit a small minority, who did teach and practice true equality. Those who represented this liberal group of reformers were visible advocates of schooling for Blacks. They, however, had little, if any, substantive impact on the type of schooling supported by the wider church.

As previously mentioned, Thomas Jefferson and other founding fathers of the new Republic never intended for common schooling to be fully accessible or optimally beneficial to anyone other than white males. Jefferson's 1779 Bill for the More General Diffusion of Knowledge was a provision of education for free white children only.

---

[5] Lawrence Cremin, *American Education: The National Experience, 1783–1876* (New York: Harper & Row, 1980) 229–30.

The increasing numbers of immigrants were also of great concern to the leaders of the Republic. It was believed that to galvanize the young Republic, an ideological and national coherency needed to be fostered.

During the early days of the Republic, the status of free Africans and the indigenous population were ill defined. The native peoples of this land were considered alien members of tribes and were afforded few benefits as legal aliens. For them Jefferson supported amalgamation, but the powers in government supported their removal. Free Blacks were neither aliens nor citizens and were denied the rights enjoyed by those who secured either status. Jefferson advocated for gradual emancipation and a limited form of education for Africans as a way of preparing them for repatriation in Africa. The level of schooling Jefferson would support for Blacks was no doubt shaped and informed by his assessment of their intellectual capacity. He made no secret of his belief in the intellectual inferiority of black people. In his *Notes on the State of Virginia* in 1787, concerning the black intellect Jefferson wrote, "Comparing them by their faculties of memory, reason, and imagination, it appears to me that in memory they are equal to Whites; in reason much inferior." Jefferson went on to write that in his experience with African people, he had never met one who "had uttered a thought above the level of plain narration," or had created or written anything deserving the "dignity of criticism."[6]

As early as the Revolutionary period, Whites in Northern colonies, and later states, moved toward the abolition of chattel enslavement. They viewed it as being irreconcilable to their affirmation of and struggle for liberty. Identifying some of the motivating factors behind the abolition of slavery in the North, Leon Litwack writes,

> If contemporary explanations have any validity, the liquidation of slavery in the North should not be considered simply on the ground of profits and losses, climate, or geography. Abolition sentiment generally ignored these factors and chose instead to emphasize one particular theme: that the same principles used to

---

[6] Thomas Jefferson, *Notes on the State of Virginia*, ed. William Peden (New York: W. W. Norton, 1982) 139–40.

justify the American Revolution, particularly John Locke's natural-rights philosophy, also condemned and doomed Negro slavery.[7]

As early as 1778, Northern states first banned the importation of enslaved Africans and then moved toward gradual abolition.

By 1830 there were approximately 319,599 free Africans in the U.S., and by 1860 the number had increased to 488,070, most living in the North. "Free," however, is a relative term. Africans were "free" from forced labor without remuneration. The so-called "free" black population could not escape the socioeconomic and political realities of a caste system. As a result, Blacks began to develop their own churches, schools, and benevolent societies long before the manumission of enslaved Africans in 1863.[8] Deborah Gray White agrees that the designation "free" is misleading. She, however, emphasizes the opportunities free Blacks had that those who were enslaved did not. White writes,

> In light of all the restrictions on free Blacks and the discrimination and prejudice they faced, it is worth remembering that they were not slaves. Although they were only semi-free, they were not in bondage. This status had real significance, significance a slave could appreciate. For, after all, free Blacks could legally rename themselves. They could marry legally, and free women gave birth to free children. They had more opportunities to learn to read and write. For instance, although only one of Sojourner Truth's five children obtained any education, at least two of her grandchildren obtained literacy during the days of slavery. William Ellison's children were more fortunate than Truth's. He sent them to Philadelphia to be

---

[7] Leon F. Litwack, *North of Slavery: The Negro in the Free States, 1790–1860* (Chicago: University of Chicago Press, 1961) 6.

[8] Cremin, *American Education*, 228–30. For a more detailed examination of the free black population in the South prior to the Civil War, see Ira Berlin, *Slaves without Masters: The Free Negro in the South* (New York: The New Press, 1974).

educated at the Lombard Street Primary School, a school run by Margaretta Forten, a free black teacher.[9]

Even though free Blacks in the North had greater access to education than Blacks in the South, they were subject to what Cremin refers to as a similar "pedagogical paradox." On one hand, they were "subjected to white efforts to teach inferiority, and, on the other hand, to black efforts to teach pride, resistance and community solidarity."[10] According to David Tyack, some Blacks argued for segregated schools. They maintained that "such systems offered opportunities for [Blacks] to obtain good jobs and claimed that black children in mixed schools suffered from the insults of white children and the cruelty and bias of white teachers." Others supported integrated schools, making the claim that separate schools were inherently unequal. Both Frederick Douglas and David Walker supported integrated schools, but for different reasons. Douglas believed black and white children would develop healthier relationships with one another as a result of getting to know each other in school. Walker was more concerned with making sure black children received the same education as white children. This, in his view, would be assured if Blacks were in the classroom together with Whites.[11]

In some Northern cities the issue of integration versus segregation caused splits within the black community. In Boston, for instance, a struggle led by integrationist Benjamin Roberts against Thomas Paul Smith, who advocated for separate education for Blacks, resulted in civil litigation. Charles Sumner argued the case for the integrationists, and Robert Morris, the first black attorney to try a case before a jury in the U.S., represented the interests of African separatists. The advocates for separate black schools lost in court, and legislative support for the integrationists was secured in 1855.

---

[9] Deborah Gray White, "Let My People Go: 1804–1860," in Robin D. G. Kelley and Earl Lewis, eds., *To Make Our World Anew: A History of African Americans* (London: Oxford University Press, 2000) 206–207.

[10] Cremin, *American Education*, 228.

[11] Tyack, *The One Best System*, 111–13.

The victory to dismantle legal school segregation in Boston was not so much the culmination of legal battles between black integrationists and segregationists, but that of a much longer struggle of black integrationists in Boston who fought to end the legacy of racist school policies that denied their children a quality education. In 1849, Roberts sued the city of Boston for denying his daughter Sarah access to the five public white schools she passed each day while walking to the school for Blacks; a school poorly funded and overcrowded. Sumner and Morris teamed to argue Roberts's 1849 case that was eventually lost. The case, however, sparked widespread protests throughout the black community and resulted in the state legislature ending segregation in 1855. States such as New York, Pennsylvania, and Ohio reacted by openly condemning any effort toward amalgamation. Other states simply let their segregated school policies quietly continue.[12]

According to Litwack, prior to the Civil War, Northern states were fairly consistent regarding their opposition to integrated schooling. There were differences, but the bottom line was segregation. Pennsylvania and Ohio provided common schools for all children and at the same time established separate schools for Blacks. In Ohio, Litwack notes violent opposition to schooling for Blacks by townspeople in and around Cincinnati who destroyed buildings and books. By 1850, most Northern states provided schools for children and at the same time condoned separate schools for Blacks. Western states opposed black education for fear of increased migration and offending constituents who migrated from Southern states.[13]

Black schools were housed in substandard buildings; had substandard materials; and had difficulty in securing qualified teachers. The state responded with some assistance for improvement, but only because of the increased demand to integrate. Interestingly, however, Litwack points out that many segregationists charged that Blacks themselves, those who started separate schools, were also

---

[12] Carl Kaestle, *Pillars of the Republic: Common Schools and American Society, 1780–1860* (New York: Hill and Wang, 1983) 179. See also Stephen Kendrick and Paul Kendrick, *Sarah's Long Walk: The Free Blacks of Boston and How Their Struggle for Equality Changed America* (Boston: Beacon Press, 2004).

[13] Litwack, *North of Slavery*, 121–22.

segregationists. Some Blacks started separate schools because this was
the only option available to them. Other black leaders who supported
separate schools saw it as an opportunity to demonstrate their equality
by producing scholars as good as or better than Whites. Litwack agrees
with Tyack that many Blacks also supported separate schools because
they wanted to prevent their children from prejudicial and
discriminatory instruction from racist white teachers.[14]

In black public schools, Blacks insisted on having black teachers.
Black teachers often opposed legislation to end race-based hiring
practices for fear of losing jobs and for fear of depriving black children
of teachers. Concerns about loss of jobs due to desegregation were
warranted because desegregation often resulted in loss of jobs for black
teachers. Additionally, economic disparity between black and white
teachers was broad. For instance, in 1853, black teachers were paid an
average of $100 less per month than their white counterparts in New
York City.[15]

According to Tyack, teaching opportunities in the North
contributed to the creation of a black middle class. Better-educated
Blacks tended to teach high school. This was primarily because there
were no other options for professional advancement in white
institutions. Black education also had positive consequences for the
sociopolitical fabric of the black community in other ways. Tyack writes
that "Black educators also provided the nucleus for a number of new
voluntary groups and stimulated social differentiation which helped
change the White communities' stereotype of Negroes." Black schools
also provided a context for political activity within the black community.
As we shall see later, the issues of segregation versus integration,
administrative control, and who taught black children were major and
divisive issues within the Christian Church.[16]

Whether or not they desired separate schools or developed them
as a result of forced segregation by Whites, Blacks found it difficult to
create and sustain their own schools due to lack of financial resources.

[14] Ibid., 136.
[15] Tyack, *The One Best System*, 119.
[16] Ibid., 118–19.

In the North, public school officials gradually absorbed the black charity schools. Most of them, however, remained segregated after being absorbed into the public school systems. The reality of depressed economic conditions within the black community would prove to be a daunting and ongoing challenge well into the twentieth century. These conditions would severely limit black education reformers within the Disciples of Christ from achieving any sustained autonomy and control over their schools. The resulting pattern was either the closing of these schools or control being handed over to the white-controlled mission agency.

As mentioned earlier, the Quakers, also known as the Society of Friends, were quite prominent among Protestant denominations that started charity schools for free Africans, and later for African Americans. Schools were established in Philadelphia in 1779 and 1787, for boys and girls respectively. A school for adults was established in 1789. In her excellent book on free black women during the period of enslavement, Wilma King writes about a school founded in 1837 called the Philadelphia Institute for Colored Youth that was a coeducational classical high school for black youth. A leading black education reformer in Philadelphia during this period, Sarah Mapps Douglas, would become head of the girls' department at the institute in 1853. She would later introduce advanced courses in the sciences to the curriculum. Douglas, according to King, "enrolled in medical classes at the Ladies Institute of Pennsylvania Medical University between 1855 and 1858 in order to introduce new subjects, including physiology, into the Institute of Colored Youth's offerings." The institute would later become known as Cheyney University of Pennsylvania.[17]

Other examples of schooling for free Blacks in the early period of the Republic include a school in New York that was run by the Manumission Society in 1787. In 1792, another school was formed in

---

[17] Kaestle, *Pillars of the Republic*, 37–39; Wilma King, *The Essence of Liberty: Free Black Women during the Slave Era* (Columbia: University of Missouri Press, 2006) 102. For more on Sarah Mapps Douglas and her work and the Institute of Colored Youth see "Sarah Mapps Douglas," in Darlene Clark Hines, Elsa Barkley Brown, and Rosalyn Terborg-Penn, eds., *Black Women in America: An Historical Encyclopedia* (Brooklyn: Carlson Publishing, 1993) 351–53.

Baltimore. As free African populations grew, so did charity school provision. Kaestle states, "By 1810, African free schools were operating in Burling, New Jersey; Providence, Rhode Island; and Wilmington, Delaware. In Boston, a group of White merchants and ministers began supporting an already existing African school in 1801. A number of Africans paid tuition in private schools in Boston and New York." During the early national period, there is no evidence that Whites in the North felt threatened by the possibility of Blacks becoming upwardly mobile as a result of schooling. They were more concerned with, and motivated by, the role of schooling in preventing criminal and other immoral behavior by Blacks and other poor and indigent children.[18]

In the Northeast during the latter part of the eighteenth century, the "Sunday" or "Sabbath" school was another type of schooling made available to Blacks. The Sunday school movement started in England earlier in the century. The initial purpose of these schools was to keep children of indigent families from being depraved of morals and manners and to provide them with rudimentary instruction. Kaestle adds that black children were attending Sunday schools in significant numbers in the Northeast, especially in Philadelphia, New York, and Boston.[19]

In 1834, the Oberlin Collegiate Institute (later Oberlin College) (white) was founded in Elyria, Ohio. Oberlin would earn the reputation of being a hotbed for abolitionist activity before the Civil War. Oberlin opened its door to Blacks during the antebellum period. By the end of the war, the school enrolled slightly more than 100 black men and women, which constituted somewhere between 2 and 5 percent of the total student population. Also of note was a normal school in Washington, D.C., run by a white New Yorker named Myrtilla Miner. Miner's Teacher's College would later become the District of Columbia Teachers College. The school offered women a classic education including scientific studies and literary studies. Milner, however, was known for her "patronizing remarks," and her

---

[18] Kaestle, *Pillars of the Republic*, 171–73.
[19] Ibid., 44.

"indifference to the hospitality offered by poor Blacks." This offended many students, some of whom chose not to remain at the school. But as King points out, the majority stayed because of the value they placed on education that "overshadowed their abhorrence of Miner's insults."[20]

More will be said about the role of Sunday schools in the South during the years following the Civil War in chapter 5; however, it's important to point out here that Sunday schools of various types were popular during the antebellum period. It became an extremely important method of religious and secular schooling for Blacks in the South before and after the Civil War. Commenting on how black access to these schools was impacted in the North and South by black insurrections and the emergence of state-supported common schools, Anne Boylan writes,

> Most black Sunday scholars were free persons of course, but slaves attended some Sunday schools during the 1820s, especially in cities. Nevertheless, their presence was controversial, especially after Turner's rebellion.... Throughout the northeast and many of the border states, Whites demanded that Blacks be removed from Sunday school classes even when they met separately.... With the spread of tax-supported public schools during the 1820s and 1830s, particularly in the North, Sunday schools eventually relinquished their function as purveyors of basic literacy.[21]

Some Sunday schools remained in operation after the black insurrections of the early1830s; however, many were forced to limit their teaching to oral instruction out of fear of the power literacy would afford Blacks. In 1831 an Alabama instruction book stated that it was "designed for the use of families, Sabbath schools, and Bible classes, and especially for the oral instruction of the colored population."[22]

---

[20] King, *Essence of Liberty*, 103.

[21] Anne M. Boylan, *Sunday School: The Formation of an American Institution, 1790–1880* (New Haven: Yale University Press, 1988) 24–26.

[22] A. W. Chambers, *The Catechetical Instructor: Designed for the Use of Families* (Montgomery: Press of the Daily Alabama Journal, 1847) quoted in Boylan, *Sunday School*, 28.

The Catholic Church established a class for black children in Baltimore in the 1820s. The class met on Sundays and was run by a French Sulpician priest named Jacques Marie Hector Joubert. Several free black women, including Marie Magdaleine Balas, Mary Elizabeth Lange, and Marie Rosine Boegue, wanted a more developed and permanent formal school than a Sunday class ran by Joubert. Their interest and commitment to the education of black children led to the establishment of the Sisters of Providence on 5 June 1829. The school became known as the Oblate Sisters of Providence upon receiving papal recognition on 2 October 1831.[23]

In the North prior to the Civil War, Kaestle points out that the primary pedagogical methodology used in African free schools was a monitorial system known as the Lancasterian system developed in 1818. This system was named after its creator Joseph Lancaster who developed this teaching method at his school in London. Lancaster later introduced this method to the U.S., where it was widely embraced in Northeastern urban centers. The Lancasterian system was characterized by competition, prizes, monitorial instruction, the use of older students as instructors and monitors, rigid forms of memorization and recitation, teachers' manuals, procedures and lesson plans, emphasis on nonsectarian moral instruction, standardization, precision, and routine. This pedagogical approach was believed to inculcate obedience, industry, and promptness in students. These of course were attributes that would be valued more and more by the business elite in the North as it became an increasingly industrialized society, a development that would have major implications for modes of production, labor, and the development of the growing relationship between schooling and industry.[24]

Although limited state funding for schools began in the late eighteenth century, Litwack reports that during this time, the Pennsylvania Society operated schools and secured limited state support

---

[23] King, *Essence of Liberty*, 92. See also Diane Batts Morrow, *Persons of Color and Religious at the Same Time: The Oblate Sisters of Providence, 1828–1860* (Chapel Hill: University of North Carolina Press, 2002).

[24] Kaestle, *Pillars of the Republic*, 40–44.

for schools for free Blacks. The society first submitted a proposal for the state to provide funding for free black education in 1790, and again in 1795. They asked the state to provide free schools for children regardless of color. It would not be until 1820 that Pennsylvania would pass legislation providing funds to support separate schools for free black children. As previously mentioned, Blacks in Massachusetts started a school and eventually secured private and state assistance. Ohio free Blacks organized the School Fund Society and started schools during this period as well. In the early 1830s, William Lloyd Garrison and Theodore Weld led Cincinnati abolitionists in the development of schools for Blacks in that city.[25]

Litwack provides other examples of white attempts to establish schools in the North that were soon met with white resistance. In 1831, there was an attempt by Garrison, Arthur Tappen, and Simeon Jocelyn to open a college for Blacks in New Haven. The citizens of New Haven opposed this effort. In August of that year, white opposition to schooling for Blacks was intensified by Nat Turner's revolt. Some were concerned that the creation of a college for Blacks would thwart the plan of colonization that sought to repatriate Blacks to Africa. They believed that providing educational opportunities in the United States would create incentives for Blacks to stay rather than return to Africa. Prudence Crandall, a Quaker, was another example. She attempted to establish a school for black girls in Canterbury, Connecticut, in 1834. It opened, but met with great opposition that culminated in legislative action and closed its doors.[26]

As support for integration increased among Blacks, abolitionists began to rethink their plans to open separate schools for Blacks. Increasingly, white Northern schools such as Dartmouth, Harvard, and Oberlin began to admit Blacks. This called into question the wisdom of opening new schools. Prior to 1861, schools such as Princeton, Union College, Amherst, Rutland, and others had opened their doors. There may have been other schools that had policies to admit Blacks; however, the number of Blacks who had the level of secondary educational

---

[25] Litwack, *North of Slavery*, 17.
[26] Ibid., 123–26.

instruction to qualify for admission to these schools was limited. According to Litwack, John B. Russworm was the first black college graduate in the U.S. In 1826, he graduated from Bowdoin College, Maine. Attaining an education, even higher education, rarely led to employment for Blacks, and as a result, Litwack claims that free middle- and upper-class Blacks in the North felt the effects of racial prejudice more acutely.[27]

Many free black women in the North were among the throngs of teachers who courageously went South to provide schooling for Blacks. Having the status of "free" did not necessarily mean easy or automatic access to formal schooling or even informal methods of literacy training. Free black women who managed to obtain such access, however, often recognized the utility literacy had not only for their own advantage, but as an indispensable tool to help other free and enslaved Africans to achieve freedom and socioeconomic upward mobility. The moral responsibility to help transform the conditions of their people embodied by many literate free black women is a point not missed by Wilma King. She writes,

> Discrimination and limited access to schools across geographical regions made it especially difficult for many free [black] women to acquire literacy. Nevertheless, they found ways to succeed, used literacy to earn a living, and made creative use of their knowledge. Once some women acquired an education, they moved beyond individual aspirations towards a social and political consciousness in the interest of empowering their people. Having accepted the challenging responsibility of serving the race, they often involved themselves in liberating their sisters and brothers in bondage.[28]

---

[27] Ibid., 139. According to "Chicken Bones: A Journal for Literary and Artistic African American Themes," Edward A. Jones, a Black man graduated from Amherst "a few days earlier" than Russworm. In 1827, Russworm became the founding editor of Freedom's Journal in New York City, becoming the first Black newspaper in the US.

[28] King, *Essence of Liberty*, 90.

Ironically, it was not unusual for black women who chose to become teachers to be the object of the ire of both white missionaries and Blacks, albeit for different reasons. Nina Silber describes the experience of some black women teachers from the North who went South prior to the end of the Civil War. After noting the high regard with which white missionaries were held by Blacks in the South, Silber writes,

> The presence of black female teachers, in contrast, often did not elicit the same responses among the freedpeople, nor did it reveal the same clashes in attitude. When Charlotte Forten arrived at last on St. Helena Island in the fall of 1862, she was the first and only black teacher there and received, at least initially, a decidedly mixed reception from the local contrabands, some of whom resented having to work for a black woman. White missionaries, too, were sometimes distant and unfriendly towards Forten.... Indeed, the fact that many black teachers often received prejudicial treatment from their white colleagues certainly would have sent signals that may have influenced how freedpeople treated and perceived African-American missionaries.... Such contempt may have encouraged certain sympathies between the former slaves and the black teachers, but also might have marked the black teachers as figures of less importance and authority when it came to aiding those who were newly freed.[29]

The unique and unfortunate existential dualism for black female teachers who traveled South to teach Blacks during the war years provides an interesting bridge between the Northern and Southern educational experience of black people in the U.S. prior to 1865.

---

[29] Nina Silber, "A Compound of Wonderful Potency: Women Teachers of the North in the Civil War South," in Joan E. Cashin, ed., *The War Was You and Me: Civilians in the American Civil War* (Princeton: Princeton University Press, 2002) 47.

The Southern Experience

In general, Southern interest in education was limited to training and apprenticeships for orphans and children of indigent families. This type of state-sponsored education did not occur on any large scale. In fact, charity and pauper schools in the South were rare during the early years of the Republic. The planter class supported pauper education as a form of benevolence but was opposed to state-supported, universal, and compulsory education. The commonly held belief among the planter class was that the state did not have the right to intervene in this way. It was believed that such intervention would usurp the functions of the church, disrupt owner/labor relations, and threaten the familial authority over children. The first viable public education system in the South would not be established until 1861 in North Carolina.[30]

Given the reality of chattel enslavement and the near universality of anti-literacy legislation for free or enslaved Blacks throughout the South, formal schooling for enslaved Africans was largely nonexistent until after the Civil War. Exceptions to this reality would include apprenticeship opportunities for a limited number of persons within the plantation system. Clandestine underground schools run by Africans, and some Whites, were also maintained throughout the South. Some examples of such schools include one that operated from 1818 to 1829 in Savannah, Georgia, which was founded and operated by a man from Santo Domingo named Julian Froumontaine; a school operated by a woman known as Deveaux from 1833 to 1865, also in Savannah; the Pioneer School of Freedom in New Orleans in 1860; the Sisters of the Holy Family school founded by Henriette Delille, a free black, in 1842 also in New Orleans; and a school run by Mary Peake in Hampton, Virginia, which began operating in the open in 1861.[31]

The story of Mary Peake is an excellent example of how opportunities given to mulattoes were used to benefit other Blacks who were denied access to any form of schooling. She was born Mary Smith

---

[30] Ronald Butchart, *Northern Schools, Southern Blacks, and Reconstruction: Freedmen's Education, 1862–1875* (New York: Greenwood Press, 1980) 182.

[31] James D. Anderson, *The Education of Blacks in the South, 1860–1935* (Chapel Hill: University of North Carolina Press, 1988) 7; King, *Essence of Liberty*, 92.

Kelsey in Norfolk, Virginia, to a free black mother and a white father. At age six she was allowed to attend a "select" school for free black children for ten years in Alexandria, Virginia. According to Joe Richardson, upon her return home to Norfolk, Mary started a Baptist-affiliated organization called the Daughters of Zion "to aid the poor and ill." In 1851, she married a formerly enslaved African named Thomas Peake. Richardson gives us a glimpse of the type of school Mary Peake was running in Hampton, Virginia, on 7 August 1861, when Confederate soldiers burned down the town. He writes, "Mrs. Peake conducted [what became an American Missionary Association school] with a strong religious emphasis, much as later association teachers would. Classes began with prayer and scriptures, and students were taught the Bible and religious songs as well as the ABC's. In addition to the day school, Mrs. Peake began night classes for adults, despite her increasing infirmity with tuberculosis."[32] The enrollment at Peake's school rose to more than fifty free and enslaved African children. Her dedication and commitment to the education of black children is reflected by her refusal to cease her teaching duties while she fell deathly ill. Lewis Lockwood, an AMA official, penned the following observation of this educator's selfless dedication: "It was beautiful, though sad, to see her...when too sick to sit, lying on her bed, surrounded by her scholars, teaching them to read."[33] Mary Peake taught until she died.

Reflecting on his experience with an underground school, Mr. Eugene Smith, an eighty-four-year-old native of Augusta, Georgia, shares this story: "Going to school wasn't allowed but still some people would slip their children to school. There was an old Methodist preacher, a Negro man named Ned Purdee, he had a school for boys and girls in his back yard. They caught him and put him in jail. He was to be put in stocks and so many lashes every day for a month. I heard

[32] Joe Richardson, *Christian Reconstruction: The American Missionary Association and Southern Blacks, 1861–1890* (Tuscaloosa: University of Alabama Press, 1980) 4–5.

[33] Lewis C. Lockwood, ed., *Two Black Teachers During the Civil War: Mary S. Peake, the Colored Teacher of Fortress Monroe, and Charlotte Forten, Life of the Sea Islands*, quoted in King, *Essence of Liberty*, 95.

him tell many times how the [jailor] said: 'Ned, I won't whip you.'"[34]
Unfortunately, Ned Purdee's good fortune of being spared physical
reprisal for violating anti-literacy laws was not the norm. An example of
the price one could pay for learning to read and write is provided by
Mr. Lewis Favors, who was born in 1855, in Meriwether County,
Georgia, near Greenville. Asked if he knew of anyone on his
plantation who could read or write, Mr. Favors said, "They was all
afraid to even try [to learn to read or write] because they would cut
these off." According to the interviewer Mr. Favors pointed to his
thumbs and index fingers as he said this. Ms. Annie Price, who was
born in 1855 in Spalding County, Georgia, shared that "If any of us
were ever caught with a book we would get a good whipping."[35]

The role of religion and of sectarian evangelical and mission-
related activity cannot be overstated regarding their impact on literacy
development in general and schooling for Blacks in particular. On this
issue, Albert Raboteau points to the influence of two Protestant
evangelical revivals known as the First and Second Great Awakenings
of 1740 and the early 1800s respectively. These revivals were pivotal
social movements that led to increased literacy instruction for enslaved
Africans. Pro-revival groups operating in the South included the New

---

[34] Eugene Smith quoted in George P. Rawick, ed., *The American Slave: A
Composite Autobiography*, 19 vols. (Westport CT: Greenwood Press, 1972) vol. 13, pt.
4, p. 231.
[35] Lewis Favors quoted in Rawick, ed., *American Slave*, vol. 12, pt. 12, p. 323;
Annie Price quoted in Rawick, ed., *American Slave*, vol. 13, pt 3, p. 182. It is quite
interesting and worthy of note that among all of the interviews I examined, none of
the interviewees claimed to be literate prior to manumission. They would speak only
of someone else they knew who could read or write; or, if they were literate at the
time they were interviewed they would be sure to point out that they developed these
skills "after freedom come." Could it be that even being removed from enslavement
for more than seventy years, these people were fearful of revealing that they learned
even the most rudimentary literacy skills during enslavement? Given the often brutal
and violent consequences suffered by many for learning to read and write during the
antebellum period, the contemporary reality of Jim Crow during the time these
interviews took place, and the racial dynamics between the interviewee and
interviewer, it is probable that these elderly formerly enslaved Blacks were reluctant
or even fearful of revealing more than they did concerning literacy development on
the plantation.

Light Presbyterians, the Separate Baptists, and the Methodist Episcopal Church. These groups emphasized the need for a person to accept Christ and repent in order to have an authentic conversion. The convert's growth in faith must be supported by subsequent reading of the Bible, which required literacy. Anglicans, according to Raboteau, placed less emphasis on literacy because they emphasized teaching the Lord's Prayer, the Ten Commandments, the Apostle's Creed (which would be memorized and not read), and moral behavior as the way to salvation. A related consequence of these early evangelical movements relative to literacy development among Blacks was the conversion of Southern Whites. According to Raboteau, the conversion of Whites in the South led to limited permissiveness on the part of some Whites regarding literacy instruction for Blacks.[36]

Margaret Washington Creel claims that Anglicans in South Carolina emphasized literacy because most clergy viewed it as a prerequisite for baptism. In the mid-eighteenth century, two Anglican-supported evangelical societies were started by Thomas Bray. These organizations had definite educational consequences for Blacks. Bray started the Society for the Promotion of Christian Knowledge and the Society for the Propagation of the Gospel in Foreign Parts. The former would give birth to the Charleston Negro School (for free Africans) in 1743. This school stayed in operation for twenty years. Creel points out that Anglican schools were tolerated by planters because the societies' missionaries promoted the belief that obedient servitude was promulgated on the principle of conscience that was informed by Christian doctrine.[37] Creel's conflict with Raboteau regarding the role of literacy in Anglican salvific doctrine is worth noting. Raboteau does point out that Anglicans were one of the few sectarian groups that required theological training for preachers and exhorters. This requirement would of course result in mandatory literacy training for

---

[36] Albert Raboteau, *Slave Religions: The "Invisible Institution" in the Antebellum South* (Oxford: Oxford University Press, 1978) 128–29.

[37] Margaret Washington Creel, *"A Peculiar People": Slave Community-Culture Among the Gullahs* (New York: New York University Press, 1988) 74–76.

Blacks seeking ordination in the Anglican tradition. Perhaps this is the point to which Creel referred.

I want to reiterate an earlier point. The very act of reading was a form of black resistance to their condition of oppression. Heather Williams reminds us of the almost seamless integration of religion, literacy development, and resistance when considering the motivational factors at play in free and enslaved Blacks' response to Christian missionary efforts. She writes,

> Christian missions to slaves attracted some converts for the very reason that church was a place in which they might learn to read. [Some] African Americans attended church in part to take advantage of the literacy offered. Once in church, many slaves placed their faith in the biblical messages of liberation. In slavery and in freedom, a desire to read the words of the Bible impelled many to seek out teachers who could help them to decipher for themselves the word that in sermon and in song kept them believing they would some day be free.[38]

Schooling and literacy development as resistance is a dynamic that must be kept in mind as we move toward an analysis of black education within the Disciples of Christ during the decades following the Civil War.

Carter G. Woodson identifies three categories of Whites interested in educating Blacks in the antebellum South: (1) planters concerned with increasing their profit margin and labor supply; (2) those moved by a sense of altruism; and (3) evangelicals who were concerned primarily with converting Blacks to Christianity.[39] Woodson also notes the common belief among many Christians in the antebellum period that one could only know God by reading the Bible, which served as a primary incentive to learn to read. Woodson further asserts that larger plantations in the South tended to be owned by Episcopalians who stressed verbal biblical and theological instruction

---

[38] Williams, *Self Taught*, 18.
[39] Carter G. Woodson, *The Education of the Negro Prior to 1861* (New York: A & B Books, 1989 [1919]) 2.

among those they owned. Woodson seems to agree with Raboteau on this issue. The diminished view of the import of literacy in relation to one's Christian experience among larger plantation owners resulted in even less literacy instruction among those they owned.[40]

Anti-literacy legislation existed as early as 1740 with Georgia and South Carolina being among the first to pass such laws. South Carolina's legislation and Georgia's—given that it shares a border with South Carolina—was in response to the Stone Rebellion in September 1739. This insurrection was led by a man named Jemmy [sic] and resulted in the deaths of twenty Whites. The law prohibited anyone from teaching enslaved Africans to write or from utilizing enslaved Blacks as scribes. This law was expanded in 1800 to include free Africans. The expansion of this law may have been influenced by a planned insurrection in Virginia in 1800 by Gabriel Prosser. Prosser's plan was aimed at massive liberation of enslaved people and the establishment of a black state. His attack was delayed by a violent storm. Before he could unleash his plan, he was betrayed and eventually hanged. According to Deborah Gray White, the impact of this failed insurrection was far reaching. She writes, "Within weeks, slaveholders as far west and south as what was then the Mississippi Territory cautioned each other to beware of suspicious behavior on the part of Blacks. On their tongues was the name Gabriel Prosser; in their minds were thoughts of what might have happened if Prosser had succeeded in leading Virginia slaves in revolt against slavery."[41]

Anti-literacy legislation became even more widespread in the South after 1830, again in response to a number of revolts by enslaved Africans, namely those led by Denmark Vesey in 1822, Nat Turner in 1831, the publication of David Walker's *Appeal* published in 1829, and the abolitionist paper, *The Liberator*, published by William Lloyd Garrison in 1831.[42] Walker's *Appeal*, which called for open rebellion by

---

[40] Ibid., 220–21.

[41] White, "Let My People Go: 1804–1860," 169.

[42] Harding, *There Is a River*, 34–35; also see Williams, *Self Taught*, 27. For an excellent treatment of David Walker's "Freedom's Journal," see Sterling Stuckey, *Slave Culture: Nationalist Theory and the Foundations of Black America* (New York: Oxford University Press, 1987) 98–137. In addition to Harding, for broader

enslaved Africans and asserted that death was a better option than slavery, caused great fear among Whites throughout the South. This 1829 Georgia statute is an example of legislative reaction to Walker's pamphlet and was designed to prevent literacy development among the black population: "If any slave, Negro or Free person of color, or any white person, shall teach any other slave, Negro, or free person of color to read or write, either written or printed characters, the said free person of color or slave shall be punished by fine and whipping or fine or whipping at the discretion of the court; and if a white person so offends, he, she, or they shall be punished with a fine not exceeding $500.00 and imprisonment in the common jail at the discretion of the court."[43]

An 1830 statute in Alabama stated that "any person or persons who shall attempt to teach any free person of color or slave to spell, read, or write, shall upon conviction...be fined in a sum of not less than $250, nor more than $500." This statute was exclusively aimed at the white population. It would be rare for enslaved Blacks to have access to money to pay fines, and, as we noted in the Georgia statute and in the testimony of Mr. Favors above, punishment for Blacks normally included physical reprisal of some sort.[44]

John W. Blassingame points out that within the community of enslaved Africans, or "quarter community," literate Blacks enjoyed "immeasurable status" because of their ability to provide information from the outside world. Blassingame states that learning to read helped

---

examinations on rebellion and resistance of enslaved Africans see John Hope Franklin and Loren Schweninger, *Runaway Slaves: Rebels on the Plantation* (Oxford: Oxford University Press, 1999); Thomas W. Higginson, *Black Rebellion* (New York: Arno Press and the New York Times, 1969); and Herbert Aptheker, *American Negro Slave Revolts* (New York: International Publishers, 1964 [1943]).

[43] 1829 Georgia statute quoted in C. T. Wright, "The Development of Education for Blacks in Georgia, 1865–1900," Ph.D. diss., Boston University, 1977, 6.

[44] Alabama statue quoted in Johnson, *Myth of Ham*, 5. Some enslaved Blacks, especially artisans, did receive remuneration when they were hired out by owners. Many would earn enough to purchase their own freedom as well as the freedom of family members. See Henry A. Bullock, *A History of Negro Education in the South from 1619 to the Present* (Cambridge: Harvard University Press, 1967) 2–5.

enslaved Blacks develop a healthier sense of self and helped them deal with the emotional and psychological challenges of chattel enslavement. To make this point Blassingame quotes Thomas Jones, who secretly learned to read while living under slavery. Jones wrote, "I felt at night, as I went to my rest that I was really beginning to be a *man*, preparing myself for a condition in life better and higher and happier than could belong to the ignorant *slave*"(italics Blassingame's). Blassingame claims that extreme opposition to black education and literacy led Blacks to value it that much more, giving it almost "supernatural status."[45]

Henry A. Bullock addresses the issue of education of Blacks from the perspective of owners. The informal educational process was one in which Blacks were socialized with the intention of producing personality types that would sustain the dominant socioeconomic and political structures along with power relations of the period. Blacks were viewed merely as tools for investment. Bullock writes that sympathy and economic interests on the part of Whites provided a "hidden passage" of educational opportunities for enslaved Africans to develop skills or the ability to read and write. Certain skills, such as Blacksmithing and masonry, were developed or taught intentionally to enhance labor production. These skills were also taught as a result of some Whites who developed sentimental concerns for those they owned. In time, according to Bullock, Whites became increasingly dependent on enslaved black labor for more complex modes of production to provide food, clothes, tools, and housing. As a result, enslaved Africans learned various skills as artisans at an increasing, albeit limited rate. A small amount of enslaved persons were eventually able to hire themselves out and earn enough to purchase their freedom. Some would go on to develop a higher degree of literacy and teach others. Children whose parents worked in the "big house" (owner's home) sometimes learned to read from instruction offered by a mistress, master, or their children. White children were both intentional and

---

[45] John W. Blassingame, *The Slave Community: Plantation Life in the Antebellum South* (Oxford: Oxford University Press, 1979 [1972]) 312. Thomas Jones's quote is from John W. Blassingame, "Status and Social Structure in the Slave Community," in Harry P. Owens, ed., *Perspectives and Irony in American Slavery* (Cambridge: Harvard University Press, 1967) 2–5.

unintentional sources of literacy training for Blacks as evidenced by the following examples.

Mr. Green Wollbanks, age seventy-seven, born in Jackson County, Georgia, related, "The biggest part of the teaching done among the slaves was by our young bosses, but, as far as schools for slaves was concerned, there was no such things until after the end of the war, and then we were no longer slaves."[46] Ms. Alice Green, age seventy-six, who grew up on a plantation in Helicon Springs, Georgia, shared this account:

> You'll be s'prised at what Mammy told me 'bout how she got her larnin'. She said she kept a school book hid in her bosom all de time and when de chillum got home from school she would ax' 'em lots of questions all about what dey had done larned dat day and, 'cause she was so proud of evvy little scrap of book larnin' she could pick up de white chillum larned her how to read and write too. All de' larnin' she ever had she got from the white chillum at de big house, and she was so smart at gettin' 'em to larn her dat atter de war was over she got to be a school teacher.[47]

Examples of owners who would provide rudimentary literacy training for enslaved Africans were not common in the antebellum South, but as we have mentioned it did occur for a variety of reasons. The following examples from the NFEAs provide excellent illustrations of literacy development resulting from white instruction. This story was shared by Mr. Charlie Hudson, who was eighty years of age at the time he was interviewed. He was born in 1858 in Elbert County, Georgia. His owner was David Bell.

> Wunst a white man named Bill Rowey, come and begged Marse David to let him teach his Niggers. Marse David had de grown mens go sweep up de cottonseed in de ginhouse on Sunday mornin', and for three Sundays us went to school. When us went on de fourth Sunday night riders had done made a shape

---

[46] Green Wollbanks quoted in Rawick, ed., *American Slave*, vol. 13, pt. 4, p. 143.
[47] Alice Green quoted in Rawick, ed., *American Slave*, vol. 12, pt. 2, pp. 33–34.

like a coffin in de dand out in front, and painted a sign on de ginhouse what read: 'No Niggers 'lowed to be taught in dis ginhouse." Dat made Marse David so mad he jus' cussed and cussed. He 'lowed dat nobody warn't gwins to tell him what to do. But us was too skeered to go back to de ginhouse to school. Next week Marse David had 'em build a brush arbor down by de crick, but when us went down dar on Sunday for school, us found de night riders had done 'stroyed de brush arbor, and dat was de end of my gwine to school.[48]

Mr. Neal Upson, age eighty-one, of Oglethorpe County near Lexington, Georgia, shares this account: "De fust school I wen to was a little one room 'ouse in our white folks back yard. Us had a whit teacher and all he larnt slave chillum was jus' plain readin' and writin.'"[49]

Bullock agrees with other scholars that literacy training was linked to the belief that one had to read the Bible for oneself in order to receive salvation. As I have noted, this belief resulted in sectarian organizations playing a critical role in the development of literacy among enslaved Africans. In terms of evangelism and literacy training, Bullock notes that Baptists and Methodists, and Presbyterians to a lesser degree, were very active in the South during the antebellum period.[50]

Eugene Genovese states that there were some Whites in the South who were not only opposed to literacy training for Blacks, but were also against literacy training for the working class in general. There was a concern that enlightenment would cause the working class to despise their position in a stratified society. This would, therefore, disrupt the predominant structure of power relations in Southern society. In addition to this concern, Genovese asserts that anti-literacy laws were rooted in a fear of enslaved Africans having the ability to

---

[48] Charlie Hudson quoted in Rawick, ed., *American Slave*, vol. 12, pt. 2, p. 226.
[49] Neal Upson quoted in Rawick, ed., *American Slave*, vol. 13, pt. 4, p. 54.
[50] Bullock, *History of Negro Education*, 2–5.

forge passes for runaways and their being able to read incendiary literature.[51]

Genovese points out that literate enslaved Africans were located mostly in towns and cities. The conditions for literacy instruction were more favorable in those locations, albeit at great risk, than they were on plantations. Cities and towns also allowed for more contact between free and enslaved Blacks. Black agency in literacy instruction was more significant than white instruction in the antebellum South, according to Genovese. He points out, however, as I have demonstrated earlier, that some Whites did provide instruction while operating illegal schools. The motives for these efforts on the part of Whites were either rooted in pecuniary gain for the owner or, in some cases, out of a sense of obligation or duty.[52]

Genovese states that larger plantations were the most restrictive in upholding anti-literacy laws. There is, however, evidence based on the records of travelers' testimony and of formerly enslaved Africans that there was at least one literate African on each plantation. This allowed for the transmission of news from the outside world on plantations throughout the South. Genovese agrees that masters, mistresses, and even children would ignore the law and teach their "favorite" enslaved Blacks to read. There is evidence, according to Genovese, that mulattoes tended to have access to literacy training to a higher degree than those who were of a darker hue. Enslaved Africans who worked in the master's house, as previously noted, received more attention because of their greater intimacy with Whites. Most attention, however, went to the children who were often not segregated from white children. For Genovese, this interaction among children represents the greatest source of literacy instruction for Blacks on the plantation. He points out that Blacks' desire to secure an education was much greater than that of poor Whites and yeomen.[53]

---

[51] Eugene D. Genovese, *Roll, Jordan, Roll: The World the Slaves Made* (New York: Vintage, 1976 [1972]) 561–62.

[52] Ibid., 563.

[53] Ibid., 564–65.

4

THE CHRISTIAN CHURCH
(DISCIPLES CHRIST):
ORIGINS AND GROWTH TO 1865

Formed on the American frontier in 1832, the Christian Church (Disciples of Christ) would eventually grow to be one of the largest indigenous Protestant religious movements in the United States. The theological and philosophical foundations of the Christian Church were influenced by numerous sources, including that of Christian Enlightenment thinkers, streams of Presbyterian and Baptist doctrine and polity, and Scottish philosophy. As a result of these streams of influence, it is not surprising that the Disciples' approach to religion was predominantly rationalistic in nature. Unlike the Methodists and Baptists who allowed for more emotional expression in worship, the Disciples stressed "head" religion rather than "heart" religion.

An axiom often quoted by early Disciples was, "In essentials, unity; in nonessentials, liberty; in all things, charity." This saying is reflective of the broader societal emphasis on liberty and religious freedom in the young Republic. It is also reflective of the movement's understanding of its mission, which was the restoration of the "primitive" or New Testament church by achieving unity in the Body of Christ, and freedom in biblical interpretation. Given these emphases, Disciples were staunchly anti-denominational and anti-creedal, seeing both of these "man made" developments as divisive, evil, and without biblical justification or authority.[1] Mark Toulouse

---

[1] According to McAllister and Tucker, this quote is attributed to Rupertus Meldenius, a German Lutheran theologian "of whom little is known." The quote is seen in a 1326 writing named *Peter Meidelin* (Lester G. McAllister and William E. Tucker, *Journey of Faith: A History of the Christian Church [Disciples of Christ]* [St. Louis: Chalice Press, 1995] 21, 92).

questions whether or not it is possible to determine which of these three principles was of the greatest importance to early Disciples. "There seems to be no solution," writes Toulouse, "to determine which of these three principles had priority." Toulouse goes on to say that "from the beginning of the movement's history, [unity] served as a formative goal. Yet early Disciples sought to set the unity of the church within the context of certain parameters. Church unity, even if it was the prior principle, seems to never have existed independently of these other two principles."[2] I argue that when understood within the context of how and why Disciples leaders responded to the issue of schooling for Blacks after the Civil War, the issue of the unity of the church took priority over both restoration and freedom in biblical interpretation. It was not the concern for unity within the church universal, but with Southern Disciples' churches, that would play a decisive role in Northern Disciples' acquiescence to Southern demands regarding schooling for Blacks in the South.

The issue of "biblical justification" is one that demands further attention. Like many evangelicals of their time, the Disciples of Christ were biblical literalists—believing that the Bible was indeed the exclusive, authoritative, and inerrant representation of the "Word of God."

According to the Disciples' founders, Christians were to refrain from any individual, organizational, or liturgical practice not clearly authorized or supported by the New Testament. This included the formation of denominations; the use of creeds; the use of terms to identify Christians such as "Presbyterians" and "Baptists"; embracing hierarchical forms of polity and church relations; and the formation of any formal representative church structures beyond the local congregation. For some, the use of instrumental music in worship was an abomination because there was no evidence in the New Testament of such music. As we shall see later, the use of instrumental music in worship proved to be an ongoing point of tension that would contribute to a division within the Christian Church. Even today, some Disciples

---

[2] Mark G. Toulouse, *Joined in Discipleship: The Maturing of an American Religious Movement* (St. Louis: Chalice Press, 1992) 10.

will quote a maxim coined by its founders by saying, "Where the Scriptures speak, we speak. Where the Scriptures are silent, we are silent." This principle proved to be a significant source of division and discord among Disciples. On this point, McAllister and Tucker write,

> Strict restorationists or scholastics argued that the New Testament provided an exact pattern for the faith and practice of the church in every age. Any deviation amounted to rejecting the Word of God and could not be tolerated. Since the early Christians organized no missionary societies and worshiped without the aid of organs, Disciples should do likewise. Moderate Disciples disagreed, insisting that Christians should resort to "sanctified common sense" in those matters where the Scriptures are silent. To restore New Testament Christianity, they saw no need to disband missionary societies and to oppose instrumental music in worship. Both scholastics and moderates accepted the principle: "In essentials, unity; in nonessentials, liberty; in all things charity." But they did not specify the same essentials.[3]

As a result of their acceptance of diversity in thought, and as a non-creedal Protestant movement, many believed the Disciples to be a church without a theology. It would not be unusual in some Christian circles to hear, "Disciples don't believe anything" or, "One can believe anything and still be a good Disciple." It was not by accident that the early Disciples leadership enjoined the popularity of newly found liberty and freedom of choice in the broader secular society with that of religious language. According to Toulouse, they learned to exploit the sensibilities toward liberty and freedom of choice by

> ...translating it into religious language and forming a community specifically designed to enhance and protect the right of individuals to interpret scripture for themselves. This early message of Disciples provided hope for people who had about given up on ever hearing the voice of God above the conflicting claims of the various denominations surrounding them. These

---

[3] McAllister and Tucker, *Journey of Faith*, 32.

types of individuals were both challenged and attracted by Disciples preachers who told them they could join a congregation that expected them to read and interpret the Bible for themselves. The early Disciples movement, with its phenomenal record of growth, no doubt owed much to precisely this set of circum-stances.[4]

During the period addressed in this book, Disciples leaders had varying theological and political ideological perspectives. They were by no means a homogenous group. Their thinking would shape and inform the educational philosophy that influenced the type of schooling the Christian Church would provide or support for Blacks. Concerning the influence of these leaders, Eugene Boring writes,

> Nonetheless, there are representative figures in each generation who serve as a legitimate point of orientation for Disciples thought of that generation. This does not mean of course, that all Disciples or even the majority of them agreed with these representative figures. It does mean that they set the agenda for Disciples theology in their times in both content and method. In each generation, these representative figures both shaped and influenced the way Disciples thought about the faith, themselves, and their role in the world.[5]

A discussion of the first generation of Disciples of Christ leaders and the streams of thought that shaped and informed the direction in which they guided their fledgling Protestant movement is vital to this study. What theological perspectives were most influential in forming the foundation of the Christian Church? What were the philosophical sources that shaped their theology? Finally, what were the features of the religious landscape in the United States during the period from which the church emerged? I will now turn our attention to an examination of these questions.

---

[4] Toulouse, *Joined in Discipleship*, 38.
[5] Eugene M. Boring, *Disciples and the Bible: A History of Disciples Biblical Interpretation in North America* (St. Louis: Chalice Press, 1997) 4.

The Protestant Landscape on the Western Frontier

Prior to the Revolutionary War, individual freedom to attend the church of their choice or whether to affiliate with a church at all was one of the ways newfound liberties were expressed in the colonies. Church membership could no longer be required by the state as it was in Europe. "Religious freedom," according to Mark Toulouse, expanded to include the right to disregard "traditional and institutional authority in religious matters."[6] This development would result in the rapid decline of church membership, and at the same time precipitate the movement of ecclesial bodies to embrace a congregational form of church polity that allowed for both local autonomy and the freedom to engage and interpret the Bible.

During the Colonial period, evangelical reaction to the sharp decline in membership, and the economic consequences of this decline, gave rise to two revival movements that would later be known as the Great Awakenings. In the Northeast around 1740, the First Great Awakening began in the form of revivals. These revivals were theologically Calvinistic in nature and spread to the middle and Southern colonies. Preachers such as Jonathan Edwards and George Whitefield gave leadership to this movement that continued to the end of the eighteenth century.

Beginning in the last quarter of the eighteenth century and into the early nineteenth century, a second revival movement emerged. While this movement traces its origins to the universities of the Northeast, its greatest impact was felt in the frontier territories of Kentucky and Tennessee, resulting in unprecedented growth among several sectarian organizations—most notably the Methodists, Baptists, and New Light Presbyterians. This revival movement, which would later become known as the Second Great Awakening, would mark the genesis of several utopian societies and cults such as the Shakers, Rappites, Adventists, and Mormons. In many ways, this period of

---

[6] Toulouse, *Joined in Discipleship*, 37.

religious decline and revival was parallel to and characteristic of social developments throughout the new Republic. David Harrell describes the religious landscape during this period when he writes,

> The religious history of the United States has been marked by recurrent cycles of decline and revival. The early religious interest which played such a major part in the founding of several of the colonies declined in the late seventeenth and early eighteenth centuries. After 1740 this decline was followed by a period of enthusiasm, the Great Awakening, which worked its way through all the colonies by the 1770's.... Around the turn of the century a second awakening stirred the American religious scene. A significant revival had erupted in the East as early as the 1740's in the universities, but more spectacular was the religious outbreak all along the American frontier known as the Great Awakening of the West. This new evangelical surge caused a significant revamping of several religious needs of the ebullient and individualistic society of the frontier....[7]

It was during this period that two distinct Protestant reform movements merged and would later become known as the Christian Church (Disciples of Christ). One group, the Disciples, was led by two former Presbyterian ministers with some Baptist connections. The other movement, the Christians, was led by a former Presbyterian minister. It could be argued, as Toulouse does, that it is incorrect to refer to this new organized Protestant religious movement as "sectarian." Some called it sectarian because its core mission was to dismantle divisions (denominationalism) within Christianity and to restore the understanding of the original or New Testament church. Toulouse argues,

> I believe it is time to question the accuracy of the wholesale depiction of early Disciples History as "sectarian." The rich theological heritage of the early days of the movement, dedicated

---

[7] David E. Harrell, Jr., *Quest for a Christian America, 1800–1865: A Social History of the Disciples of Christ*, vol. 1 (Tuscaloosa: University of Alabama Press, 2003 [1966]) 2.

as it was to the wholeness of the church and the importance of apostolic faith for that wholeness, seems to call at least some aspects of sectarian analysis into question. I believe it is more accurate to understand the commitments of early Disciples as part and parcel of a struggle toward wholeness in church life, one lacking in maturity and often naïve, one often affected by the fluctuations of American culture, but nevertheless one that was inclusive in intent and, therefore, hardly sectarian.[8]

Within the framework of strict theological and sociological definitions, Toulouse's argument concerning the early days of the Disciples movement is correct. What is also true, however, is that, over time, the rigid and staunch commitment to restoration and unity within the church would, ironically, result in the Christian Church becoming by definition and by practice a Protestant sectarian denomination.[9]

The ideological and theological foundations of the Christian Church's commitment to Christian unity and restoration can be traced directly to its founders. And as we shall later see, this commitment played a central role in the church's response to the needs of schooling for free and formerly enslaved Africans throughout the South.

The Founders, Theology, and Polity

According to historians, Thomas Campbell, his son Alexander Campbell, Barton Stone, and Walter Scott, are considered the founding fathers of the Christian Church. Arguably, the most influential of the four are the younger Campbell and Stone. They are consistently credited with being the foundational architects of what is today known as the Christian Church (Disciples of Christ). The theological agenda that would be most influential in guiding the Disciples of Christ was

---

[8] Toulouse, *Joined in Discipleship*, 6.

[9] Throughout the years, and even today, many Disciples reframe from referring to the Christian Church as a "denomination." These individuals prefer the term "movement" as an institutional descriptive. This preference of one term over the other reflects a commitment not so much to the "restoration" of the New Testament church; rather, it reflects a commitment to the contemporary ecumenical movement and Christian unity, both of which find their roots in the theological perspectives of the church's founders.

clearly set by the elder Campbell. According to Stephen Sprinkle, Thomas Campbell "set the theological agenda for his son and through him the whole movement for nearly fifty years. While Alexander Campbell made it his own in his editorial work, his preaching, and public debating, all the major architectonic features of the Disciples way were set by his father."[10]

The theological and ideological origins that shaped and informed Alexander Campbell's thinking can be traced to his father Thomas, to Scottish philosophical traditions, and to one of the preeminent Enlightenment thinkers, John Locke. Thomas Campbell, who served as a local church pastor in Ireland, was an Old Light Anti-Burger Seceder Presbyterian. His son would also become one. In 1807, leaving his family in Ireland, the elder Campbell traveled to the United States to establish a new life for his family. He became formally affiliated with the Associated Synod of North America, which was the organizational manifestation of the Anti-Burger Seceder Presbyterians in North America. According to McAllister and Tucker, "[The Presbyterians were] a particularly rigid body in both doctrine and polity. They characteristically opposed every innovation designed to meet the peculiar needs or problems of the new country. Unlike the Methodist circuit rider and the Baptist farmer-preacher, who served all frontier communities equally, the Presbyterian preacher ministered primarily to people of his own background."[11]

Campbell argued that the Church of Christ on earth is "essentially, intentionally, and constitutionally one," and became so frustrated by the rigid exclusivity of the Presbyterian Church that he renounced all creedal statements.[12] In 1809 he withdrew from the Chartiers Presbytery Synod, moved to Southwestern Pennsylvania, and established the Christian Association of Washington. It was during this period that Campbell and a group of reformers wrote the *Declaration and Address of the Christian Association of* Washington, which is the

---

[10] Stephen Sprinkle, *Disciples & Theology: Understanding the Faith of a People in Covenant* (St. Louis: Chalice Press, 1999) 9.

[11] McAllister and Tucker, *Journey of Faith*, 105.

[12] Ibid., 24.

oldest foundational document of the Christian Church. McAllister and Tucker provide a summary of this important document:

> Campbell's thirteen propositions identify specific principles and may be summarized as follows:
>
> First, the essential unity of the Church of Christ.
>
> Second, the supreme authority of the scriptures.
>
> Third, the special authority of the New Testament.
>
> Fourth, the essential brotherhood of all who love Christ and try to follow him.
>
> Sixth, that if human innovations can be removed from the church, the followers of Christ will unite upon the scriptural platform.[13]

The year 1809 also marked the arrival of Alexander Campbell and the rest of the Campbell family in North America. On his way to America, the younger Campbell was shipwrecked for nine months in Scotland. During this period he studied under James and Robert Haldane at the University of Glasgow. Robert Haldane brought twenty men and four women from Africa to educate them for the purpose of sending them back to Africa to serve as missionaries. "It seems quite likely," writes John Long, "that [Campbell's] attitude toward Negroes was formed by his acquaintance with those men and women."[14] Many years later Alexander Campbell actively supported the African colonization movement that sought to repatriate Africans to their homeland. His experience at Glasgow may have influenced such support.

Following his father's footsteps, Alexander Campbell became a Presbyterian minister, and like his father before him, withdrew from the Seceder Presbytery. The motivation for this departure was to return to New Testament Christianity. He was later licensed to preach by the Brush Run Church. This church was formerly the Christian

---

[13] Ibid., 112.

[14] John C. Long, "The Disciples of Christ and Negro Education," Ph.D. diss., University of Southern California, 1960, 34.

Association of Washington and constituted in 1811. The younger Campbell's identification with "Believers baptism" played an influential role in his association with the Redstone Baptist Association from 1815 to 1830. In 1823, Campbell started a publication called *The Christian Baptist* with the goal of restoring original Christianity. Through this medium, which was discontinued in 1830, Campbell articulated his controversial ideas about reform, which were met with considerable opposition from Baptist clergy. Campbell would succeed, however, in attracting numerous Baptists to his ideas about restorationism. Concerning the impact of the *Christian Baptist*, Harrell writes,

> During his year as a Baptist, Campbell founded his first paper, the *Christian Baptist*, which he used from 1823 to 1830 with devastating proficiency in gaining followers among the Baptists of western Pennsylvania, western Virginia, Ohio, and Kentucky. The fundamentals of the restoration plea, as well as the basis of separation from the Baptist church, appeared in the pages of the *Christian Baptist*. Campbell mercilessly attacked the clergy, creeds, and authoritative councils and pled for a "restoration of the ancient order of things." By 1830 the Campbell movement was rapidly crystallizing and thousands of converts were being gained yearly.[15]

Many argue, as I do, that of the four founders, Alexander Campbell emerged to be the primary and most influential voice of the Disciples of Christ movement. Through the *Millennial Harbinger*, which he established in 1830 and edited for more than thirty years, Campbell influenced the direction of the Christian Church for decades to come. Of the four founders, Campbell was the most learned and most conversant with the scholars of his time. He would later become founder of Buffalo Seminary (1818–1823) in Western Pennsylvania, and played a central role in the founding of Bethany College in 1841, serving as its first president. Campbell has been credited with being the "chief architect of higher education philosophy for the Disciples in

---

[15] Harrell, *Quest for a Christian America*, 7.

the 19th century...."[16] Known as an eloquent orator and skillful debater, Campbell would become the most visible national leader of the early movement. Commenting on Campbell's emergence as a leader, McAllister and Tucker write, "As Disciples moved through this eventful period of rapid expansion, [people] asked over and over: 'What does Mr. Campbell think?' It was a natural question, for the Sage of Bethany was by all odds their most prominent spokesman and influential leader."[17]

Born in Maryland in 1772, and the only American-born of the four founders, Barton Stone spent his formative years in North Carolina and Virginia. He initially set out to practice law, but through a turn of events, he began study for Christian ministry. Stone was licensed to preach in the Presbyterian Church in 1796 and began serving in Kentucky. He too had a growing theological opposition to hierarchical polity and authority and to the church's adherence to "man-made" creeds. Stone believed that each congregation should govern itself and affirmed that the only sure way to heaven was the Bible. At his ordination, he reluctantly accepted the *Westminster Confession of Faith*, stating that he embraced it only as it was "consistent with the Word of God."[18]

During the Cane Ridge camp meetings of 1803 in Kentucky, Richard McNemar, a prominent Presbyterian minister and a central figure of the camp meeting, came under fire from the Synod of Kentucky "for deviating from the Westminster Confession and violating church discipline." It seems that the "acrobatic Christianity" that was characteristic of the worship at Cane Ridge was met with strong disapproval from Presbyterian authorities. Stone and three other clergy, along with McNemar, broke away from the Synod of Kentucky and started the *Springfield Presbytery*. Within a year, this group disbanded and published *The Last Will and Testament of the Springfield Presbytery*. This document is second only to the *Declaration and Address*

---

[16] D. Duane Cummins, *Disciples Colleges* (St. Louis: Christian Board of Publications, 1976) 30.

[17] McAllister and Tucker, *Journey of Faith*, 155.

[18] Ibid., 23.

of the Christian Association of Washington in terms of its influence on the theological foundation of the Disciples of Christ. The *Last Will and Testament* expressed the core issues for which Stone had a growing frustration. The document, according to McAllister and Tucker, "insisted that each congregation should govern itself; argued that the Bible is the 'only sure guide to heaven;' and expressed a desire to 'sink into union with the Body of Christ at large.' Having renounced the name 'Presbyterian' as sectarian, they agreed henceforth to call themselves Christians."[19]

Church historians often refer to the Christian Church as the "Stone-Campbell movement." Such a reference implies that Walter Scott played a less influential role in the founding of this church; however, his contribution to the Disciples of Christ movement should not be minimized. Born in Moffat, Scotland, and educated at the University of Edinburgh, Scott moved to the United States in 1818. He initially taught school in Pittsburgh and was later ordained as a frontier Presbyterian minister in Kentucky. Scott soon became fed up with denominationalism and was interested in establishing "the ancient order of things." He, therefore, joined the Protestant reform movement. It is said that Scott's itinerate evangelical preaching method, used in the Western Reserve, proved to be a catalyst for the Protestant restorationist movement. It is likely that Scott's interest in the Protestant frontier restoration movement was sparked by his association with a congregation of "primitive Christians" led by George Forrester. It was here that Scott was exposed to John Locke, James Glas, Robert Sandeman, and James and Robert Haldane. The influence these men had on the Disciples of Christ and other Protestant reformationists will be addressed below. Scott first met Alexander Campbell in Pittsburgh in winter 1821–1822. He later also met Thomas Campbell. Scott soon discovered that he shared common views with the Campbells concerning Christian union.

Scott was an anti-emotionalist, and like many Presbyterians, he sought to counter the emotional fervor of the revivals. He developed the "five-finger exercise," which for him was a rational and logical

---

[19] Ibid., 24.

process to become a Christian. Summarizing this process of conversion, Toulouse writes, "The first three steps involved human action: (1) confess faith; (2) repent sins; (3) undergo baptism. The last two steps belonged to God and were associated with the third step: as baptism is completed, (4) God forgives; and (5) the Holy Spirit is granted (as is eternal life)."[20]

The founders of the Christian Church each shared common theological and philosophical antecedents. Citing the European origin of these antecedents, McAllister and Tucker write, "The European backgrounds of the Disciples are found in Northern Ireland, Scotland, and England. These backgrounds were shaped by nonconformist and Free-Church movements in the last part of the eighteenth century. Through them the Disciples relate directly to the full history of Christianity."[21]

The Disciples founders held in common a disdain for creeds and ecclesial authority; an affinity toward the integration of reason and faith; a rigid affirmation of the absolute authority of the Holy Bible; and a desire to restore what they believed to be the form and function of the New Testament church. Each of these principles can be traced to the influence of several Enlightenment thinkers, but none had more impact than John Locke.[22]

The larger Protestant evangelical sectarian groups of the American frontier espoused a theology and doctrine that were primarily either Calvinistic or Lutheran. In contrast, according to John Long, the Disciples "were grounded in the philosophy of the father of the Enlightenment, John Locke. The course of American democratic institutions and the inception and growth of Disciple of Christ

---

[20] Toulouse, *Joined in Discipleship*, 30.

[21] McAllister and Tucker, *Journey of Faith*, 89.

[22] For an expanded examination of the Enlightenment see Louis K. Dupre, *The Enlightenment and the Intellectual Foundations of Modern Culture* (New Haven: Yale University Press, 2004). For a discussion on the Enlightenment's influence on seventeenth- and eighteenth-century North American theological and political thought see Henry Farhman, *The Enlightenment in America* (New York: Oxford University Press, 1976) and Peter Harrison, *Religion, and the Religions in the English Enlightenment* (New York: Cambridge University Press, 1990).

churches were shaped greatly by the spirit and ideas of Locke."[23]
Locke's writing had such a profound influence on Disciples' theological
and philosophical formation that Long refers to him as the "patron
philosopher of the Disciples of Christ."[24]

Of particular literary influence are Locke's *Essay on Human
Understanding* and his *Letters on Toleration*. Here Locke elevated the
Bible over and above human creeds while rejecting metaphysical and
theological theories. Locke denounced emotionalism and argued for the
"reasonableness of Christianity." He also was an advocate for tolerance.
This would become a critical principle for Disciples who would later
champion the cause for the unification of the church. McAllister and
Tucker point out that "portions of the *Declaration and Address* could be
almost direct quotations from John Locke." This is especially true as it
relates to Thomas Campbell's views concerning the integration of
reason and faith; the concept of voluntary association; and an
individual's right to organize a church and to worship God as one sees
fit. McAllister and Tucker add that "before Campbell, Locke
emphasized the sole authority of the Scriptures, the needless divisions
of the church, and the essential requirements for the church
membership."[25]

Concerning Locke's influence on the founders' understanding of
the gospel message, Toulouse writes that their mutual interest in Locke
"led them to affirm that the gospel was eminently reasonable. They
believed that preachers should simply present the biblical evidence
supporting the fact of Jesus' messiahship. Any rational person would be
persuaded of the gospel's truth." Harrell acknowledges the impact of
Enlightenment thinkers on the Disciples as well as the wider frontier
religious community when he writes,

> The rationalistic and optimistic philosophy of the
> Enlightenment was simply a sophisticated expression of the spirit
> that prevailed in the American West. If many of the first-
> generation leaders of the Disciples of Christ were influenced by

[23] Long, "The Disciples of Christ and Negro Education," 23.
[24] Ibid., 17.
[25] McAllister and Tucker, *Journey of Faith*, 114.

the writings of Locke, Reid, and Bacon, the practical rationalism of the frontier reached into the pulpits and pews of every country church. The self-confident American frontiersman lacked respect for all authority, especially ecclesiastical and clerical, and his individualism led him to believe that every man had the innate ability to discover religious truth simply by a rational investigation of the Scriptures.[26]

As I have already noted, the restoration of "primitive" or "New Testament" Christianity was a central component of the Disciples of Christ understanding of mission. According to Toulouse, restorationism was based on two presuppositions: (1) the nature of the Bible and (2) the nature of the church. Nineteenth-century Disciples "viewed the Bible, particularly the New Testament, as a 'constitution' enabling them to reproduce the primitive and unified church in all times and all places."[27] Early Disciples leaders believed that anyone who approached the Bible without bias would arrive at a common understanding of truth. Thus, the belief and hope in Christian unity lay firmly on this approach to biblical interpretation.

Concerning the nature of the church, Toulouse writes,

> Disciples of the nineteenth century believed that all local gatherings of Christians in the first and second centuries were perfectly unified in all essential matters of faith and organization. This presupposition [concerning the nature of the church] was central to early Disciples commitment to restoration.... Early [Disciples theologians] were convinced that Christ had successfully communicated to his apostles what God intended for the establishment of the church. They also were convinced that

---

[26] Toulouse, *Joined in Discipleship*, 31; Harrell, *Quest for a Christian America*, 28–29. For a summary and analysis of John Locke's religious and political thought, see Greg Forster, *John Locke's Politics of Moral Consensus* (New York: Cambridge University Press, 2005); Victor Nuovo, *John Locke and Christianity: Contemporary Responses to the Reasonable of Christianity* (Dulles: Thommes Press, 1997); and John Marshall, *John Locke: Resistance, Religion, and Responsibility* (New York: Cambridge University Press, 1994).

[27] Toulouse, *Joined in Discipleship*, 60.

these apostles recorded accurately God's vision of the church in the Bible, just as it had been communicated to the apostles by Christ.... Finally, nineteenth-century Disciples believed the "primitive" church had followed these instructions to the letter. They affirmed, therefore, that all Christian congregations in the earliest era of Christianity were united around one common purpose and according to one uniform understanding of the church. Restoration movements in the British Isles during the eighteenth and nineteenth centuries represent precursors of the Christian Church's emphasis on the restoration of "primitive" or "New Testament" Christianity.[28]

Harrell points out that restoration for the Disciples was based on simple reforms. These included "the abandonment of names except such biblical terms as Christian and Disciples; regular participation in the Lord's Supper every first day of the week; and the establishment of independent congregations with biblically authorized officials."[29] Baptism by immersion for the forgiveness of sins would also be included among these reforms.

As it relates to this thesis, the importance of grasping the Disciples' commitment to restorationism and the presuppositions that informed this commitment cannot be overstated. Based on their reading of Scripture, it is the Disciples' understanding of God's mandate that the church must be united at all costs. The absolute urgency and necessity to dismantle divisions within the church and maintain unity is revealed by this quote from Thomas Campbell's 1809 *Declaration and Address of the Christian Association of Washington*:

> [The] division among the Christians is a horrid evil; fraught with many evils. It is anti-Christian, as it destroys the visible unity of the body of Christ; as if it were divided against Himself, excluding and excommunicating a part of Himself.... In a word, it is productive of confusion and of every evil work.... Although the Church of Christ upon earth must necessarily exist in particular

---

[28] Ibid., 63.
[29] Harrell, *Quest for a Christian America*, 3–4.

and distinct societies, locally separate one from another; yet there
ought to be no schisms, no uncharitable divisions among them.[30]

The source of the pervasive disunity within the church was the
authority given to human-created creeds or theological treaties and
doctrines. It was creeds and "human inventions" that caused the church
to be split into denominational and ecclesial factions, weakening its
witness in the world. Addressing the source of divisiveness within the
church and its cure, Campbell wrote,

> Moreover, being well aware, from sad experience, of the
> heinous nature and pernicious tendency of religious controversy
> among Christians; tired and sick of the bitter jarrings and
> janglings of a party spirit, we would desire to be at rest; and,
> were it possible, we would also desire to adopt and recommend
> such measures as would give rest to our brethren throughout all
> the churches: as would restore unity, peace, and purity to the
> whole Church of God.... Our desire, therefore, for ourselves and
> our brethren would be, that, rejecting human opinions and the
> inventions of men as of any authority, or as having any place in
> the Church of God, we might forever cease from further
> contentions about such things; returning to and holding fast by
> the original standard; taking the Divine word alone for our rule;
> the Holy Spirit for our teacher and guide, to lead us into all
> truth; and Christ alone, as exhibited in the word, for our
> salvation; that, by so doing, we may be at peace among ourselves,
> follow peace with all men, and holiness, without which no man
> shall see the Lord.[31]

Barton Stone was equally as zealous about Christian union. In 1826
he wrote, "It is frequently asked, Why so much zeal in the present day
against the authoritative creeds, party names, and party spirits? I answer
for myself: because I am assured they stand in the way of Christian

---

[30] Thomas Campbell, "Declaration and Address of the Christian Association of
Washington," in Charles A. Young, *Historical Documents Advocating Christian Union*
(Chicago: Christian Century Co., 1904) 79.
[31] Ibid., 72–74.

union, and are contrary to the will of God.... If we oppose the will of
believers, we oppose directly the will of God, the prayer of Jesus, the
spirit of piety, and the salvation of the world."[32] Stone's understanding
of the need for church unity, its meaning, and the source of its disunity
is reflected earlier in his ministry when he broke away from the
Presbyterian Church. In the *Last Will and Testament of the Springfield
Presbytery*, of which Stone was a signatory, we find these words:

> We *will*, that this body die, be dissolved, and sink into union
> with the one Body of Christ as large; for there is but one Body,
> and one Spirit, even as we are called in one hope of our
> calling.... We *will*, that our power of making laws for the
> government of the church, and executing them by delegated
> authority, forever cease; that the people may have free course to
> the Bible, and adopt *the low of the Spirit of life in Christ Jesus*....
> We *will*, that the people henceforth take the Bible as the only
> sure guide to heaven; and as many as are offended with other
> books, which stand in competition with it, may cast them into the
> fire if they choose; it is better to enter into life having one book,
> than having many to be cast into hell.[33]

The primacy Alexander Campbell placed on Christian unity, and
his understanding of what that meant, is consistent with that of his
father. The younger Campbell's emphasis on church unity and sources
of its antithesis is made clear in his book, *The Christian System: in
Reference to the Union of Christians and a Restoration of Primitive
Christianity as Plead in the Current Reformation*. The fact that Alexander
Campbell dedicates an entire book to this topic speaks volumes about
the degree of importance he placed on it. In the book, Campbell asserts
that two propositions have been "proved." The first is "That the union
of Christians is essential to the conversion of the world...." The
second proposition is "That the word or testimony of the Apostles [the
Bible] is itself all-sufficient and alone sufficient to the union of all

---

[32] Barton Stone, "Of the Family of God on Earth," *The Christian Messenger* 1/1
(November 1826): 15–16.
[33] Barton Stone et al., *The Last Will and Testament of the Springfield Presbytery*, in
Young, *Historical Documents Advocating Christian Union*, 20–22, italics theirs.

Christians...." Underscoring the disruptive and destructive impact of creeds and "human inventions," Campbell goes on to write,

> Therefore, all the defenses of creeds, ancient and modern, while they assert that the Bible alone is the only perfect and infallible rule of faith and morals, not only concede that these symbols called *creeds* are imperfect and fallible , but also that these creeds never can achieve what the Bible, without them, can accomplish.... To say nothing of the lesser schisms in the party that once formed one communion on the platform of the Westminster creed, we can now enumerate no less than nine separate communions, all professing the Westminster Articles in substance or in form.... It were useless to furnish other evidence in proof that human opinions, inferential reasonings, and deductions from the Bible, exhibited in the form of creeds, can never unite Christians; as all their fruits are alienation, repulsion, bickering, and schism.[34]

Simply put, in the minds of Disciples leaders, a divided church represented sin and would undermine a strong and convincing apology for the Christian faith to nonbelievers. I argue that it was this belief that informed the Disciples' radical commitment to the unification of the church; a belief that would play a critical role in adversely influencing the movement's response to Southern secession and to its educational mission with and among Blacks.

Ironically, the Christian Church's emphasis on restorationism also provides a partial explanation for why some Blacks would identify with this movement after the Civil War—a movement that supported a limited and conservative educational philosophy when it came to schooling for Blacks. I will address this in more detail in the section below titled "Black Presence in the Christian Church."

Manifestations of Protestant restorationism in North America during the Colonial period, and into the days of the new Republic, are

---

[34] Alexander Campbell, *The Christian System: In Reference to the Union of Christians and a Restoration of Primitive Christianity as Plead in the Current Reformation* (Salem: Ayer Company Publishers, 1988 [1866]) 108–109.

directly associated with opposition to European forms of control and governance being expressed throughout the land. Again, Harrell writes,

> The flourishing of restorationist thinking in America contributed to the establishment of a number of new sects and influenced the thought of others. The idea of restoring New Testament Christianity to its original purity seemed a perfect corollary to the secular understanding of the meaning of the new nation. As American democratic society represented a stripping away of unjust and unreasonable restraints of feudalism and monarchy, so the return to simple New Testament Christianity was an attack on religious privilege and ecclesiastical tradition. As the post-revolutionary generation of Americans lionized reason as the divine path to the discovery of natural law, so restorationists believed that man's reason would reveal the primal truth in divine law. The secret in both cases was honest investigation and an open mind. As the political democratization of the nation challenged the remaining remnants of privilege and class distinction...so the restoration movements of the early nineteenth century were religious challenges to the churches of the elite.[35]

More specifically, restorationist thinking in the Disciples of Christ can be traced directly to the influence of movements led by John Glas and his son-in-law Robert Sandeman in the Church of Scotland. It can also be traced to James and Robert Haldane who led small independent churches in Scotland. Concerning their influence on the Disciples of Christ, Harrell writes,

> The movement begun by Glas and carried forward by Sandeman elaborated many of the ideas adopted later by American reformers. Sandeman came to America in 1763 and established a congregation in Danbury, Connecticut, that later

---

[35] David E. Harrell, Jr., "Restoration and the Stone-Campbell Tradition," in Charles H. Lipp and Peter W. Williams, eds., *Encyclopedia of the American Religious Experience*, vol. 2 (New York: Charles Scribner and Sons, 1988) 845.

became a Disciples church. The Haldanes were important leaders of small Scottish independent churches of the early nineteenth century and they had direct contact with several American restoration leaders. Their ideas where widely known in America as well as Scotland.[36]

Prior to coming to the United States, Thomas Campbell was affiliated with an independent church that was associated with Glas's and Sandeman's movement. He also joined the Society for the Propagation of the Gospel at Home (SPGH) in Northern Ireland. The SPGH was organized in 1797 by James Haldane as an agency "for the promoting of the evangelical cause."[37]

A large and influential group among the Disciples leadership believed the church was mandated by the New Testament to be a purely spiritual and apolitical body. Later, this will become more evident when the Disciples' response to Southern secession is examined. Presently, it is of interest to note the Scottish influence of this position. According to McAllister and Tucker, "Glas distinguished between the Old and New Testaments. In the former, he held the state and the church to be identical while in the latter, he saw the church as purely a spiritual community. The aim of his movement was to restore primitive New Testament practices."[38]

Another example of Scottish influence on the Disciples of Christ is the manner in which the sacrament of the Lord's Supper or Communion is practiced. Unlike most of the so-called "mainline" Protestant denominations, which celebrate the Lord's Supper on the first Sunday of each month, the Disciples are widely known for their rather unique practice of celebrating this sacrament each Sunday. Again, the Scottish influence through Sandeman seems apparent as McAllister and Tucker point out that "[Sandeman] advocated the weekly observance of the Lord's Supper." The Haldanes also seem to have been influential in this practice as "they adopted congregational

---

[36] Ibid.
[37] McAllister and Tucker, *Journey of Faith*, 95–96.
[38] Ibid., 95.

independency as being the order of the New Testament churches and introduced the weekly observance of the Lord's Supper."[39]

The Disciples founders were postmillennialists. Like other Christians during this period, their reading of Scripture, which informed their mission of restoration and unity, convinced them that God was going to usher in the Kingdom, i.e., the thousand-year period of peace (millennium), through the church. For Disciples, "the church" was not merely divided Western forms of Protestant Christianity; God's mission could only be fulfilled through a united and restored New Testament church. Under Alexander Campbell's leadership, Sprinkle writes that the Disciples "became convinced and convicted that through them God was calling together all the 'People of the Book' into a new Pentecost of Christian unity that would begin theologically where the first Pentecost left off. Alexander Campbell called this the 'Millennial Church' whose task was thoroughly eschatological: That is, the conversion of the world in preparation for God's consummation of all things in Christ."[40]

Like many of their evangelical contemporaries, Alexander Campbell and Walter Scott believed that democratic republicanism and Christianity were almost, if not entirely, synonymous. This "native Protestant ideology," as I previously mentioned, was embraced by most religious and secular thinkers of the day and would inform the emergence of the doctrine of *manifest destiny*. Related to this point, Boring writes, "Campbell and Scott were postmillennialists and saw the U.S. and Britain as messianic nations that God would use to 'spread the influence of the Christian faith and the democratic government, and Christian civilization throughout the world,' which would gradually lead to the millennial Kingdom."[41]

In 1831, Barton Stone was the widely accepted leader of a loosely organized group of about 12,000 reformers in Kentucky and Ohio known as the "Christians." Additionally, Alexander Campbell, already in association with Walter Scott, was deemed to be the controversial

---

[39] Ibid., 95–96.
[40] Sprinkle, *Disciples & Theology*, 2.
[41] Boring, *Disciples and the Bible*, 47.

leader and spokesman of a group of "Disciples" that had split from Baptist associations in Virginia and Ohio. This group, also known as "Campbellites," had a loosely held membership of about 12,000. Formal conversations, worship, and fellowship between Christian and Disciple congregations began as early as 1828 in Cooper Run, Kentucky.

Barton Stone and Alexander Campbell met for the first time at Georgetown, Kentucky, in 1824. The two were already quite familiar with each other's restoration movements. Through published and private correspondence on the subject of uniting their movements, debate and dialogue among various clergy as well as inter-congregational worship and fellowship among Disciples and Christian churches throughout Ohio, Kentucky, Virginia, and Pennsylvania took place. In 1831, after a period of heated exchanges between Stone and Campbell, the Disciples and Christians were poised for unification.

Barton Stone developed a relationship with John T. Johnson, who was a highly respected Disciples minister from Georgetown, Kentucky. McAllister and Tucker describe what ensued:

> Under their leadership two Georgetown congregations, one Disciples and the other Christian, agreed to worship together. The experience convinced them that they ought to be one people. Subsequently, a small group of Disciples and Christians met in Georgetown for a four-day conference, beginning on Christmas Day, 1831, at which Johnson and "Raccoon" John Smith played prominent roles. This meeting was followed by a larger one at the Hill Street Church in Lexington, Kentucky, on January 1, 1832. There the chief spokesmen were Stone and Smith. Smith urged the assembled no longer to be "Campbellites or Stoneites, New Lights or Old Lights, or any other kind of lights," but to come together on the basis of the Bible which would yield "all the light we need." In hearty agreement with the position stated by Smith, Stone extended his hand as a pledge of full fellowship. A handshake sealed the commitment to unite Christians and Disciples.... Alexander Campbell was not present at the Lexington meeting. In view of his serious reservations about moving too quickly without giving due regard to all factors

involved, it is not surprising that his response to the news was hardly enthusiastic. He did expressed guarded hope for the success of the venture. Stone was elated; the union for him was the fulfillment of a dream. "This union," he reflected, "I view as the noblest act of my life."[42]

This union did not represent the formal coming together. "National" organizations as national structures did not exist within these movements. Union among the core leadership was now in place. A more complete union of the Christians and Disciples movements would occur over a period of time, primarily through the building of relationships between local congregations in cities and towns throughout the frontier.

A common belief in a core set of theological, biblical, and philosophical principles made the union of the Disciples and Christians possible. These groups, however, were by no means ideologically homogenous. Stone and Campbell's differences are summed up by McAllister and Tucker:

> Christians tended to emphasize unity at the expense of full-blown primitivism whereas Disciples were less willing to compromise their understanding of New Testament faith and practice for the sake of unity.... Disciples equated immersion with baptism; hence immersion was a prerequisite for membership in their congregations.... The Christians were immersionists, too, but exercised patience and tolerance in their dealings with "the pious unimmersed." ...Disciples observed the Lord's Supper weekly...but the Christians only gradually modified their practice of corporate worship accordingly.... The Christians had a higher conception of the office of the ministry and were less anticlerical than the Disciples.... The two movements differed substantially in their respective programs of evangelism. The Christians in the West emerged from the fires of camp-meeting Christianity on the raw frontier.... Disciples

---

[42] McAllister and Tucker, *Journey of Faith*, 151–52.

were more inclined to stress "reasons of the head" than "reasons of the heart" in winning converts.[43]

Perhaps it is this last point that substantially contributed to the rapid growth of this movement. The Disciples of Christ seemed to stand between the two extremes of rigid rationalism of the eastern churches and the emotional revivalism of the American frontier. It is not unreasonable to conclude that such balance was attractive for many.

Another area of tension for the fledgling restorationist movement was agreeing on a name by which they would be known. Both Stone and Campbell presented biblically based arguments to support their claim that the name of their respective group was the most appropriate. This was an area of disagreement that would not be settled until more than a century later. During that span of time the movement was known by those in and outside of the church as Disciples, Disciples of Christ, Christians, Churches of Christ, and the Christian Church. In 1957, the church changed their corporate name to the Christian Churches (Disciples of Christ), and in 1968 adopted the name it goes by today, the Christian Church (Disciples of Christ).

Despite their doctrinal differences, the Stone and Campbell movements held a common belief in the absolute authority of the Bible, especially the New Testament, and a fervent disdain for divisions with the Body of Christ. In the early years of the unified movement, what the Disciples and Christians held in common provided a strong enough foundation to work through their differences.

At its inception, the Christian Church was primarily a lower-class movement with a membership of 22,000. Its message of Christian union; restoration of the "ancient order of things"; freedom in biblical interpretation; and opposition to authoritative creeds and hierarchical structures was apparently one with which many on the American frontier could identify as evidenced by its phenomenal rapid growth. To appreciate the rapid growth of the Disciples of Christ movement, Harrell places it in the broader context of Protestantism in the U.S. during this period. He writes,

---

[43] Ibid., 148.

The eruption of fervent and revivalistic religion in the West and the urban centers of the East produced an extraordinary shuffling of the American religious census. In 1800 the largest American denomination was the Congregationalist, the Presbyterians were second, and Baptists, Episcopalians, Lutherans, Reformed, Quakers, German Sectaries, and Methodists followed in that order. By 1850, the Methodists were first with 1,324,000 members; Baptists second with 315,000; Presbyterians third with 487,000; Congregationalists fourth with 197,000; Lutherans fifth with 163,000; the Disciples of Christ, after only about twenty years of independent existence, sixth with 118,000 members; and the Episcopalians seventh with only about 90,000 members.[44]

By 1860, the Disciples of Christ's membership increased to between 195,000 to 200,000. It included 5,000 members who were black, 2,070 congregations (829 in the South and 1,070 in the North), and 1,800 licensed ministers.[45] As with any organization of this magnitude, tensions rooted in ideology, theology, and human response to socioeconomic and political developments in the broader society would lead to fragmentation.

The church resisted formal organizational structure beyond the local congregation because it was not, in the opinion of its leaders, biblical, and to do so might lead to division. However, national, regional, and statewide organizations did emerge. These organizations laid the groundwork for divisions within the church. In addressing this issue Harrell writes, "The church slowly coalesced into factions around such institutions such as missionary and state societies, periodicals, schools, and benevolent agencies. The diversity within the church was more profound than most church leaders in the late nineteenth century realized."[46] Ideologically, Darwinism and higher criticism would eventually play a divisive role between the liberal and moderate factions

---

[44] Harrell, *Quest for a Christian America*, 3.
[45] McAllister and Tucker, *Journey of Faith*, 188. McAllister and Tucker place the membership at 195,000 in 1860, and Harrell estimated 200,000.
[46] Harrell, *Quest for a Christian America*, 7.

of the church. By the end of the nineteenth century, for all intent and purposes, the "moderate" elements of the church were evangelical and conservative. Three-fourths of the most influential leaders of the movement could be located among the moderate group. Before and after the Civil War, they were located both north and south of the Mason-Dixon Line. A relatively small group of Disciples were considered politically "progressive" because of their outspoken position on the issues of the day such as secession and slavery. Below, I will discuss an outspoken but even smaller group of liberal Disciples and their relation to the church's response to the educational needs and demands of Blacks.

Black Presence in the Christian Church

Beginning as a handful of believers in the early nineteenth century, Disciples placed heavy emphasis on evangelism and expanded rapidly until about 1900. The heart of their numerical and financial strength lies in the Midwest and the Southwest. Slightly more than one-third of all Disciples in the United States and Canada can be found in Indiana, Missouri, Ohio, and Texas. Another third of the participating membership is located in the six states of California, Illinois, Iowa, Kansas, Kentucky, and Oklahoma.[47]

The above quote from McAllister and Tucker provides a snapshot of the Christian Church (Disciples of Christ), which began as an amalgamation of two distinct Protestant reform movements in 1832 at Lexington, Kentucky. Missing from this picture is the location of the largest concentration of African-American Disciples, who in addition to the locations named were also concentrated in Georgia, North Carolina, Tennessee, and Virginia.

Reacting to my rather negative assessment of the Christian Church's response to the educational needs and demands of Blacks before and after the Civil War, a professor of Hebrew Scriptures at the Interdenominational Theological Center in Atlanta, Georgia, posed

---

[47] McAllister and Tucker, *Journey of Faith*, 20.

this question: "Given the conservative nature of schools supported by the Christian Church for Blacks, what motivated African-American people to join this movement in the years following the Civil War?"[48] The professor's question gave me pause to reflect and carefully consider an informed response to his inquiry. The answer is complex and must begin by addressing black presence in the Disciples of Christ prior to the Civil War.

Blacks were associated with the Stone-Campbell movement from its earliest beginnings. Similarly with Protestant churches throughout the South, black church membership generally came about as a result of Blacks' association with a white owner or overseer. In his seminal monograph on black Disciples congregations, Hap Lyda writes,

> Blacks were members of the Christian Church (Disciples of Christ) almost from the beginning of the denomination in the early nineteenth century. By 1820 there were Black members in the two oldest Christian Church congregations, Cane Ridge, Kentucky, and Brush Run, Pennsylvania. Some of these members from the Cane Ridge church, notably Alexander Campbell[49] and Samuel Buckner, were given ordination and were encouraged to preach to Blacks and to establish churches among them in Kentucky and North Carolina.[50]

Thomas Campbell provided religious instruction for black children at Burlington, Kentucky, as early as 1819. Campbell's son Alexander baptized and received into membership Blacks in Pennsylvania, Western Virginia, and Ohio. "[Black] participation," writes Lyda, "in White-controlled churches was limited. Sometimes colored persons served as custodians. Occasionally Negroes filled the office of Deacons,

---

[48] The professor's name is Dr. Randall Bailey.

[49] This Alexander Campbell was black. It is not clear if his name was the result of some intentional identification with one of the Disciples' founders or if this was simply a coincidence. Lyda points out that both of his sons, Alexander II and Stafford, were Disciples ministers.

[50] Hap Lyda, "A History of Black Christian Churches (Disciples of Christ) in the United States Through 1899," Ph.D. diss., Vanderbilt University, 1972, 1.

although they served only Negro members. There were no Negro Elders or board members of record."[51]

Robert Jordan states that the early attraction for Blacks to Disciples congregations was quite simple: the message that was preached offered a vision of a better world than the hell that represented their lived experience. "They were already in Hades," writes Jordan, "and to hear a man of God tell them how they might secure peace and sit down at the welcome table pleased them very much."[52] For some, exposure to the preached word came as a result of driving Whites to church. On the other hand, some plantation owners simply allowed those they enslaved to attend, albeit in segregated seating. Again, Jordan writes, "[Blacks] occupied the rear seats in balconies in the churches where many heard the Word, believed it, confessed Christ, and were baptized. Although they had designated seats, whether in the rear, in the basement, or in the balcony, they were members just the same."[53]

According to Lyda, black membership in the Disciples of Christ totaled 7,000 in 1862 with approximately 1,500 Blacks belonging to segregated congregations; 20,000 members in 1876; and 48,250 by 1899. According to the 1897 yearbook of the Christian Church, by 1870, the total membership of the Disciples of Christ was 250,000.[54] Elmer Lewis points out that these numbers indicate a steady increase of black participation in the Disciples of Christ between 1865 and 1890. Black membership, however, began to experience a sharp decline after this point. In 1950, Leland Tyrrell, president of Winston-Salem Bible College, a black Bible college established by the Christian Churches/Churches of Christ in 1945 in North Carolina, attributed this decline to the lack of opportunities for theological education for Blacks within the Disciples of Christ. Tyrrell stated, "The white church provided no adequate facilities for the training of a faithful and enlightened Negro ministry and the Negro was not yet in a position to provide the facilities for himself. As a result we have lost over three

---

[51] Ibid., 8–9.

[52] Robert Jordan, *Two Races in One Fellowship* (Detroit: United Christian Church, 1944) 23.

[53] Ibid., 25.

[54] Lyda, "A History of Black Christian Churches," 37, 173.

hundred preachers, and churches in proportions, since 1890."[55] Lyda's
analysis and Tyrell's lament are supported by the 1887 writings of E. F.
Henderson, a black Disciples minister. Henderson describes conditions
that resulted in the exodus of Blacks from the Disciples of Christ toward
the close of the nineteenth century.

> We had not a single, solitary ordained preacher, or even an
> educated preacher among us. We had no place except in groves
> and private quarters in which to meet for worship. Many of our
> white congregations refused us, or manifested an unwillingness
> for us to take membership in their local congregations.... Thus
> you see plainly that we were either forced to stand still, organize
> into bodies without any reasonable possibility or success, join the
> denominations to be in some church or go back into the world....
> Many of our most active men and women in our church have
> gone into either the Methodist or Baptist church because these
> churches seem to them to be more prosperous than ours.[56]

During the first decade following the Civil War, black churches
experienced considerable growth. The black and white response to
manumission within the Disciples, as summarized here by McAllister
and Tucker, was not unlike that of Protestant sectarian groups after the
war.

> At the end of the Civil War the former slave states of
> Kentucky, Tennessee, Georgia, Virginia, and North Carolina
> had the largest number of Negro Disciples. There were few
> black congregations in Northern states. Most Negro Disciples
> were members of predominantly white congregations, but within
> a few years of emancipation this pattern was broken. Where a
> sufficient number of black Disciples existed, they were

---

[55] Lewis Tyrrell, "Promotional Bulletin," (Winston-Salem Bible College, 1950)
in Elmer C. Lewis, "A History of Secondary and Higher Education in Negro
Schools Related to the Disciples of Christ," Ph.D. diss., University of Pittsburgh,
1957, 25.
[56] E. F. Henderson, "The Cause of the Colored Brethren," *Christian Evangelist*
24/44 (3 November 1887): 699.

encouraged to form their own congregations and were often aided financially by the Whites to do so.[57]

There seems to be some disagreement regarding the date and location of the first predominantly black Disciples congregation. Edward Kolbe states that the oldest black congregation was the Old Liberty Christian Church established in 1846 in Collin County, Texas. In a paper written in circa 1943, R. H. Peoples, who served as the General Secretary of Negro Churches in the early 1940s, states, "The oldest record of one of these Colored churches is the membership roll of the Lexington African Christian Church. It was written in 1858 and lists the names of forty members."[58] Interestingly, Jordan writes, "The history of the Disciples of Christ from 1809–1860 is correct in omitting Colored churches for there were none on record."[59] More recently, in an article published in the *Encyclopedia of the Stone-Campbell Movement*, Lyda offers the following revisions concerning the earliest churches established by black Disciples.

> The earliest African American congregations were the Colored Christian Church, Midway, Kentucky, constituted in 1834; Pickerelltown, in Logan County, Ohio (1838); Lexington, Kentucky (1851); Hancock-Hill Church, Louisville, Kentucky (early 1850s); Free Union Church of Christ, Disciples of Christ, Uniontown/Union Community, North Carolina (1854); Grapevine Christian Church, Nashville, Tennessee (1859); Little Rock Christian Church, in Bourbon County, Kentucky (1861); and other congregations in Washington, Johnson, and Wilkinson Counties in Georgia.[60]

Lyda adds that Alexander Campbell (black) was purchased for $1,000 to become the pastor of this church, and that the first school for

---

[57] McAllister and Tucker, *Journey of Faith*, 294.

[58] R. H. Peoples, "The Disciples of Christ Negro Churches" (Indianapolis: United Christian Missionary Society, ca. 1943).

[59] Jordan, *Two Races in One Fellowship*, 25.

[60] Douglas A. Foster, Paul Blowers, Anthony L Dunnavant, and D. Newell Williams, eds., *The Encyclopedia of the Stone-Campbell Movement* (Grand Rapids: William Eerdmans Publishing Co., 2004) 11.

black pupils (probably a Sunday school) was started in this church. According to McAllister and Tucker, the Midway church started as an "interracial congregation." Once it grew, "money was provided by the whites to erect a building for black members so that they might meet separately." Alexander Campbell, they add, was "converted at Cane Ridge meetinghouse and freed to preach; who took the name of Alexander Campbell as his own. He obtained a job as a porter at Lexington, [and] attended Transylvania University."[61] Concerning other early black Disciples of Christ congregations, Lyda writes,

> By the mid–1830's there were large congregations of Disciples including both Black and White members in [Kentucky]. In Woodford County the churches at New Union, Grassy Springs, Georgetown, and Midway comprised so many Black members that the leaders of the churches thought it appropriate to organize a Negro Christian church.... [The Midway church] was also given the privilege of ministry by its own elders and the right to conduct its own business affairs.... There were, however, three additional churches founded before 1863. In 1851 the Lexington Colored Christian Church was organized...the Hancock-Hill church was constituted in Louisville about 1860.... Samuel Buckner, a member of the Cane Ridge Church and a particularly effective Negro evangelist, organized the Little Rock [Kentucky] Christian Church in 1861.... A "Christian Disciples Church" composed of Negroes was begun in Pickerelltown, Logan County [Ohio], in 1838. Henry Newson served as the first pastor. The church also functioned as an Underground Railroad station. In 1856 it was disbanded.... In 1842 Negro Disciples in Morrow County [Ohio] formed a congregation.... A number of Colored Disciples constituted a church at West Liberty on the Mad River in Logan County [Ohio]. In 1847 a meeting house was erected by the congregation.[62]

---

[61] McAllister and Tucker, *Journey of Faith*, 186.
[62] Lyda, "A History of Black Christian Churches," 23–35.

McAllister and Tucker locate the first black Disciples congregation in the South at Nashville, Tennessee, as late as 1859. According to them, in 1849 a white congregation maintained two black Sunday schools with a total membership of 125 pupils. "Ten years later," write McAllister and Tucker, "in 1859, one of these Sunday schools was organized into a congregation. Located in West Nashville and called Grapevine Church, it is considered the first black congregation of the Disciples in the South."[63] According to Lyda, the Grapevine church "was constituted in Davidson County near Nashville on the Harding plantation. Peter Lowery, a Negro businessman and devoted churchman, was selected as leader of this new Grapevine Christian Church."[64] Peter Lowery is also the founder of Tennessee Manual Labor University, the first school for African Americans of any type established by the Christian Church (Disciples of Christ). Much more will be said about the establishment of this school and its eventual demise later in chapter 7.

Finally, McAllister and Tucker write the following text concerning early black Disciples congregations and black presence in the Disciples movement prior to 1860:

> For the most part in the period from 1830 to the Civil War, any Negro members of the Disciples were slaves enrolled by their masters as members of a particular congregation. However, a small number of black Disciples, preachers and people, were free…. Sometime before 1838 there is record of a congregation in Savannah, Georgia, led by Andrew Marshall, a mulatto, who was a convert from the Baptists to "Campbellism." He bought freedom for himself and his family, built a large congregation, and was an able and popular preacher…. Under white Baptist pressure Marshall later rejoined the Baptists.[65]

Concerning this Georgia church, Lyda states that "…Between 1832 and 1837 Andrew Cox Marshall, pastor of the 3,000 member

---

[63] McAllister and Tucker, *Journey of Faith*, 186.
[64] Lyda, "A History of Black Christian Churches," 35
[65] McAllister and Tucker, *Journey of Faith*, 179.

Negro Baptist Church, became convinced of Alexander Campbell's views and tried to take his church into the Restoration movement. The White leaders of the Sunbury Baptist Association forced Marshall to recant and return to the Baptist fold, and exacted a promise from him to quit stirring up free discussion of religious issues, especially in the church."[66]

The question posed by the professor in Atlanta specifically addressed black attraction to the Disciples of Christ during the post-war period. Having the opportunity to exercise their newly acquired freedom and some semblance of organizational autonomy made the Christian Church and its congregational polity very appealing to African Americans after the war. It is not surprising that as black membership increased, Whites were more than willing to assist them in setting up separate congregations. Moreover, it is not a surprise that Blacks desired to control their own church. The opportunity to control their own churches made Disciples membership, particularly for preachers, quite attractive to black people. Securing such control was one of the immediate and accessible opportunities many Blacks had to exercise the fruit of manumission as they struggled to define freedom after the war. Commenting on this aspect of black reaction to freedom, Vincent Harding makes a key point. He writes, "In thousands of individual and collective actions black men and women persistently experimented with freedom, tentatively creating its forms and content. Working at the communal bedrock of their religion, Blacks made it clear that freedom meant independence from white control of their churches, of their organized religious lives."[67]

The Disciples believed in the absolute authority of the Bible and staunchly affirmed the freedom each individual had to interpret the Scriptures for herself or himself. Additionally, as reflected in its congregational polity, the Disciples were opposed to hierarchical ecclesial authority as a method of church governance. I argue that these distinctive traits made the Christian Church attractive to African

---

[66] Lyda, "A History of Black Christian Churches," 33.
[67] Vincent Harding, *There Is a River: The Black Struggle for Freedom in America* (New York: Harcourt Brace Jovanovich, 1992 [1982]) 278.

Americans. These traits were so appealing that many Blacks embraced the movement and its message even though it offered an industrial school model, which was a much less attractive form of schooling. It must be kept in mind, however, that the limitations and conservative nature of Disciples of Christ-supported schools for Blacks were not immediately apparent. After the war, access to any type of schooling met the immediate needs of Blacks, who historically had no access at all. Later, many Blacks became aware of other models of schooling being provided by sectarian and secular philanthropic organizations. Now Blacks attending Disciples' schools had a basis for comparison and critique.

The Disciples' polity of local church autonomy requires further attention. Church autonomy would later prove to be a paradoxical issue for black Disciples. While it is true that the opportunity to control their own churches was attractive to black Christians, the same opportunity financially to sustain and control schools would be far more difficult. Blacks, who formed schools in historically black denominations, such as the African Methodist Episcopal Zion Church, were able to maintain control over their schools because their national denominational structure provided financial support. Over time, Blacks who started schools in predominantly white churches, such as the Baptists and Disciples of Christ, lacked the organizational structure to sustain them financially and eventually were forced either to give control of their schools to Whites or to close their doors. These problems occurred because the governance of their denomination was based on congregational polity. To support this point, Eric Anderson and Alfred Moss argue that churches belonging to historically black denominations "were better prepared to enter the educational arena because they possessed denominational structures that facilitated the establishment and systematic funding of institutions."[68]

Other factors played a role in Blacks identifying with the Disciples of Christ. Some of these include plantation-based relational, even

---

[68] Eric Anderson and Alfred A. Moss, Jr., *Dangerous Donations: Northern Philanthropy and Southern Black Education, 1902–1930* (Columbia: University of Missouri Press, 1999) 17.

familial, ties with white Disciples, and lack of access to other churches because of challenges caused by geographic location. The idea of having the freedom to interpret the "Word of God" and the power to govern one's own church affairs without the control of outsiders (Whites) must have seemed alluring to black people. This would be especially true for a people whose lived experience for nearly two and a half centuries had been one of control and violence by Whites professing to be Christians.

Some of these attractive elements were also present in other sectarian groups. The Methodists and Baptists attracted the largest number of Blacks before and after the Civil War. Both of these groups allowed for more emotional expressions of faith in worship and offered opportunities for both industrial and higher education for Blacks. The issue of "emotional expression" of faith should not be minimized. The Disciples' emphasis on rationalism likely turned off many Blacks who embraced religion holistically with the "head and the heart." Unlike many European traditions, African cultures embraced and experienced a dialectic relationship between feeling and thinking, reason and faith. The dominant European tendency to dichotomize these realities was outright rejected by a large number of Blacks and many Whites.[69]

It would be a gross understatement to say that freedom in church worship was important for Blacks. Before and after manumission, worship provided a great many Blacks with one of the few opportunities to express fully—with mind, body, and spirit—the pain wrought from the brutality of chattel enslavement. It also enabled them to express the pain of other forms of racial, class, and gender oppression as well as vocal moans born of unimaginable emotional, psychological, and physical pain. Conversely, worship also provided the opportunity for

---

[69] It needs to be said also that many Blacks embraced this Eurocentric notion of the superiority of reason over emotion. In an effort to gain acceptance in a white-dominated culture, some Blacks rejected outright all forms of emotional expression in worship seeing such expression as a "heathenistic" and inferior behavior associated with their African past; a past from which many Blacks wanted to be disconnected. Such rejection by Blacks was due in part to self-defeating efforts to gain white approval and acceptance, but also an embracing—consciously or unconsciously—of racist interpretations of African history and culture.

many to express the joy born of experiencing the evidence of God's grace and love in the midst of seemingly insurmountable circumstances, a joy that surpasses rational understanding. To be able to engage in such expression without fear of white reprisal or judgment is a point often missed by historians and other religious scholars. Church was where Blacks could express their hope for a better day while living in ostensibly hopeless situations. It was hope rooted in the belief that God could make a way when there seemed to be no way at all. This form of worship required a rational decision to believe and trust in a God that could not be seen, yet it also embodied a faith that transcended the dimension of reason.

The manner in which African American Disciples interpreted and understood the concept of "unity"—so central to Disciples of Christ restorationism—needs to be explored in terms of the role it played in causing many to remain with this movement. It is likely that many black Disciples applied their commitment to racial justice to the biblical conceptualizations of unity in ways white Disciples did not. I will examine this aspect of why black people remained in the Christian Church more fully in chapter 8.

Although white Disciples tended to be more rationalistic than most Christians, they were not totally bereft of affirming expressions of emotion associated with their faith. In a footnote, Harrell states, "Among Disciples the rationalistic emphasis was more unmixed than in most evangelical sects. Disciples almost completely rejected emotion and 'experience,' although they inherited some of this emphasis through Stone."[70] Stone's ministry, of course, was shaped and influenced by the powerfully emotional environment of the frontier revival movement known as the Second Great Awakening, which was referenced earlier.

As I have pointed out, Blacks were present at Cane Ridge and Brush Run. Without question, they made up a portion of those exposed to the frontier revivals. Revivals would allow Blacks to worship more freely and completely, using their heads and their hearts. Describing

---

[70] Harrell, *Quest for a Christian America*, 27.

the cultural complexity and expression of enslaved Africans within the context of the camp meeting, Albert Raboteau writes,

> The increasing numbers of second-, third-, and even fourth-generation slaves born and raised in America meant that the linguistic and cultural barriers of earlier days were no longer so overwhelming. Moreover...there were situations which allowed for cultural adjustment and reinterpretation. The powerful emotionalism, ecstatic behavior, and congregational response of the revival were amenable to the African religious heritage of the slaves, and forms of African dance and song remained in the shout and spirituals of Afro-American converts to evangelical Protestantism. In addition, the slaves' rich heritage of folk belief and folk expression was not destroyed but was augmented by conversion.[71]

Here, it is important to reiterate that the Disciples were not a theologically or even liturgically monolithic group. When Toulouse and other historians speak of diversity within the early church, they are primarily talking about ideological differences and, to a lesser extent, differences in worship and sacramental styles among the leadership in white churches. Viewing the early Disciples of Christ movement, historians often neglect to acknowledge the diversity of the cultural depth and breadth of worship (in prayers, preaching, and music) and biblical interpretation made possible by the presence of Africans, and later African Americans. When given the opportunity to worship apart from white control, and undoubtedly when they formally separated from white congregations, Blacks worshiped in ways that gave expression to their cultural makeup. Freedom to worship allowed them to express their lived experiences in a way that was responsive to their socio-emotional and spiritual needs. Furthermore, early on throughout the South, black Christians were an extremely ecumenical group. It was not unusual for black Disciples, Baptists, Methodists, and others to have

---

[71] Albert Raboteau, *Slave Religions: The "Invisible Institution" in the Antebellum South* (Oxford: Oxford University Press, 1978) 149.

pulpit exchanges and to attend each other's worship services. Surely both emotion and reason would find full expression in these services.

Issues of autonomy, control, and freedom to interpret Scripture are indeed factors that attracted Blacks to the Disciples of Christ and Baptists. With these similarities one must ask why Blacks gravitated toward Baptist churches in numbers that made the Disciples' black membership seem miniscule. By 1890, of all African Americans who claimed church membership, 53 percent listed themselves as Baptists and 44 percent listed themselves as Methodists.[72] Given the similarities with the Baptists in polity and freedom to interpret the Scriptures, why was there such a disproportionate attraction to the Baptists? Given the Methodists' use of an Episcopal polity that is a hierarchical and authoritative model of church governance, what was the attraction for such large numbers of Blacks? Three key factors are instructive in an attempt to address these questions. First was the predominance of a conservative ideology among the Disciples leadership. Second was the Disciples' unwavering commitment to church union. Third is the manner in which the first two reasons informed the restrained Disciples' evangelistic and educational mission among Blacks compared to the more progressive approach of the Methodists and Baptists.

Arguments to support my hypothesis will be presented below. For the moment, it is instructive to point out that unlike the Methodists, Baptists, Presbyterians, and others who experienced splits within their communions over the issue of slavery, the Disciples tempered their involvement in the debate in an effort to avoid a schism for the sake of Christian unity. Northern manifestations of the major Protestant sectarian groups were actively involved in the abolition movement. They called for immediate emancipation of enslaved Africans. These

---

[72] Anderson and Moss, *Dangerous Donations*, 47. The Methodist figures include the African Methodist Episcopal Church, African Methodist Episcopal Zion Church, and the Colored (now Christian) Methodist Episcopal Church that are historically black denominations. The same can be said concerning national black Baptist groups such as the Consolidated American Baptist Missionary Convention and the National Black Convention that separated themselves from white-controlled Baptists in the North and South. Still, black membership in the white-dominated Methodist groups exceeded that of the Disciples of Christ.

same groups developed and implemented aggressive strategies aimed at the provision of literacy development and schooling for Blacks in the South before, during, and after the Civil War. These factors coupled with the aggressive mission efforts, in comparison to Disciples of Christ, by Methodists and Baptists played a considerable role in larger numbers of Blacks connecting with these Protestant movements.

By no means were these sectarian efforts devoid of policies and practices informed by racist ideology and practice. By comparison, however, they provided better options than those offered by the Christian Church. By 1868, in various degrees, through the efforts of both Blacks and Whites, the Methodist Episcopal Church had established fifty-nine elementary and three normal schools in the South.[73]

By 1867, the Congregational Church, through the American Missionary Association, supported 451 teachers and missionaries who were providing instruction for 38,718 students throughout the South. During this same period, white members of the Disciples of Christ had yet to establish the group's first school for Blacks, and at the same time they failed to provide any substantive financial aid toward missionary and evangelistic support among Blacks.

During this period, however, there was one established Disciples of Christ-supported school for Blacks. It was the aforementioned Tennessee Manual Labor University founded in 1868 by Peter Lowery, a black minister near Nashville. White Disciples did not establish a school for Blacks until 1873, the Louisville Bible School. Increased Disciples of Christ efforts in the area of schooling for Blacks would be forthcoming, but as we will see in chapter 5, these efforts were a comparatively late response with questionable motives.

The rapid growth of African-American membership in the Disciples of Christ by 1876 was due in large part to the work of several black evangelists. Mostly self-supported, and receiving assistance from local hosts, these itinerate pastors and preachers started numerous churches and baptized thousands. Prominent among these evangelists in Kentucky were Samuel Buckner, mentioned earlier, Leroy Reed,

---

[73] Richardson, *Christian Reconstruction*, 35.

Alpheus Merchant, George Williams, and R. Elijah Hathaway. Due in part to significant financial support from white Disciples, growth in North Carolina was prolific as a result of the work of persons such as Joe F. Whitley, Alfred (Offie) Pettiford, Demus Hargett, R. Esom Green, Yancy Porter, William Anthony (Bill Ant'ly), Charles Randolph, B. J. Gregory, and Davis Whitfield. E. L. Whaley, George Linder, and Joe Corbett were active in Georgia. In Tennessee, notable evangelists were Rufus Conrad and Hesike Hinkel. Other evangelists during this period include Charles C. Haley in Texas; Eleven (Levin) Woods in Mississippi; and Thomas Cross in Michigan.[74]

For reasons I have already outlined, before and after the war there was almost nothing more important to black people than learning to read and having access to schooling. Immediately following the Civil War, white Disciples placed little to no priority on evangelizing Blacks, arrived rather late on the scene to establish schools for Blacks, and developed a conservative and limited variety of schools once they were established. Given these factors and the comparatively aggressive education reform initiatives of Northern sectarian groups in the South, the low number of Blacks who joined or remained with the Disciples of Christ should come as no surprise.

The Disciples' Response to and Participation in the Enslavement of Black People

Like most white Protestant assemblies between 1832 through 1863, within the Christian Church there existed a measure of diversity on the position and response to the wretched and dehumanizing institution of chattel enslavement. Putting it simply, as an institution, the Disciples of Christ were not unlike most if not all predominantly white religious groups at that time—they were racist. According to David Harrell, "Disciples shared with their fellow Americans not only a rationalistic view of providence, but also a racist view. A belief in Anglo-Saxon superiority was never far beneath the surface in Disciples thought."[75] Supporting this view is the appeal for financial assistance to

---

[74] Foster et al., eds., *The Encyclopedia of the Stone-Campbell Movement*, 11–12.
[75] Harrell, *Quest for a Christian America*, 4.

the Northern church from a Disciples evangelist in Mississippi.
Describing those who were the object of his ministry in Mississippi,
he writes that the "[white] citizens are of the same superior race as
yourselves."[76] In chapter 5, I will provide a closer examination of white
Disciples of Christ leaders concerning the anthropological and
ontological assumptions both of themselves and of black people.

On the issue of slavery, like other communions, the Christian
Church was composed of members who both supported and opposed
this institution. Without question their staunch commitment to
Christian union figured prominently in their decision not to take any
extreme position on the question of slavery. Writing in 1845,
Alexander Campbell made clear his priority: "to preserve unity of spirit
among Christians of the South and of the North is my grandest object."
Of course, it was critical that he justify his neutral position on the issue
of slavery—an issue that divided national sectarian religious bodies as
well as the nation. Based on his reading of Scripture, Campbell
concluded that the institution of slavery was permissible in God's eyes.
McAllister and Tucker summarize Campbell's position on slavery and
the biblical interpretive rational he presented. They write,

> [Campbell] placed great emphasis on the Apostle Paul's
> insistence that every man should "abide in the same calling
> wherein he was called" (1 Corinthians 7:20). Instead of hedging,
> he stated that "the simple relation of master and slave" is *not*
> "necessarily and essentially immoral and unchristian."
> Concluding the series, he summarized his position in three
> propositions: (1) The master-slave relation is not "in itself sinful
> and immoral." (2) Slavery, nevertheless, is "inexpedient." (3) No
> Christian community "governed by the Bible can constitutionally
> and rightfully" make slavery "a term of Christian fellowship or a
> subject of discipline."[77]

---

[76] B. F. Manire, "Mississippi State Meeting," *Millennial Harbinger* 39/10
(October 1868): 583.
[77] McAllister and Tucker, *Journey of Faith*, 194.

Commenting on Campbell's response to slavery, Toulouse states that Campbell never condemned slavery, adding, "If anything the biblical witness seemed to allow for it. Hoping to hold the movement together, Campbell relegated the matter to the realm of private opinion."[78]

As a whole, the Christian Church was proportionately one of the largest holders of enslaved Africans among all Protestant communions in the United States. Commenting on the 1851 annual report of the American Foreign Anti-Slavery Society, Garrison and DeGroot note that "the 'Campbellites' owned 101,000 slaves, the Methodists twice that number and the Baptists only a few more. If this is true, the Disciples, on a per capita basis, constituted the leading slave-holding church in the nation."[79]

Both Barton Stone and Campbell were owners of enslaved Africans. Stone inherited a six-year-old black child and freed him at the age of twenty-five. He summarily arranged for him to be sent to Liberia through the Georgetown Colonization Society. Historians are quick to point out that once the enslaved persons reached their mid- to upper twenties, Campbell and Stone emancipated those they owned "out of conscience." Interestingly, neither Stone nor Campbell chose to manumit their "property" while they were children. Stone and Campbell were not opposed to abolition, but neither supported immediate emancipation. Like Stone, many Disciples actively supported the African colonization movement that sought to repatriate Africans to their native land. This was viewed as a viable option to the slavery issue.[80]

Stone eventually became outspoken in his opposition to slavery. Concerning his changed opinion, leading to the release of those he held in captivity, Stone credited his experience during the revivals at Cane Ridge as a turning point in his life. He later wrote, "This revival cut the bonds of my poor slaves; and this argument speaks volumes in

---

[78] Toulouse, *Joined in Discipleship*, 150.
[79] Winfred E. Garrison and Alfred T. DeGroot, *The Disciples of Christ: A History* (St. Louis: Christian Board of Publications, 1948) 468.
[80] McAllister and Tucker, *Journey of Faith*, 192.

favor of the work. For what avail is a religion of decency and order, without righteousness."[81]

Like Campbell, Scott did not believe slavery to be a moral evil, but thought it to be a political issue having nothing to do with religion. According to Lyda, Scott's congregation at Carthage, Ohio, "passed resolutions against partaking communion with liquor dealers, but insisted with Scott that slavery was not a religious issue."[82] Scott was opposed to abolition yet "took issue with the argument that one must be proslavery if he rejects abolitionism."[83]

There were Disciples who were actively involved in the abolition movement. An Indiana preacher named Pardee Butler moved to Kansas in 1855 to help stem the spread of slavery in the Western territories. Pro-slavery activists tarred and feathered him and threatened to hang him if he persisted in his work. In 1858, Butler requested financial support for his work in Kansas, which included an effort to provide schooling for Blacks. The request was sent to the American Christian Missionary Society (the ACMS will be examined in chapter 5). Isaac Errett, the ACMS corresponding secretary at the time, made a recommendation concerning Butler's request that reflects the prevailing neutrality and acquiescence to Southern sensibilities that would prove influential in addressing the issue of black education after the war. Errett's recommendation stated, "It must...be distinctly understood that if we embark in a missionary enterprise in Kansas, this question of slavery and anti-slavery must be ignored." In response to what amounts to being a gag order, Butler sent this reply:

> For myself, I will be no party, now or hereafter, to such an arrangement as that contemplated in your letter now before me. I would not make this "Reformation of the nineteenth century" a withered and blasted trunk, scattered by the lightnings of heaven, because it took part with the rich and powerful against

---

[81] Quoted in John Rodger, *The Biography of Elder Barton Warren Stone, Written by Himself with Additions and Reflections* (Cincinnati: J. A. and U. P. James Publishers, 1947) 44.

[82] Lyda, "A History of Black Christian Churches," 18.

[83] McAllister and Tucker, *Journey of Faith*, 192.

the poor and oppressed, and because we have been recreant to those maxims of free discussion which we have ostentatiously heralded to the world as our cherished principles.[84]

In protest to the ACMS position, in 1858, Ovid Butler (not related to Pardee), founder of North-Western Christian University (now Butler University), a Cincinnati preacher named John Boggs, and several others organized an anti-slavery convention in Cleveland, Ohio, and founded the Christian Missionary Society the following year. This society provided modest funding in support of Pardee Butler's work and ceased operations in 1863.[85]

Two Disciples-sponsored anti-slavery literary efforts are worthy of note. One was an abolitionist publication called the *North-Western Christian Magazine* first published in Cincinnati, Ohio, in 1854. The publication was edited by John Boggs and was renamed the *Christian Luminary* in 1858. This magazine was the primary outlet for antislavery writers within the Stone-Campbell movement until it ceased publication in 1863. Among this group of Disciples abolitionists were Matthew Clapp, who was a brother-in-law of Alexander Campbell; William D. Stone; John Kirk; Jane Campbell McKeever, Campbell's sister; and Jonas Hartzel. Kirk, of Ohio, openly challenged Campbell's support of the 1851 Fugitive Slave Law. McAllister and Tucker share this written exchange:

> Kirk wrote to Campbell: "I have come to the conclusion that I will neither patronize priest nor paper that is not strictly anti-slavery. Your position to American Slavery I very much dislike." A smoldering Campbell replied tersely: "I wish you were emancipated from the tyranny of opinionism. Were I to form my opinion of you from this communication, I would say that you are a very good miniature Pope. You are infallibly right, and every one that differs with you is infallibly wrong."[86]

---

[84] Quoted in ibid., 199.
[85] McAllister and Tucker, *Journey of Faith*, 199–200.
[86] Ibid., 197–200 ; also see Foster et al., eds., *The Encyclopedia of the Stone-Campbell Movement*, 573.

The other noteworthy literary effort was initiated by John Fee who was the founder of an interracial school in Berea, Kentucky. In 1848, Fee wrote an anti-slavery manual that attacked the myth that the Bible sanctioned the institution of slavery, and supported immediate emancipation.[87]

James Shannon was a prominent Disciples scholar who served as president of the University of Missouri, of Bacon College, and of Christian University (now Culver-Stockton College). This quote, from an address he delivered to a pro-slavery convention in 1855, is representative of Northern and Southern Disciples of Christ who were proponents of slavery: "And if, as we have seen, right of property in slaves is sanctioned by the light of Nature, the Constitution of the United States, and the clear teaching of the Bible, a deliberate and persistent violation of that right, even by government, is as villainous as highway robbery; and when peaceable modes of redress are exhausted, is a just cause of war between separate states, and of revolution in the same state."[88]

Among Disciples, opinions concerning the appropriateness of Christians being involved in the political issues of the broader society ran the gamut of the ideological spectrum. Walter Scott's notion of the church being an apolitical institution was by no means an isolated one. David Lipscomb was a major voice of the conservative branches of the church who opposed Christian involvement in politics, social activism, and civil government. According to Harrell, Lipscomb advocated an extreme position that demanded total noninvolvement in civil government and social activism. "Generally," writes Harrell, "he concluded 'Christians engaging in politics injure religion, hurt themselves, and never elevate the politics.'"[89]

Benjamin Franklin, editor of the *American Christian Review*, a Disciples periodical first published in 1856, reflects a more moderate position among Disciples. He wrote, "If a man has a favorable political

---

[87] *The Encyclopedia of the Stone-Campbell Movement*, 197.
[88] Ibid., 196.
[89] Quoted in David E. Harrell, Jr., *The Social Sources of Division in the Disciples of Christ, 1865–1900* (Atlanta: Publishing Systems, Inc. 1973) 27.

scheme let him declare it, publish a paper advocating it, or maintain it in public addresses; but not under the name of Christian; not in the name of the Lord, nor under the pretense of preaching Christ; for this would be a manifest imposition, no matter how good the political doctrine."[90]

Disciples belonging to the ideological camps of Franklin and Lipscomb regarding social activism and political engagement represented the prevailing sentiment among Southern Disciples. They believed that the Civil War and the issue of slavery drew Northern Disciples into social activism and thrust them toward liberalism. Isaac Errett and others representing a more liberal perspective on the subject of political and social activism believed that a Christian was called to engage and was to be a reformer and not an observer. Quoting Errett, Harrell writes, "An embattled Isaac Errett wrote in 1866 that the 'question of slavery,' while a political one, was also a 'question of involving domestic relations, social progress, the rights of man, civil and religious liberty,' and insisted that Christians could not avoid becoming involved in such issues."[91]

Already having embraced the principle to "speak where the Scriptures speak, and be silent where the Scriptures are silent," Campbell sought to justify political and moral neutrality on the issue of slavery by pointing out that the New Testament did not explicitly prohibit or condemn slavery. Even though, as McAllister and Tucker point out, Campbell "consistently refused" to support the pro-slavery position of the Southern churches, I believe it can be successfully argued that Campbell's position amounts to a defense of slavery. Not to oppose the Southern position is to support it. This pattern of acquiescence to Southern demands played an active role in shaping the Disciples' educational philosophy for Freedpeople in years following the war. Further evidence of Campbell's capitulation to Southern demands is the position he took to uphold the Fugitive Slave Law of 1851. This law gave Southerners the legal right to capture enslaved Africans who escaped to the North and return them to the South. The

---

[90] Ibid., 29.
[91] Ibid., 26.

bottom line for Campbell was unity of and within the church at all costs. At the end of the day, Campbell's bias was made clear when he wrote, "Much as I sympathize with a Black man, I love a White man more."[92]

Several colleagues have queried as to whether or not Alexander Campbell or Barton Stone ever related the principle of Christian unity to racial unity or if they ever applied this principle theologically to race relations. I've demonstrated above that for Campbell "unity" or "union" related exclusively to a relationship between and among churches and Christians. One could argue that there is an inference to racial unity when recognizing or affirming the reality of racial diversity within the church at that time. To conclude their principle of unity was intended to encompass, even by extension, race relations or racial unity, however, would be anachronistic. Given the well-entrenched practice of socioeconomic and political inequality based on race during the period, Campbell had every opportunity to live out explicitly the principle of unity in a manner that encompassed racial unity or race relations, but he did not. Responding in 1845 to the growing tension between opponents and proponents of slavery within the church, Campbell's singular focus regarding unity is made clear. He wrote, "Christian union and communion are not in the least to be affected by such parties, any more than by any other political denominations…. To preserve unity of spirit among Christians of the South and of the North is my grand object and for that purpose I am endeavoring to show that the New Testament does not authorize any interference of legislation upon the relation between master and slave, nor does it either in letter or spirit authorize Christians to make it a term of communion."[93]

As we have mentioned, Stone, and many of his followers in Kentucky, were outspoken in their opposition to slavery. Even though there was no clear demonstration that social equality in their contemporary setting was a goal, it can be argued that "unity" ultimately

---

[92] Alexander Campbell, "Our Position to American Slavery," *Millennial Harbinger* 2/5 (5 May 1845): 234.
[93] Ibid, 194.

had direct implications for race relations if not racial unity. Richard Hughes observed that the "Stoneites" generally gave more attention to issues of social justice, a reality that was informed by the apocalyptic worldview of Stone, which found its genesis in the theology of the revivals of Cane Ridge. Hughes writes,

> ...the Stoneites' abhorrence of slavery also grew from their overarching apocalyptic worldview, which focused on the sovereignty of God and the future triumph of his kingdom.... This means, quite frankly, that the early Stoneites wove a commitment to social justice into the very fabric of their faith. They believed that social justice belonged to the very essence of the Christian gospel.... One's attitude toward race, therefore, became for many early Stoneites a test for Christian fellowship.[94]

Stone and others were willing to include the ownership of human beings as a criterion for church membership, a position to which Campbell responded with great concern. For Campbell, at the end of the day, when it came to Christian unity his concern was primarily and exclusively the restoration of the "primitive" or New Testament church.

Clearly, Stone understood the institution of slavery to be incompatible with the gospel message and the reestablishment of the New Testament church. One should not conclude, however, that Stone's opposition to slavery pointed toward any affirmation of the principle of racial equality. Christian unity for Stone forbade a Christian owning another human being, but race relations and its impact on socioeconomic and political access and equity was entirely something else. As late as 1835 Stone would write, "Let your charity condescend to men of low estate, and treat them with respect, even the poor African slave. The salvation of their souls is equal to that of the kings of the earth. In death—in heaven, the distinction is lost." Even though Stone calls for "charity" and "respect" to be given to Blacks and acknowledges there will be no distinction of the souls of Whites and

---

[94] Richard T. Hughes, *Reviving the Ancient Faith: The Story of Churches of Christ in America* (Grand Rapids: William B. Eerdmans Publishing Co., 1996) 271–72.

Blacks (kings or formerly enslaved persons) "in heaven," he stops short of addressing or affirming racial equality in this world.[95]

Earlier in his ministry Stone did not support immediate abolition, preferring instead the repatriation of the free African. His participation in the African Colonization Movement through the American Colonization Society was fueled by his desire not to live among a free black populous. Writing in 1829, Stone states, "To free them [Blacks] among us, and let them live among us, is impolitic, as stubborn facts have proved. Were those now in slavery among us to be thus emancipated, I would instantly remove to a distant land beyond their reach."[96] Harrell observed, "In 1835 Stone wavered between the alternatives of becoming a radical abolitionist or accepting the permanence of slavery and becoming a supporter of moderation and compromise. . . . By 1845 the slavery issue had become too dogmatic and divisive for the expansive and tolerant mind of Barton Stone." [97]

In fairness to Stone there are indications that his position to consider only repatriation for enslaved—or formerly enslaved—Africans if they were manumitted, had shifted to a more progressive stance by 1835. My former professor in church history, Dr. D. Newell Williams, makes the following statement concerning Stone's opposition to slavery:

> Examination of Stone's antislavery pilgrimage indicates an abiding opposition to slavery over a period of more than forty years; discloses Stone's consistent respect for the African as a human being; and shows that the driving force of all of his anti-slavery activities, no matter how wrongheaded his support of the

---

[95] Barton Stone, *Christian Messenger*, (January, 1844), 259, quoted in D. Newell Williams, *Barton Stone: A Spiritual Biography*, (St. Louis: Chalice Press, 2000), 246.

[96] Barton Stone, "An Humble Address to Christians, on the Colonization of Free People of Color," *Christian Messenger*, (June 1829), 199, quoted, in Harrell, *Quest for a Christian America* , 98.

[97] Harrell, *Quest for a Christian America* , 98-99.

colonization scheme, was not "Negrophobia" or the welfare of Whites, but rather justice for the African slave.[98]

As evidence of Stone's shift from supporting the colonization scheme to supporting immediate emancipation, Williams points to his publication of William Lloyd Garrison's "Address to the People of the United States" in the *Christian Messenger*, edited by Stone, in 1835. The "Address"—originally published by the New England Anti-Slavery Society founded by Garrison in 1832—was a controversial tract calling for the immediate manumission of all enslaved Africans. Williams also points out that later that year, Stone reproduced two other articles in the *Christian Messenger* written by writers seeking to demonstrate how formerly enslaved Africans lived civilly with Whites after they were emancipated in British and French territories in the Caribbean.[99] Stone's decision to print these tracts does suggest a shift in his thinking concerning abolition, but if one is looking, as I have, for Stone's own voice—not simply printing the position of others—in supporting immediate abolition, one will not find it. One can only wonder if the divisiveness of the issues surrounding immediate emancipation versus gradual manumission and colonization—an issue fiercely debated among abolitionists—played a role in the lack of Stone's own voice and pen in support of immediate emancipation. If in fact Stone's reluctance to personally voice his support of immediate manumission of enslaved Africans was rooted in his concern for attaining Christian unity, his silence would represent yet another example of *the cost of unity*. It is interesting to note, as Harrell points out, that the *Christian Messenger* ceased giving any attention to the slavery issue after 1835, and in fact remained silent on the issue until the year of Stone's death in 1844.[100]

At the end of the day, it seems, for both Campbell and Stone, the primacy placed on Christian unity, understood narrowly, was to be

---

[98] D. Newell Williams, "The Pursuit of Justice: The Anti-Slavery Pilgrimage of Barton W. Stone," *Encounter*, 62, 1 (Winter 2001), 2.

[99] Williams, *Barton Stone: A Spiritual Biography*, 218-219. Also see Williams, "Pursuit of Justice," 17-19.

[100] Harrell, *Quest for a Christian America*, 99.

protected at all costs from anything that was determined to be too "divisive," including racial equality and unity "in this world." Clearly, however, Barton Stone's critique of and opposition to chattel enslavement was much more progressive than that of Alexander Campbell.

In the years leading to the attack on Fort Sumter, virtually every major Protestant denomination experienced a schism between their Northern and Southern churches over the issue of slavery. On the surface, it appeared that Campbell's effort to hold the church together during the years leading to and during the war had paid off. Little did he know that in 1863, three years prior to his death in 1866, the seeds of the eventual schism that would take place in 1906 had been planted by the formal position on Southern secession taken by the American Christian Missionary Society. At the same time, countless numbers of Blacks, enslaved and free, were completely unaware of how compromises made by the Disciples of Christ leadership to secure Christian unity would adversely impact Disciples-supported schools for black people for years to come.

The Missionary Enterprise and Southern Secession

Struggling to honor their commitment to restore primitive Christianity, the Disciples of Christ found themselves with a dilemma. They wanted to resist the temptation to develop any formal organizational structures beyond the local church that they deemed to be without biblical justification. By the 1840s, however, the home and foreign missionary enterprise was in full swing within Protestantism. Throughout North America, the millennial impulse to evangelize the world had taken on formal organizational dimensions. Several sectarian groups had developed domestic and international missionary societies in response to real and perceived human needs. The American Baptists' American Baptist Home Missionary Society and the Congregational Church-affiliated American Missionary Association are examples of such organizations. Furthermore, they all had begun major efforts to evangelize Native Americans, free and enslaved Blacks, various immigrant groups new to the United States, and people in various parts of Asia, the Caribbean, Africa, the Middle East, and the Pacific Islands.[101]

In response to internal pressure to join the Protestant missionary enterprise, the Disciples of Christ reluctantly and controversially responded to the call. The American Christian Missionary Society (ACMS) was organized at the First National Convention of the Disciples of Christ in Cincinnati, Ohio, 24–28 October 1849. The ACMS was both a home and foreign missionary society whose organization was met with great opposition because many believed there was no biblical basis for such an organization.

As with all national missionary organizations, this group's financial support depended heavily on donations generated at the local level. The controversy surrounding the biblical legitimacy of the existence of the ACMS severely impaired efforts to raise funds for its work. Between 1849 and 1869, average receipts for the work of the ACMS totaled just under $7,000. These limited funds were to support all of its domestic and international missionary work. Funding of missionary societies associated with other Protestant organizations was supplied primarily by the liberal arms of these groups that actively supported evangelistic and educational mission initiatives for and among black populations in the South. In addition to the controversy surrounding biblical legitimacy, ACMS's opposition to black education and their silence on the slavery issue also contributed to the meager financial support the organization received.[102]

Disciples who opposed the formation of a national organization within the Disciples of Christ took exception to the language of "society" being attached to their missionary organization. The very

---

[101] Unlike other Protestant missionary organizations, the ACMS gave little attention to evangelistic activities among North American indigenous communities. For further examination of nineteenth-century Protestant missionary societies see Daniel H. Bays and Grant Wacker, eds., *The Foreign Missionary Enterprise at Home: Exploration in North American Cultural History* (Tuscaloosa: University of Alabama Press, 2003); and William Hutchinson, *Errand to the World: American Protestant Thought and Foreign Missions* (Chicago: University of Chicago Press, 1987).

[102] Also see Lewis, "A History of Secondary and Higher Education in Negro Schools," 26–27.

word "society" was language used by the missionary organizations of Protestant denominations, and Disciples wanted to avoid any association with sectarianism. In 1869, a compromise was struck to address this issue. As a result, the word "society" was replaced with "convention." Concerning the founding and growth of ACMS, Lyda writes, "The white-controlled national missionary organization of the Disciples of Christ was called American Christian Missionary Society from 1849–1869. It was then integrated into the General Christian Missionary Convention from 1869 to 1895, then reorganized under the former name from 1895 to 1920. The names are sometimes used interchangeably in Christian Church literature regardless of the year designated."[103]

James Washington adds, "...the terms 'association' and 'convention' imply the voluntary consultative nature of the organizations."[104] This distinction would be important for Disciples who would be opposed to compulsory membership, which would then imply a biblical precedent or mandate to associate with such an organization.

Response to Pardee Butler's request for support, mentioned earlier; the AMCS's ongoing silence on the issue of slavery; and the group's lack of effort to evangelize among enslaved Africans caused the ACMS to come under heavy criticism by Disciples abolitionists. Controlled at the time by moderates who were committed to neutrality, the ACMS chose instead to concentrate its missionary efforts on overseas missions. Commenting on the tension resulting from ACMS's missionary agenda, Harrell writes,

> In 1859 [Pardee] Butler became the central figure in the agitation for the formation of an antislavery missionary society among the Disciples of Christ. Disciples abolitionists had criticized the American Christian Missionary Society from its inception because of the appointment of Dr. James T. Barclay as a missionary to Jerusalem at the first meeting of the society in 1849. Barclay was a Virginian slaveholder and although he

---

[103] Lyda, "A History of Black Christian Churches," 110.
[104] James M. Washington, *Frustrated Fellowship: The Black Quest for Social Power* (Macon GA: Mercer University Press, 1986) 78.

disposed of his slaves when he received his missionary appointment, he was never acceptable to Disciples radicals. Throughout the decade of the fifties the abolitionists in the church continued to attack the Barclay mission as an example of the "*Legree* theology" which dominated the missionary society.[105]

The next missionary would not be sent out by the ACMS until 1854. Perhaps in response to the criticism being lodged by Disciples' abolitionists, the ACMS sent Alexander Cross, a black man, to Monrovia, Liberia. Cross, an enslaved African, was described as being "well known to the church as a pious and orderly member, and as possessed with extraordinary gifts as a public speaker." Alexander's freedom was purchased at a price of $550.00 by the Hopkinsville, Kentucky, church from a "Mr. Cross of Todd County" for the purpose of engaging in missionary work in Liberia, West Africa. Alexander, his wife, and their young son James departed for Liberia 5 November 1853, arriving in January 1854. Tragically, James died during the voyage across the Atlantic. Two months after his arrival in Monrovia, Alexander Cross died of what is believed to have been malaria. None of the sources I've accessed concerning Alexander Cross provide the first name of Mrs. (a title she undoubtedly would have used) Cross, or indicates what became of her after the deaths of her son and husband.[106]

---

[105] Harrell, *Quest for a Christian America*, 116. "Legree" is a reference to Simon Legree, an extremely cruel dealer of enslaved Africans in *Uncle Tom's Cabin*.

[106] "They Went to Africa: Biographies of Missionaries of the Disciples of Christ," booklet (Indianapolis: United Christian Missionary Society, 1945) 5, on file at the Disciples of Christ Historical Society, Nashville; McAllister and Tucker, *Journey of Faith*, 258. Also see Richard Chowning, "A Brief History of the Churches of Christ in Africa," on the Churches of Christ website, http://www.africamissions. org/africa/cochist.htm, November 1991. Robert Jordan erroneously makes this statement: "Alexander Cross was sent out from the Cane Ridge Church (White) in Kentucky as a foreign missionary to work among the Negroes of Jamaica " (*Two Races in One Fellowship*, 35). Actually, it was Julius O. Beardslee (white) who was sent to Jamaica by ACMS in 1858. See also "Our First Missionary to the Heathen," *Christian Standard* 33/27 (3 July 1897): 851. Jacob Kenoly was the second black Disciples of Christ missionary. Kenoly, from St. Louis, studied for a short time at SCI. In 1905, without CWBM support, he worked his way on ships to Liberia where he served from 1905 to 1911. CWBM eventually provided for the mission he began at Schieffelin, Liberia. Kenoly drowned in 1911 while fishing with his students on

While tensions rooted in slavery and states rights increased, the Disciples of Christ as a national movement continued to hold fast to its policy of neutrality for the sake of maintaining union among its churches. Without question, Disciples laity and clergy from both the North and South took strong and diverse stances on the issues of slavery and states rights. The extremes ran from pro-slavery positions like that of the aforementioned James Shannon of Missouri to that of a pro-Union reaction as represented by James A. Garfield. In 1861 Garfield was serving as principal of Western Reserve Eclectic Institute (later to become Hiram College), a Disciples-related school in Ohio. At the outbreak of the war, he resigned to join the Union Army. Garfield, of course, would become the twentieth president of the United States in 1881.[107]

As war broke out between the Union and the Confederacy, the most influential spokesperson of the Disciples, Alexander Campbell, held his ground on neutrality. Commenting on the Christian Church's response to the war and its aftermath, Kenneth Henry writes, "Disciples of Christ made no dramatic witness during the Civil War, and tended to conform to the prevailing views wherever they were located: In the North, there were Disciples abolitionists, and in the South, there were pro-slavery advocates. Consequently, Disciple programs to aid the Freedmen were varied and dependent upon local initiative and dedicated individuals."[108]

While the ACMS remained virtually non-responsive to the issue of slavery, they eventually took a stand on the issue of Southern secession. Historians would later conclude this position to be the seeds of a formal schism that occurred in 1906.[109] During the General

---

the coast of Liberia. For more on Cross and Kenoly, see "They Went to Africa: Biographies of the Disciples of Christ," an undated pamphlet on file at the Disciples of Christ Historical Society, Nashville. Also see C. C. Smith, *Jacob Kenoly and His Work in Africa* (Indianapolis: Christian Women's Board of Missions, 1911) also on file at DOCHS.

[107] McAllister and Tucker, *Journey of Faith*, 202.

[108] Kenneth Henry, "Unknown Prophets: Black Disciples Ministry in Historical Perspective," *Discipliana* 46/1 (Spring 1986): 5.

[109] McAllister and Tucker, *Journey of Faith*, 252.

Convention of October 1861, the ACMS considered and rejected the following resolution: "Resolved, that we deeply sympathize with the loyal and patriotic of our country in their present efforts to sustain the government of the United States, and we feel it our duty as Christians to ask our brethren everywhere to do all in their power to sustain the proper and constitutional authorities of the Union." The fact that such a resolution was even considered caused a great deal of tension among Disciples in the North and the South, but the fact that it didn't pass was considered a victory for moderates.[110]

As the conflict between the states intensified, the ACMS took a bold and decisive position on the war at the Cincinnati convention of 1863. By now, Northern radicals and those from the border states who sympathized with their cause were now in control of the ACMS. Furthermore, Southern church representatives decided not to cross the Mason-Dixon Line to attend the gathering. Those who did attend the deliberations of the ACMS overwhelmingly passed the following resolution:

Whereas, "there is no power but of God," and "the powers that be are ordained of God;" and whereas, we are commanded in the Holy Scriptures to be subject to the powers that be, and "obey magistrates," and whereas an armed rebellion exists in our country, subversive of these divine injunctions; and whereas, reports have gone abroad that we, as a religious body, and particularly as a Missionary Society, are to a certain degree disloyal to the Government of the United States:
therefore—
Resolved, That we unqualifiedly declare our allegiance to said Government, and repudiate as false and slanderous any statement to the contrary.
Resolved, That we tender our sympathies to our brave and noble soldiers in the fields, who are defending us from the attempts of armed traitors to overthrow our Government, and

---

[110] Quoted in Lyda, "A History of Black Christian Churches," 19.

also to those bereaved, and rendered desolate by the ravages of war.

    Resolved, That we will earnestly and constantly pray to God to give our legislators and rulers, wisdom to enact, and power to execute, such laws are [as] will seedily bring to us the enjoyment of a peace that God will design and bless.[111]

According to Harrell, by the end of the war, the membership of the Christian Church had united around three sectional oriented positions. First was Northerners who were primarily "preachers who had condemned slavery, supported the war, and instigated the passage of the war resolutions by the American Christian Missionary Society...." Second was the Southern churches where "there was a seething deep resentment against the actions of the missionary society during the war." And third was a faction made up of border state churches "built around the nucleus of those who had opposed the war; had especially tried to forestall the involvement of the church; and were determined to try to reconcile the discordant elements in the church by reverting to the old time-tested principles of moderation and repression of the controversial."[112] As we shall see, this third group will play a central and influential role in shaping the Disciples of Christ's form and function of schools for the newly freed African Americans of the South.

---

[111] *Report of Proceedings of the Fifteenth Anniversary Meeting of the American Christian Missionary Society, Held in Cincinnati, October 20, 21, 22, 1863* (Cincinnati: E. Morgan and Sons, Printers, 1863) 24, quoted in Harrell, *Quest of a Christian America*, 163.
[112] Ibid.

5

RACIAL ASSUMPTIONS, ATTITUDES, AND
THE U.S. LANDSCAPE, 1865–1914

The Freedmen's effort to educate themselves and their children provide one of the most moving chapters in American social history.... [The] extent to which Blacks without resources and little experience scraped to pay for schools and teachers stand but like a miracle.... The desire for education everywhere exploded. For the Freedmen, as for the slaves before them, it represented the keys of the Kingdom.[1]

No other area of black life received a higher priority from black churches than education.... First of all literacy was the key to the scriptures, the Word of God, but education was also a rebuttal of the prevailing allegation that black people were a different order of human being, incapable of learning and manipulating the master's language.[2]

In order to gain an in-depth and critical understanding of the establishment, evolution, challenges, and demise of black schools supported by the Disciples of Christ, and to gain a more accurate understanding of black and white participation in this process, it is necessary to examine the socioeconomic and political context of the broader society during this period. Additionally, to assist in our understanding of why white Disciples supported the type of schools

---

[1] Eugene D. Genovese, *Roll, Jordan, Roll: The World the Slaves Made* (New York: Vintage, 1976 [1972]) 565.

[2] C. Eric Lincoln and Lawrence H. Mamiya, *The Black Church in the African American Experience* (Durham: Duke University Press, 1990) 251.

they did, the prevailing racial assumptions and attitudes held by influential members of the Disciples of Christ will be examined.

The Reconstruction Era (Presidential and Congressional)

The end of hostilities between the states and black manumission gave birth to the Reconstruction Era—a period that marks what is arguably the most radical period in African-American education reform. Blacks' belief in self-improvement and self-determination was intense and not to be denied. "After the war," writes Noralee Frankel, "a sense of having shared interests and goals strengthened collective efforts in education, religion, and politics, widening Freedpeople's vision of the meaning of community. Despite fierce white opposition that included violence, African Americans persevered to establish their own churches and schools."[3]

African-American agency during this period was often shaped and informed by an ideological perspective bent on the defense of the emancipation of enslaved Africans and to challenge the dominant planter regime that sought to keep them locked into a second-class status. The black agenda was to ameliorate the status quo through education. They sought to develop skills to change their own status and place in society; develop businesses, leaders, and organizations designed to respond to their needs; and demonstrate to the dominant group their ability to function as responsible and productive citizens of the Republic. To accomplish this, Blacks needed to have access to higher or classical education as well as industrial education.

The Sunday or Sabbath schools, which played a vital role in literacy development and religious instruction in the antebellum South, continued their dual function long after the war ended. In the history of African-American education, one cannot overstate the importance of this institution. Commenting on function of Sunday schools during the Reconstruction Era and beyond, Sally McMillen writes,

---

[3] Noralee Frankel, "Breaking the Chains: 1860–1880," in Robin Kelley and Earl Lewis, eds., *To Make Our World Anew: A History of African Americans* (New York: Oxford University Press, 2000) 279–80.

One cannot consider the South in the Post-Civil War period without considering the impact of the religious institution that touched so many lives. Northerners and Southerners black and Whites alike came to view the Southern Sunday school as central to their efforts to rebuild the region out of the ashes of the Civil War…. Northern missionary societies and almost all of the active Protestant denominations operating in the South identified the Sunday school as the best means to expose children to the Bible and lead them toward conversion, attract new church members, strengthen their denomination, and mold the next generation into pious, purposeful adults.[4]

Higginbotham emphasizes the role of women and the dual educational function of Sunday schools in the black church tradition:

Sabbath Schools constituted another example of independent efforts to promote black literacy during and after the Reconstruction and Progressive Eras. Products of the black church, these schools were usually run by women in the evening and on weekends and provided instruction in both religion and reading. Sabbath Schools and other church-housed sponsored schools continued to offer needed academic and industrial training as public schools literally lost ground throughout the late nineteenth and early twentieth centuries.[5]

Using the Sunday school as a primary tool for evangelism after the war, unlike the Disciples of Christ, major Protestant organizations poured large amounts of human and financial resources into missionary initiatives in the South. On this point, McMillen writes,

In addition to concerns for moral development, and developing methods of social control for five million Blacks who are now free, a key factor for the proliferation of Sunday schools

---

[4] Sally G. McMillen, *To Raise Up the South: Sunday Schools in Black and White Churches, 1865–1915* (Baton Rouge: Louisiana State University Press, 2001) xi–xiii.

[5] Evelyn Brooks Higginbotham, *Righteous Discontent: The Women's Movement in the Black Baptist Church, 1880–1920* (Cambridge: Harvard University Press, 1993) 54.

in the South was evangelism. The American Baptist Home Missionary Society placed sixty-eight missionaries in the South within one month of the war's end, and by 1868 Northern Presbyterians had placed one hundred seventy-nine. The White Northern Methodists were active along the border states. The African American Methodist Episcopal and African Methodist Episcopal Zion churches were also active in building a network of Sunday schools in the South after the war.[6]

Concerning the black Methodists, McMillen states, "These Black denominations needed and wanted to expand their influence naturally. Like Whites, they saw the Sunday school as a most effective evangelical agency to achieve these goals."[7] Through the Sunday school, black Disciples later established the first schools for African Americans associated with the Christian Church.

It is true, as McMillen states, that "Sunday schools helped strengthen and expand African-American churches and communities and gave Blacks additional resolve and strength to stand on their own. The institution became a place where lessons in racial pride were taught." Without question, Sunday schools provided a space to rethink, deconstruct, and reconstruct biblical interpretations given to them by Whites. It gave Blacks the opportunity to reinterpret the Scriptures and to articulate an understanding of the gospel message in light of their own experiences. It is also true, however, that Sunday schools in the black church served as a mechanism for the reproduction of Eurocentric theological constructions and biblical interpretative traditions. Such views of reality, more often than not, relegated or associated the very blackness of the people themselves to that of evil, cursedness, and God-ordained servitude. Unfortunate as it was, the Sunday schools served to reinforce within the minds of Blacks, Whites, and others the notion of an inferior position of black people within the human family in general, and in the American social structure in particular.[8]

---

[6] McMillen, *To Raise Up the South*, 32.

[7] Ibid., 32.

[8] For excellent examinations of biblical interpretive traditions that demonize the color black and the utilize the Bible to "justify" the enslavement of black people see

Primarily under the leadership of women, the Sunday school movement would serve as a catalyst for the development of statewide and national organizations throughout the black church. In chapter 6, I examine the manifestation of this phenomenon as it existed in the Disciples of Christ.

The availability of adequate supplies for black schools during this period was scanty at best. Books often used by AMA schools included the *Freedmen's Primer*, *Lincoln's Spelling Book*, and the *Freedmen's Spelling Book*, were designed specifically for black children and depicted Blacks in subservient roles. The main purpose of these books was to inculcate within the students the belief of black inferiority. Anderson argues that it is doubtful these books had long-term impact because the AMA schools were not sustained over time. In 1870, they had 157 schools throughout the South, 70 in 1871, and only 13 common schools by 1874. By the mid 1870s, Northern aid societies had little involvement in common schooling for Blacks in the South.[9]

Scholars generally agree that the Reconstruction Era was from 1865 to about 1877, which marks the end of the Civil War to the withdrawal of Federal troops from the Southern states. Henry Bullock states that Presidential Reconstruction, which was started by Abraham Lincoln in 1865 and continued by Andrew Johnson until 1867, was a series of amnesty initiatives toward Southerners designed to "cater to the traditional needs of those still in rebellion" in the South. Southern Whites (planter class) used Johnson's leniency toward the South as an opportunity to reestablish the Southern social order and in effect reinstitute a slave system. State constitutional conventions acted quickly during this period to enact laws aimed at severely limiting Blacks with

---

David M. Goldenberg, *The Curse of Ham: Race and Slavery in Early Judaism* (Princeton: Princeton University Press, 2003); and Stephen R. Haynes, *Noah's Curse: The Biblical Justification of American* Slavery (New York: Oxford University Press) 2002. Also see Cain Hope Felder, *Race, Racism, and the Biblical Narratives* (Minneapolis: Fortress Press, 2002).

[9] James D. Anderson, *The Education of Blacks in the South, 1860–1935* (Chapel Hill: University of North Carolina Press, 1988) 30. Also see Joe Richardson, *Christian Reconstruction: The American Missionary Association and Southern Blacks, 1861–1890* (Tuscaloosa: University of Alabama Press, 1980) 35–54.

regard to access to education and full-fledged citizenship (suffrage). "Black Codes" were legislated throughout the South, and they included limitations placed on the type of work in which Blacks could engage, vagrancy laws (anyone not lawfully employed would be imprisoned), prohibitions against assembling, the requirement of special passes to travel across county lines, and anti-slavery laws that functioned to close schools that were established. Congressional action moved to nullify the Johnson plan and passed the Freedmen's Bureau Bill in February 1866. This legislation, according to Bullock, marks the genesis of Congressional Reconstruction.[10]

During the early years of Reconstruction, several constitutional amendments designed to secure the civil liberties of formerly enslaved Africans were enacted. These included the Thirteenth Amendment (1865), which abolished slavery; the Fourteenth Amendment (1868), which granted citizenship to the Freedpeople; and the Fifteenth Amendment (1870), which granted the right for African-American males to vote. It was under Congressional Reconstruction that Blacks were able to vote for new state constitutions, a development made possible by the Fourteenth and Fifteenth Amendments. Even though Blacks never received the promised "forty acres and a mule" as ordered by General Douglas Sherman's "Field Order number 15" in Savannah, Georgia, the power to vote offered much hope.

During Reconstruction and beyond, the school and the church were the primary instruments through which Blacks tried to develop a sense of community and to achieve economic and political goals. The idea of African inferiority, widespread in the North and South, was fueled by the belief that at no time in history had Africans developed higher forms of civilization. To educate Blacks would be a waste and would ruin them as laborers. Such attitudes were prevalent among Disciples. "The attitudes of white church leaders," writes Harrell, "on questions of civil rights and segregation confirmed Black suspicions that racism persisted in Disciples thought.... Much more common among Northern and Southern Disciples was an overt racist approach. Social

---

[10] Henry Bullock, *A History of Negro Education in the South from 1619 to the Present* (Cambridge: Harvard University Press, 1967) 35–45.

segregation was defended by virtually every important leader in the church."[11] Underscoring Harrell's point are these comments by Disciples of Christ clergy: "The Negro does not take well to our plea; it has too much reason and not enough animal excitement; it appeals too much to the brain, and too little to the flesh."[12] Speaking at the Jubilee Convention of the Christian Church at Cincinnati, Ohio, in 1899, B. A. Jenkins described the African-American past and present during a presentation to the plenary: "Add to this character of the people. Tropic in their natures, sprung of a line that had doted [sic] the centuries away in the shadows of a dark continent, fed by the droppings of the trees, roused to action only by wars or games or passion; is it strange that such as these produced the careless, happy, fickle, shiftless ebon child of the cotton and the cane? ...These very qualities, which make him easy to control, only add to the complications of the present problem."[13]

Some Northern abolitionists believed formerly enslaved Africans could be educated and that socially deviant behavior was the result of conditioning under chattel enslavement and not biological inferiority. Education, they believed, would foster virtue, frugality, industriousness, and citizenship.

While African Americans were motivated to read and write because of its utility regarding their salvation, they did not lose sight of education's utility regarding social, economic, and political upward mobility. In 1869, the National Negro Labor Union emphasized the importance of education to develop skills in the various trades and because they realized that an educated laborer would earn higher wages than an illiterate laborer. According to Robert Cruden, generally speaking, Southern white laborers and farmers tended to shun educational opportunities made available to them during this period, a

---

[11] Harrell, *Sources of Division*, 203–204.

[12] M. M. David, "Texas Letter," *The Christian Standard* 31/32 (28 November 1895): 760.

[13] Address by B. A. Jenkins, "The Way Out of Egypt," in *The Christian Standard* 35/42 (28 October 1899) 1376.

fact that would play a role in the slow development of state-supported public education in the South.[14]

Northern black aid societies were active in the South during this period. Their societies included Black Methodists, Black Baptists, the African Methodist Episcopal Church, the African Methodist Episcopal Zion Church, and secular groups such as the African Civilization Society. Unitarians organized Freedmen's Aid Societies in Boston, New York, and Philadelphia. Many Blacks in the Union Army received instruction through black and white chaplains and other black soldiers who were literate. Other soldiers started schools for free and formerly enslaved Blacks in newly occupied areas of the South. Examples of this system of schooling were those directed by Major General Nathaniel Banks who started schools in New Orleans. He used Northern abolitionists to start a system that by 1865 numbered 126 schools with 230 teachers and 15,000 students.

The Bureau of Refugees, Freedmen, and Abandoned Lands, often referred to as the Freedmen's Bureau, was established on 3 March 1865 by an act of the War Department. President Johnson vetoed the bill to establish the bureau, but his veto was overturned by Congress. Under the direction of General Oliver Otis Howard, the Freedmen's Bureau was an experiment in social policy and was responsible for developing "a free labor system in the South; establishing schools for freedmen; providing aid to the destitute, aged, ill and insane; adjudication of disputes among Blacks and between the races; and attempting to secure for Blacks and white unionists, equal justice from the state and local governments...." It can be argued, as Foner does, that this system was beneficial for both Blacks and Whites. Planters' aspirations were met because a labor force, albeit free, was put into place and operating on plantations. Black aspirations were fulfilled by the establishment of schools for Blacks, protection from violence, removal of coercive labor

---

[14] Robert Cruden, *The Negro in Reconstruction* (Englewood Cliffs: Prince Hall, Inc., 1969) 56–58.

practices, and the dismantling of legal barriers that prohibited black socioeconomic and political advancement.[15]

The bureau wasted no time in providing what many agreed was the most important need of the Freedpeople—schooling. The bureau's educational arm was directed by John W. Alvord who was appointed as General Superintendent of Schools in September 1865. Immediately after the war, 740 schools were established and supported by approximately 1,000 teachers. By 1869, 3,000 schools with a total enrollment of 150,000 students reported to the Freedmen's Bureau. Initially teachers for these schools were mostly white females from New England; however, emphasis was soon placed on training black teachers, and by 1869, of the 3,000 Freedmen's Bureau teachers Blacks outnumbered Whites for the first time.

Some of the white teachers were college educated, but most were not educated beyond normal school. Those living in cities often had comfortable living conditions in space rented by aid societies. Rural teachers had a tougher time. They had to deal with being ostracized by local Whites and had to live with black families. Other hardships included poor facilities, books, and materials. By 1870, the Freedmen's Bureau had spent more than $5,000,000 on education and operated 4,239 schools with 9,300 teachers and more than 247,000 students. This amount represented only half of the total expenditures for education. The rest came from Northern aid societies and the Freedmen themselves who contributed an estimated $785,000. Cruden states that many Whites kept their children away from schools because they were integrated and teachers taught republican politics and social equality. Some teachers were assaulted and denied access to worship.[16]

Many scholars attribute the development of universal, free, and state-sponsored public education in the South to African Americans' desire and insistence for formal education. W. E. B. Du Bois makes this point when he states, "The first great mass movement for public

---

[15] Eric Foner, *Reconstruction: America's Unfinished Revolution, 1863–1877* (New York: Harper & Row, 1988) 142–44.
[16] Cruden, *Negro in Reconstruction*, 61–63; Foner, *Reconstruction*, 144; and Frankel, "Breaking the Chains," 274.

education at the expense of the state, in the South, came from Negroes. Many leaders before the war had advocated general education, but few had been listened to. Schools for indigents and paupers were supported, here and there, and more or less spasmodically. Some states had elaborate plans, but they were not carried out. Public education for all at public expense, was, in the South, a Negro idea."[17]

For Du Bois, the crowning work of Reconstruction was education. The demands and agency of Southern Blacks; the benevolence and commitment of Northern sectarian and non-sectarian philanthropists and aid societies; and the presence and provisions of the Freedmen's Bureau laid a foundation that eventually led to universal, state-funded, free public education in the South. According to Du Bois, in a climate of great opposition to education from Southern Whites, it was the presence of the Freedmen's Bureau that helped galvanize the efforts of others to establish free public schooling in the South. It is ironic that the Freedmen's Bureau did not initially have as one of its functions the creation of schools for Blacks. Du Bois writes,

> In the midst of these efforts of Negroes and the general opposition of Whites came the Freedmens' Bureau. The Freedmen's Bureau found many schools for freedmen already in existence maintained by tax commissioners, by Negroes, and by the army. The original Freedmen's Bureau act made no provision for Negro education; but notwithstanding this, the funds derived from the rent of abandoned property was used for education, and government buildings were turned into schoolhouses. Transportation was given to teachers and subsistence granted.... The efforts thus begun in the army and by philanthropists, and taken up later by the Freedmen's Bureau, expanded into a system which penetrated the whole South....[18]

The socioeconomic and political advancement of African Americans suffered a tremendous blow when the Freedmen's Bureau was officially

---

[17] W. E. B. Du Bois, *Black Reconstruction in America, 1860–1880* (New York: Antheneum) 1992 [1935]) 638.
[18] Ibid., 647–48.

dismantled in 1869, and its school operations terminated three years later. The impact of this decision was dramatic with planters moving swiftly to reestablish control. Lyda observed that "Tennessee, Virginia, Georgia, and North Carolina were among the first states to restore their governments; Mississippi, Alabama, Arkansas, and Texas were soon 'redeemed.' By 1876 only Florida, Louisiana, and South Carolina were still under control of the radical Republicans [governments installed under Reconstruction]."[19] The state governments were restored to white Southern control as part of compromises associated with the election of Rutherford B. Hayes to the presidency in 1876. This period was followed by intensified violence against Blacks; the establishment of Jim Crow laws to solidify segregation; and measures aimed at reducing, if not eliminating, African-American access to quality education. Du Bois was convinced that if the black public school system were maintained in the South, literacy among Blacks would have surpassed that of several European nations by the time his manuscript on Reconstruction was first published in 1935.[20]

As mentioned earlier, black education after the Civil War was supported by Northern benevolent societies, the Freedmen's Bureau, and, after 1868, state governments. But the driving force behind it all, according to Foner, was black agency and initiative. Northern church groups and Freedmen's officials often spoke of finding schools started by Blacks throughout the South right after the Civil War such as Mary Peake's school, previously mentioned. Some communities developed a self-taxation system to fund education. Blacks, according to Foner, took pride in self-help efforts to provide themselves an education, but extreme poverty of the newly freed African Americans forced them to get support from outside. As a result, the issue of control rose quickly. AMA missionaries noted the incompetence of Blacks teaching in schools run by the Savannah Education Society, which was created by Blacks. In response to AMA complaints of substandard teaching, the Freedmen's Bureau withheld money. Blacks could not afford to run

---

[19] Hap Lyda, "A History of Black Christian Churches (Disciples of Christ) in the United States Through 1899," Ph.D. diss., Vanderbilt University, 1972, 82.

[20] Du Bois, *Black Reconstruction in America*, 637.

schools alone and AMA teachers took over. Black teachers had the
burden of having multiple roles in the community. Many helped the
Freedmen's Bureau work out contract disputes.[21] Ron Butchart points
out several factors that impeded the effort of Blacks to control their own
schools. He writes,

> Control of the schools never was a reality for long, however.
> Effective continuous control presupposed community solidarity
> and group proximity. The dispersal of the freedmen onto isolated
> plantations, their further isolation onto individual tenant farms of
> the plantation, the refusal of the denominational societies to
> provide access to control over the schools, and the creation of
> white-controlled public education in the Southern states
> destroyed the vital community power base in education.
> Nonetheless, the Southern Blacks had struck out vigorously for
> their alienated right to equality and liberty through their attempt
> to control their own schools.[22]

Black leadership in Reconstruction education societies often came
from those who were free prior to the war, either from the North or
the South. Galvanizing free and newly freed Blacks was smoother in
the upper Southern states, but more difficult in the lower South and
coastal cities where affluent mulatto elites lived. According to Foner,
this was because many Blacks, who were previously free, were
concerned with losing their unique status now that slavery had ended.
Large mulatto populations existed in New Orleans and other coastal
areas such as the eastern Carolinas. In an effort to create divisions
between mulattoes and Blacks of darker hues, white planter elites often
provided certain economic, material, and social privileges to those of a
lighter hue. The instigation and management of class divisions and
tensions among Blacks served as a method to protect and maintain
Whites' position of power and privilege. Despite these efforts by

---

[21] Foner, *Reconstruction*, 99. In *Christian Reconstruction*, Joe M. Richardson
makes reference to the "Savannah Education Association" (Tuscaloosa: University of
Alabama Press, 1980, p. 237).
[22] Ronald Butchart, *Northern Schools, Southern Blacks, and Reconstruction:
Freedmen's Education, 1862–1875* (New York: Greenwood Press, 1980) 175.

Whites, political and cultural fusion among free and formerly enslaved Blacks occurred during Reconstruction, giving birth to new social arrangements in the black community and serving as a catalyst for the "explosion" of new institutions. Some black officials within fledgling organizations were illiterate, but a larger number could read and write; some studied law in the North. In order to attain and sustain socioeconomic and political advancement, Blacks were clear that access to schooling was essential.[23]

A decline in access to state-supported schools took place in nearly all Southern states toward the end of Reconstruction. Responding to the depression and loss of funds, cutbacks took place in the area of state-supported services including education. Texas began charging fees to attend school, while some states like Alabama and Mississippi abolished statewide school taxes altogether. Rates of illiteracy actually began to rise from 1880–1900, and Blacks suffered as gaps in state expenditures between Blacks and Whites widened.[24]

The Freedmen's Bureau helped societies establish the first black colleges whose primary goal was to train teachers. Among these schools were Fisk, Tougaloo, and Hampton. Foner describes these schools as "amalgams of benevolent uplift and social control" aimed at assisting Blacks to become industrious, self-reliant, and good citizens. AMA and Freedmen's Bureau schools such as Hampton emphasized industrial education and encouraged Blacks to eschew politics. This approach was an area of great contention. Many people, black and white, believed Blacks needed access to higher or classical education if they were ever to develop the political and economic sophistication to move their race toward true equity in society. This would also be an area of tension among Disciples. Indeed, during this period, education was not divorced from the idea of equal rights and protection under the law as societies had among their membership merchants, railroad men, and manufacturers who wanted to infuse republicanism in the South. Equal

---

[23] Ibid., 100.
[24] Ibid., 541, 589.

rights under the law, however, did not necessarily result in integration of public schools.[25]

The issue of establishing integrated versus segregated schools presented a serious challenge to reformers during this period. The AMA and other groups wanted to establish integrated schools, but local hostility prevented this from occurring on a broad basis. Some mixed schools did exist but these were not common. Most states did not mandate segregated schools during Congressional Reconstruction. In fact, South Carolina and Louisiana actually had legislatively mandated integration during this period. In practice, however, in South Carolina only the university was integrated, and in Louisiana only the schools in New Orleans were integrated. Most Blacks were not concerned with integrated schools during this period. Early on, their primary concern was getting an education and having opportunities for Blacks to secure jobs as teachers. Attempts by states to require separate schools through legislation, which would legally secure an imposed segregation, were met with great opposition by black leaders. During Presidential Reconstruction, even though Blacks were taxed, most states moved legislatively to secure segregation and make black access prohibitive to all public facilities. Texas and Florida were the only states to provide education for Blacks during Presidential Reconstruction. These states, however, levied a special (additional) poll tax and tuition fees on Blacks to pay for it. North Carolina, during this same period, moved to abolish its state-supported, public education system to avoid having to support black education with tax revenues. The legislature moved to empower locals to support private academies that would exclude poor Whites as well. Repression of state-supported education for Blacks often became violent. In 1870, Whites, believing their taxes provided education for Blacks and the propagation of republican politics and social equality, went on a rampage in eight counties, burning schools and torturing and killing teachers.[26]

The decision to discontinue the educational function of the Freedmen's Bureau in 1872 marked the beginning of educational

---

[25] Ibid., 144.
[26] Ibid., 367.

decline for Blacks in the South. This withdrawal brought about an increase in their dependency on the financing, and thereby control, of Northern aid societies and the philanthropy of the "new rich" business elites. The AMA continued with integrated coeducational work at Berea College in Kentucky, and several schools throughout the South. After 1878, the Freedmen's Aid Society of the Methodist Episcopal Church broadened its support to extend beyond secondary schools and colleges and included two medical schools and three seminaries.

Primary sources for nonsectarian philanthropic educational funds were the Peabody Education Fund (George F. Peabody), the John F. Slater Fund, the General Education Board (John D. Rockefeller), the Anna T. Jeanes Fund, the Julius Rosenwald Fund, and the Phelps Stokes Fund. Prior to the close of Reconstruction in 1877, George Peabody was the only significant nonsectarian Northern philanthropist to invest in black education in the South, having given $2.5 million in 1867 specifically for "the promotion and encouragement of intellectual, moral, or industrial education among the young people of the destitute portions of the Southern and Southwestern states." Beginning in 1882, with John Slater taking the lead, a .proliferation of Northern nonsectarian largesse began.[27]

Motivation for Northern giving, according to John Hope Franklin, was varied. Sectarian giving was fueled by authentic acts of benevolence in response to social needs. Financial giving by these groups was also a method of providing support to agencies that could advance the theological perspectives of denominations. Nonsectarian groups were more interested in establishing the principle of self-help for individuals and the state; promoting the development of a disciplined and moral work force to support the factories, railroads, steel mills, and textile mills they were building in the South (a development that would also allow the South to provide a larger share of the tax burden); and

---

[27] John Hope Franklin, *From Slavery to Freedom: A History of Negroes in America* (New York: Alfred A. Knopf, 1974 [1947]) 278. For further discussion of the impact of Northern philanthropic organizations on black education during the period addressed in this study, see William H. Watkins, *The White Architects of Black Education: Ideology and Power in America, 1865–1954* (New York: Teachers College Press, 2001); and Anderson, *The Education of Blacks in the South*, 1988.

educating both Blacks and Whites to play one against the other in an effort to keep wages at a minimum. "Thus," says Franklin, "[Northern business elites] were at least interested in the improvement of the common schools; some even contributed to the improvement of higher education." Franklin allows for the possibility that another motive could have been a sense of duty.[28]

Watkins refers to this pattern of Northern benevolence after the Reconstruction Era as the *charity movement*. Informed by the missionary impulse found in Protestant sectarian movements, the charity movement, he further asserts, was a response to the lack of government action to social ills during economic crisis. "The charity movement had its ideological roots in both long-standing missionary outlooks and the populist discontent following Reconstruction. While many in the charity movement were socialists or otherwise situated left of center, they did not challenge American industrialism at its root." Watkins identifies Jane Addams as an exemplary figure of this movement.[29]

The ability to act free of legislative constraints as well as the freedom to exercise absolute control over the schooling of Blacks made what Watkins refers to as *race philanthropy* an attractive enterprise for many Northern philanthropists. Commenting on this targeted form of philanthropy, Watkins writes, "It was quick, avoided the slow deliberative processes of law making, and could be expeditiously and unilaterally started and/or halted at will. Race philanthropy was ideally suited to educating Blacks as well as other minorities. The building and support of schools, the training of teachers, and, very important, the construction of curriculum could be accomplished handily by corporate philanthropies."[30]

Franklin's commentary on Northern philanthropy during this period implies that improvement of black schooling controlled by Northerners would be almost ubiquitous. Anderson points out, however, that it would be a mistake to conclude that Northern

---

[28] Franklin, *From Slavery to Freedom*, 278–80.

[29] Watkins, *White Architects*, 17.

[30] Ibid., 19.

philanthropic support of black education represented a radical shift from the second-class schools for Blacks controlled by Southerners. Anderson writes,

> Thus historians have revealed only a half-truth in arguing that it was the white South that insisted on a second-class education to prepare Blacks for subordinate roles in the Southern economy. The Northern philanthropists insisted on the same. White supremacists themselves, Northern reformers were not perturbed by the Southern racism per se. They also viewed black Americans as an inferior and childlike people. [George Foster] Peabody maintained that black people were "children in mental capacity."[31]

These almost seamless racist anthropological and ontological assumptions about African Americans and the ideology that informed the type of schools provided for them by white Northerners and Southerners was evident among white reformers within the Disciples of Christ. Evidence of such thinking within the Christian Church will be presented in chapter 6.

Northern philanthropists had little impact on the distribution of public funds for education in the South. Southerners reasoned that since black education was being funded by Northern philanthropists, then tax money should be used on Whites; or, Blacks were not entitled to benefit from tax-supported education since they did not pay much in taxes.

The Progressive Era

The latter quarter of the nineteenth and the first decade and a half of the twentieth centuries are commonly referred to by historians as the Progressive Era. This was a period of rapid socioeconomic and political change in the United States. Indeed, this was a period of paradoxes. It was a time of rapid economic growth and depression, social reform and access to fulfilling the American dream for massive numbers of European immigrants, while at the same time, increased violence,

---

[31] Anderson, *The Education of Blacks in the South*, 92.

political repression, and disfranchisement for African Americans. There was also unprecedented industrial growth and expansion while workers labored under deplorable conditions and unfair wages. These inequalities led to the organization of industrial workers and farmers and to massive education reform.

Even though the U.S. experienced economic depressions in the 1870s and again between 1893 and 1897, the decade of the 1890s was marked by substantial economic growth. According to Nell Painter, "Between 1889 and 1900, production of raw steel doubled from 5,865,000 tons to 11,227,000 tons. Total manufacturing capital soared from $5,697,000,000,000 in 1889 to $8,663,000,000,000 in 1900."[32] As is the case in capitalist America today, the distribution of wealth in the final decade of the nineteenth century was, as Painter points out, grossly uneven. She writes, "The wealthiest 1 percent of families in 1890 owned 51 percent of the real and personal property, the 44 percent of families at the bottom owned only 1.2 percent of all the property. Together, the wealthy and well to do (12 percent of families) owned 86 percent of the wealth. The poorer and middle classes, who represented 88 percent of the families, owned 14 percent of the wealth."[33] The Civil War served as a major catalyst to the ensuing industrial boom. Prior to the war the United States was primarily an agricultural economy, but according to Harold Bradley, "By 1890 manufacturing had surpassed agriculture in its contribution to the gross national product and in its share of national income, but ten years later 35 percent of the American people were still dependent upon agriculture for their livelihood and more persons were employed on farms than in factories.... Industry centered in the northeast, and around the Great Lakes. Southern mills provided only 10 percent of the country's manufacturing by 1900. [the same as it did in 1860]."[34]

Between 1865 and 1915, twelve million new jobs were created by industry in the U.S., and American dependence on industry increased

---

[32] Nell Painter, *Standing at Armageddon: The United States, 1877–1919* (New York: W. W. Norton, 1987) xvii.

[33] Ibid., xx.

[34] Harold Bradley, *The United States from 1865* (New York: Charles Scribner's Sons, 1973).

five-fold. "In terms of commodity prices and real wages, the financial position of skilled workers improved substantially. Unskilled workers were less fortunate."[35]

Industrial expansion and technological advancement shared a kind of dialectic relationship, each influencing development in the other. According to Bradley, there were 62,000 patents issued in the U.S. before 1860. From 1865 to 1900, 500,000 were issued with another 500,000 being issued by 1915. Inventions during this period include the telephone, typewriter, Kodak camera, bicycle, cash registers, gasoline-powered motor, fountain pen, refrigerated freight cars, phonograph, incandescent light, the Bessemer process (converting iron to steel), airbrakes for trains, linotype (typesetting), and the advances in steam boilers that enhanced steam power and resulted in increased demand for coal.[36]

The use of coal during this period was dramatic. In 1860, 20,000,000 tons of coal were used in the U.S.; 270,000,000 tons in 1900; and 500,000,000 tons in 1910. Bradley states that technological advances "dramatically modified the daily routine of the American people; added new conveniences for the conduct of business; facilitated the diffusion of information and goods; and formed the basis of thousands of new industries."[37] In 1910, there were 1,500,000 firms in the U.S.; 250,000 manufacturing enterprises; 25,000 banking institutions; and 1,000 railroads. For the first time, the impact of the railroad system alone, with greater speeds and refrigerated cars, allowed for the creation of a truly nationwide market.[38] Production of manufactured goods in the U.S. exceeded the demand of the national market by 1900, which spawned a greater interest by industrialists to expand the development of markets abroad. According to Bradley, "By 1900 flour, meat, and petroleum products joined cotton, wheat, and tobacco as major exports of the U.S." Iron, steel, cooper, and machinery would be added to this list after 1900. U.S. exports experienced a

---

[35] Ibid., 36.
[36] Ibid., 31–33.
[37] Ibid.
[38] Ibid., 36.

phenomenal increase during this period, from 316 million tons in 1860 to more than 2.4 billion tons in 1913.[39]

The population in the U.S. exploded during the Progressive Era, growing from 35 million people in 1865 to more than 100 million in 1910. Of this number, 11 percent was black, with 90 percent of this group living in the Southern states. Fourteen percent of the population was born outside the U.S. In 1910, there were approximately 200,000 people of Chinese or Japanese ancestry living in the far West. The Chinese had been brought to the U.S. to work on railroads and in mines prior to the completion of rail lines in 1869. The depression of the 1870s played a role in increased violence toward Chinese people, many of whom had migrated to U.S. cities in search of work. The U.S. took steps to reduce the socioeconomic impact of Asian presence during this period. Bradley states, "In violation of the Sino-American Treaty of 1868, the U.S. reached an agreement with China to prohibit Chinese immigration to the U.S. for two to ten year periods beginning in 1887." In 1902, the U.S. made the prohibition permanent.[40]

From pre-colonial population estimates as high as 10 million, Native Americans north of Mexico had been reduced to about one-half of 1 percent of the U.S. population by 1900. The majority of Native American communities were concentrated on reservations throughout the Northern Plains, South, and Southwest. Expansion of the West was stimulated by rapid population increases in the East; the discovery of gold; the establishment of rail lines; and other market influences. Land previously "given" to indigenous groups as tribal holdings were redistributed to individual Native Americans through the Dawes Act or General Allotment Act of 1887. This act provided that allotments could be sold after a twenty-five-year period. At that time, land that was considered "surplus" was opened up to settlers. The majority of Western tribal lands were in the hands of Whites by the end of the Progressive Era.[41]

---

[39] Ibid., 36–40.
[40] Ibid., 143.
[41] Ibid., 134.

Virtually no one was unaffected by the rapid socioeconomic and political changes brought on by industrialization in the U.S. during this period. This was a time when men and women moved into public life to defend or advance a variety of private interests. This was the era of "progression" when many people, according to Richard McCormick, "supplemented their private decisions with public efforts to withstand and, where possible, benefit from the new economic and social forces around them."[42] As a result of industrial growth, many American families shared common problems such as defense of their families and communities from outside forces. But as McCormick points out, "Yet whatever the commonalities, the conditions were experienced by diverse, often antagonistic groups with unequal capacities for shaping public choices."[43] As we will see, McCormick's depiction of "antagonistic groups with unequal capacities for shaping public choices" accurately describes the relationship between white and black members of the Disciples of Christ during this period as they struggled to carve out effective modes of schooling for African Americans.

The last decade of the nineteenth century was particularly difficult for African Americans. This was a period when Southern Whites intensified violent methods and legislation in an attempt to reestablish white supremacy and retrench themselves in the old Southern social order. Lynching was occurring at an unprecedented rate and other forms of violence were used to deny or control African-American suffrage. Thousands were beaten and killed as a result of white resistance to black socioeconomic and political advancement. On the issue of black suffrage, Harrell points out how Disciples leaders both North and South revealed their tendency to lean on the conservative

---

[42] Richard L. McCormick, "Public Life in Industrial America, 1877–1917," in Eric Foner, ed., "*The New American History* (Philadelphia: Temple University Press, 1997) 93. For additional analysis and commentary on industrialization and the Progressive Era, see Kevin Hillstrom and Laurie Collier Hillstrom, eds., *The Industrial Revolution in America* (Santa Barbara: ABC-CLIO Publishers, 2005); David W. Southern, *The Progressive Era and Race: Reaction and Reform, 1900–1917* (Wheeling IL: Harlan Davidson Pub., 2005); and Michael E. McGerr, *A Fierce Discontent: The Rise and Fall of the Progressive Movement in America* (New York: Free Press, 2003).

[43] McCormick, "Public Life in Industrial America, 1877–1917," 95.

side of a political issue. After commenting on the expected Southern opposition to black suffrage, Harrell quotes the editor of an Okaloosa, Iowa, and Chicago-based Disciples periodical called the *Evangelist*. Harrell writes,

> Nor were Northern Disciples preachers convinced that Negro suffrage was an unmixed blessing. During reconstruction a leading editor confided that he had "always believed that the general government acted unwisely in bestowing suffrage upon the emancipated slaves." During the late 1880's and 1890's when the Southern states were systematically disfranchising Negro voters, Northern Disciples editors frequently supported the actions. Few openly defended racial discrimination in voting, but they repeatedly characterized the Negro as an irresponsible voter and supported educational qualifications.[44]

A common method of white resistance to black advancement during this period was lynching. Between 1884 and 1900, there were more than 2,500 lynchings of African Americans, mostly in Mississippi, Alabama, Georgia, and Louisiana.[45] Here again, a conservative Disciples editor of a St. Louis-based periodical seems to rationalize this violent act. Harrell writes,

> An 1899 editorial in the *Christian-Evangelist* came perilously close to justifying lynching. People "not acquainted with the conditions which prevail in certain regions of the South" had little understanding of the "terrible crimes" which goaded Southerners into lynchings, wrote the editor. "The sudden emancipation of the negro race, together with their enfranchisement, has precipitated a condition of things in many parts of the South which is responsible for these appalling crimes," he continued. As a result, the "women of the South" had suffered "brutal abuse by the negroes" and Southerners were

---

[44] David E. Harrell, Jr., *The Social Sources of Division in the Disciples of Christ, 1865–1900* (Atlanta: Publishing Systems, Inc. 1973) 205.

[45] Franklin, *From Slavery to Freedom*, 323.

"doing what they can with their limited means" to help the Negro and preserve their society.[46]

In an effort to justify the lynching, Whites accused black men of engaging in a consistent pattern of raping white women. According to John Hope Franklin, this accusation of sexual abuse of white women by black men is a myth that continues to exist. He points out that "the record does not sustain this impression. In the first fourteen years of the twentieth century, only 315 victims [of lynching] were accused of rape or attempted rape. While more than 500 were accused of robbery, insulting white persons, and numerous other 'offenses.'"[47]

Numerous laws regarding land ownership, taxes, and small business ownership aimed at serving the interests of Whites were established throughout the Southern states. Statutes were designed to lock African Americans into a class of landless agricultural workers. To a large extent, the aims of these codes were realized at the turn of the century when nine out of ten African Americans lived in the South, and of these, three-fourths were tenants or sharecroppers. Painter describes the economic condition of African Americans during this period:

> Blacks, who constituted about 40 percent of the Southern population, had bought one-eighth of the region's farms. Even so nearly all Afro-Americans, even the landowning minority, were poor. The most oppressed lived as peons, tied to planters by long-term contracts that deprived them of the right to change employers for as much as ten years.... These Southern Blacks, who earned subsistence and often died before earning their freedom, represented the worst paid workers in this country.[48]

For African Americans, this was also a period of abandonment by the federal government. The Supreme Court weakened federal ability to act on infringements of individual civil rights by saying Congress could only act on actions of the state. In 1883, the Court ruled that the

[46] Harrell, *Sources of Division*, 205.
[47] Franklin, *From Slavery to Freedom*, 323.
[48] Painter, *Standing at Armageddon*, xxi.

Civil Rights Act of 1875 was unconstitutional, which opened the way for legalized discrimination in public accommodations. In 1896, the Court approved racial segregation in the *Plessey v. Ferguson* case, and in 1898 in *William v. Mississippi*, the Court ruled against an African-American man who claimed the state constitution of 1890 was racist because of disfranchisement.[49] In 1899 in *Cummings v. the Board of Education*, the Court ruled, "The education of people in schools maintained by state taxation is a matter belonging to the respective states."[50] This of course allowed states legally to exclude Blacks from accessing state-supported public education.

The Progressive Era was a period that witnessed further entrenchment and expansion of many of the education reforms such as consolidation and bureaucratization, addressed in chapter 2. In 1890, responding in many ways to expanding markets and modes of production, colleges and universities entered into a new era. The Morrill Act of 1890, also known as the Land Grant College Act, stipulated that states that maintained segregated colleges and universities and used funds granted by the first Land Grant Act of 1862 exclusively for white institutions would either have to integrate these schools or provide separate institutions of equitable value and quality. As a result of this act, state-supported higher education became available for African Americans for the first time.

American colleges and universities were also becoming more dependent on high schools as feeder institutions during this period. By 1890, Midwest state universities were almost entirely dependent on them. By 1895, 41 percent of all those entering colleges or universities were graduates of public high schools. This upswing in high school graduates was due mostly to the high school movement in the East and Northeast, an institutional consequence of industrialization and urbanization.[51]

Access to higher education for women, mostly white, increased rather dramatically during this period. In 1870, there were an estimated

---

[49] Ibid., 8.
[50] Quoted in Bradley, *The United States from 1865*, 146.
[51] Ibid., 284.

11,000 women enrolled in institutions of higher education nationwide. These women represented 21.7 percent of all students attending a college or university at the time. In 1890, there were 56,000 women enrolled, representing 35.9 percent of all students attending college. By 1910, the number of women enrolled in a college or university totaled 140,000, or 39.6 percent of all college and university students nationwide.[52] A contributing factor to this dramatic increase between 1870 and 1910 was the professionalization and certification of teachers, which became a more widely accepted norm throughout the country during this period.

By 1890, a system of certification had been adopted by most states, and by 1900, 42 states and 150 private institutions had developed systems of certification and accreditation. In 1879, Harvard began offering courses to women under the auspices of "The Society of the Collegiate Instruction of Women." By 1893, this effort would evolve into Radcliff College, which was considered an annex of Harvard at the time. Though most colleges and universities continued to exclude women, institutions such as Smith, Wellesley, Vassar, and Bryn Mawr were established during this decade for the higher education of women.[53]

Whatever the challenges for white teachers, the conditions for black teachers in general and black female teachers in particular were magnified many times over. At the end of the war, black teachers who tried to earn a living by running private schools were often forced into other work to make a living because of the proliferation of free schools offered by Northern missionary societies that preferred white teachers. White mission agencies preferred to commission white teachers, thereby forcing black teachers into domestic service. Jacqueline Jones points out, however, that many Southern Blacks preferred black teachers and opted to pay. Commenting on the burden of black teachers, Jones writes,

---

[52] Barbara Miller Solomon, *In the Company of Educated Women: A History of Women and Higher Education in America* (New Haven: Yale University Press, 1985) 63.

[53] Frederick Rudolph, *The American College & University: A History* (Athens: University of Georgia Press, 1990 [1962]) 284, 318–20.

The lot of black teachers was a particularly difficult one, for she [sic] relied upon either hostile white administrators or poverty-stricken black parents for her livelihood.... Compared to her white Southern counterpart, the black instructor taught more children (an average of ninety-five as opposed to forty-five) in a smaller school. She had to do with less in the way of essential equipment (books, pencils, and slates) and classroom time (a three-to-four-month rather than a five-to-six-month school year).... She also made an average of 25–35 dollars per month which was about 45 percent less than whites.[54]

Teaching for Blacks was more than simply a way to make a living; it was a form of political activism, Christian mission, and resistance. Black teachers likely engaged their work with a racial self-consciousness. Black Southerners were demanding more black teachers at all levels of education, an issue that became a national concern toward the end of the nineteenth century. This was a major theme at the 1895 meeting of the American Association of Educators of Colored Youth. During one session, Charles Gradison of Delaware expressed his preference for black teachers, saying that he "would rather have men of my own race...teach my children than a white man who is not in sympathy.... [The] man who holds that all I need is to be a good servant is not fit to teach me."[55] Having a black teacher was of such great importance to some Blacks that they were willing to use some of the little money they had to pay for black instruction. Jones relates the story of an AMA missionary, who in 1866 observed that "many (or should I say some) parents now prefer to send their children to colored teachers and pay a dollar a month for tuition than to send them to our schools for free."[56]

---

[54] Jacqueline Jones, *Labor of Love, Labor of Sorrow: Black Women, Work, and the Family from Slavery to the Present* (New York: Basic Books, 1985) 144.

[55] Eric Anderson and Alfred A. Moss, Jr., *Dangerous Donations: Northern Philanthropy and Southern Black Education, 1902–1930* (Columbia: University of Missouri Press, 1999) 22–23.

[56] Jacqueline Jones, *Soldiers of Light and Love: Northern Teachers and Georgia Blacks, 1865–1873* (Chapel Hill: University of North Carolina Press, 1980) 70.

Delineating the political dimension of teaching for black women during this period, Jones writes,

> Teaching constituted a special category of black women's work during this period in American history. For it implicitly involved a commitment to social and political activism.... After emancipation, the schooling of black children continued to have sinister connotations in the minds of white Southerners; the caste system generated its own forms of social control, and education was not one of them.... [I]t is not surprising that the period's outspoken national black female leaders (among them Fannie Jackson Coppin, Lucy Laney, Charlotte Hawkins Brown, and Fannie Barrier Williams) began their careers of lifelong service as Southern elementary school teachers.[57]

By 1900, church-supported colleges and universities were as old as the American college itself. Most of the older universities had either direct or indirect sectarian affiliation at their inception. Examples of this include Harvard (1650) and Yale (1745), both founded by the Congregational Church, Brown (originally College of Rhode Island, 1764) by the Baptists, and the University of Pennsylvania (originally the Charity School in 1740), which was established by Anglicans (Church of England). During and immediately following the Civil War, many sectarian groups turned their attention toward establishing schools of "higher learning" for African Americans throughout the South, and to a lesser extent the North. By the turn of the century, African-American higher education served a much broader constituency than the more established colleges and universities for Whites. In the final decade of the nineteenth century, the course of instruction at many of these schools ranged from elementary education through the college degree.

In terms of the quality of higher educational institutions for Blacks during the first decade of the twentieth century, Frederick Rudolph offers this assessment: "After the war the Freedman's Bureau and Christian impulse of the stronger caste led to the founding of a great

---

[57] Jones, *Labor of Love, Labor of Sorrow*, 143–44.

number of institutions which, while collegiate in name, did not remotely resemble a college in standards or facilities. By 1917, two institutions alone, Howard in Washington and Fisk in Nashville, approximated what was coming to be known as an American college."[58]

Despite this assessment, Protestant organizations were committed to developing institutions that offered the best possible education for Blacks to include, but not be limited to, industrial education. Unlike the Disciples of Christ, many sectarian organizations demonstrated their preference for and commitment to liberal arts education over and above the industrial model. This commitment is demonstrated by James Anderson's commentary on the existence of church-related institutions for Blacks at the turn of the century. Anderson writes,

> Those institutions supported by the various religious denominations continued to regard academic or literary education as the most important facet of their work and strongly objected to the notion that academic subjects should be subordinated or correlated to industrial training. In 1900 the American Missionary Association supported five major black colleges—Fisk, Talladega, Tougaloo, Straight, and Tillotson—along with forty-three normal schools for black youth. The Methodist Episcopal church operated one theological seminary, ten colleges, and twelve secondary schools for Blacks in the South. The Presbyterian church, U.S.A., maintained two colleges for men, five normal and graded schools for women, and eighteen coeducational graded and normal schools. The American Baptist Home Mission Society controlled twelve colleges and fourteen secondary schools. The African Methodist Episcopal church supported Wilberforce University in Ohio, Turner Normal School in Tennessee, Campbell College in Mississippi, Kittrell College in North Carolina, Allen University in South Carolina, and Central Park Normal and Industrial School, Payne College, and Morris Brown University in Georgia. The Colored Methodist Episcopal church established and sustained Miles

---

[58] Rudolph, *The American College & University*, 488.

College in Alabama, Lane College in Tennessee, Holsey Normal and Industrial Institute in Georgia, and the Mississippi Industrial College.[59]

The relationship between industrialization and education reform for and by Blacks during this period is important to address here. The interests and influence of Northern industrialists and business elites resulted in an emphasis and preference being placed on industrial education as opposed to classical or liberal arts college curricula. Motivation for such a strategy by Northern industrialists was twofold. First, they needed to maintain a secure and steady stream of skilled and semi-skilled laborers to sustain industrial expansion in the North. Second, they needed to maintain a pool of black skilled and semi-skilled laborers to compete with white workers, which would allow the industrial business elites to keep wages down to a minimum, thereby maximizing their profit margin. Such a strategy played a central role in the "epidemic" of race riots that erupted throughout the country during the early part of the twentieth century. Major riots occurred in Philadelphia; Atlanta; Springfield, Illinois; Springfield, Ohio; and New Orleans.

Most of the Northern sectarian organizations that were already well entrenched in supporting both classical and industrial education for Blacks throughout the South soon became prime targets for reform. The Northern philanthropic foundations established by industrialists moved to convince sectarian groups to transform institutions that were not using the industrial model exclusively. Commenting on this development, Anderson writes,

> In pursuing this course the philanthropists found moderate success and a great deal of opposition. Those institutions supported by various religious denominations continued to regard academic or literary education as the most important facet of their work and strongly objected to industrial training.... The power and prestige of the great philanthropic foundations could not influence the denominations to abandon their primary

---

[59] Anderson, *The Education of Blacks in the South*, 134–35.

commitment to classical liberal education, even though this commitment meant losing badly needed money such as the funds contributed by philanthropists to Hampton, Tuskegee, and Fort Valley.[60]

In addition to being motivated by self-interests, the strategy of Northern philanthropists also reflected their response to Southern sensibilities, which was rooted in the state of race relations in the South at the turn of the century. Much like their response to the educational mission of Northern sectarian organizations, Southerners reacted with great indignation to Northern philanthropic efforts along these same lines. Commenting on the strategy of Northern philanthropists, Eric Anderson and Alfred Moss write,

> Black education, and anyone who supported it, came under particularly strong attack after 1900, as the white South sought to enforce white supremacy and segregation in all areas of life. In response to this crisis in race relations, Northern philanthropists were forced to consider a new approach to the South. The familiar phrases about the importance of tact and caution took on added urgency, of course, in an environment of increasing Southern white intransigence and fading Northern interest in "the Negro question" and other vestiges of Reconstruction. But more importantly, key Northern leaders began to challenge the policy of focusing Northern philanthropy upon black education. Beginning about 1900, a new group of philanthropic leaders developed a strategy for changing the South—and sought to impose this strategy on all supporters of African American education.[61]

Below, I will demonstrate how white Disciples, motivated by self-interests rooted in a perceived threat by free black masses as well as their acquiescence to Southern demands for the sake of church union, by 1900 and for almost twenty-five years, had already been thoroughly and almost exclusively committed to an industrial model of education. In

---

[60] Ibid.
[61] Anderson and Moss, *Dangerous Donations*, 40.

a kind of morbid sense, one could say the Disciples of Christ were "way ahead" of the Northern philanthropic strategy to industrialize black education at the turn of the century.[62]

Competing philosophical perspectives on education during the Progressive Era would instigate the mythical "debate" between W. E. B. Du Bois and Booker T. Washington. This "debate," known as the "Du Bois/Washington debate," centered on the emphasis each man placed on the educational needs of African Americans. Their respective curricular emphases, however, were not total rejections of the other's preference as is often projected by historians. Washington emphasized industrial education for Blacks. His educational philosophy was shaped and informed by his days as a student, and later instructor, at Hampton Normal and Agricultural Institute in Virginia. Washington would later replicate this model in the Tuskegee Normal and Industrial Institute that he founded in 1881. Louis Harlan states, "Booker T. Washington believed all of his life that Hampton had given him a better education than he could have secured at Harvard or Yale. This was because of its industrial features which gave students both the skill to improve themselves and the means of usefulness to the community that would improve race relations."[63]

Responding both to the needs of black people and to the desires of white segregationists, Washington, in his famous Atlanta address in September 1895, stated, "In all things that are purely social we can be as separate as the fingers, yet one as the hand in all things essential to mutual progress."[64] According to Anderson, this Atlanta address "set in motion the ideological struggle between the industrial philanthropists and the black intelligentsia to determine the social purpose of training

---

[62] It would seem that the common interest in industrial education shared by Disciples leaders and Northern philanthropists would have resulted in some form of collaboration or partnership. My research, however, has not revealed any such partnership or collaboration between these groups. Given the Disciples' conservative theological and biblical traditions, it would not be surprising if they responded negatively to overtures by secular Northern philanthropic organizations.

[63] Louis Harlan, *Booker T. Washington: The Making of a Black Leader, 1865–1901* (New York: Oxford University Press, 1972) 65.

[64] Quoted in Harlan, *The Making of a Black Leader, 1865–1901*, 218.

Afro-American leaders and teachers."[65] The philosophy reflected in Washington's words must have been like music to the ears of Disciples leaders who were responsible for black education and who were present in Atlanta immediately to embrace Washington. They later not only lifted up the Hampton-Tuskegee model as exemplary and worthy of replication, but they also extended Washington an invitation, one that he would accept, to deliver a keynote address at the General Convention at Indianapolis in 1897. Disciples of Christ leaders embraced Washington's educational philosophy as ideal. The Disciples' intense identification with and embracing of Washington's analysis of the African-American situation and their educational needs is reflected by an editorial written in the *Christian-Evangelist*, which says in part,

> His address on the subject of the negro problem in the South was one of the most remarkable speeches, in its point, power and pathos, to which we have ever listened.... Mr. Washington seems to be a philosopher, an orator, a teacher, a prophet, and a practical philanthropist, all in one. He has remarkable powers of oratory, and a clear grasp of the situation and its needs. He understands the possibilities and the weaknesses of his race, and is doing a work among them which no one else is doing, or perhaps could do.[66]

Washington was also clear regarding his support of the integration of industrial training and Christian education. He wrote in the *Gospel Plea* in 1903,

> You will find one of the problems that is going to press more seriously upon you for solution in the near future than in the past, is the one of employment of our people, especially in the Northern cities. Competition is becoming more and more severe. The Negro who comes to Philadelphia, for example, from the South, naturally finds more competition in the matter of industry, but then finds himself surrounded by temptations on

---

[65] Anderson, *The Education of Blacks in the South*, 103.
[66] "Indianapolis Convention," *Christian-Evangelist* 34 (28 October 1897) 674, in Harrell, *Sources of Division*, 179.

every hand, and between competition and temptations a very large proportion of the race is likely to go down unless they are guided carefully and wisely by the ministers.... We can only hold our own in the world of labor and industry by teaching our people to do a thing as well as anyone else, by teaching them to perform common labor in an uncommon manner.[67]

Washington's rhetoric and his practice demonstrated his bias toward the preeminent place of industrial education; however, he did not deny the utility of classical or higher liberal arts education for African-American advancement. During an address to the Young Men's Forum of Cambridge in October 1904, Washington said, "We need not only the industrial school, but the college and professional school as well for a people so largely segregated, as we are, from the main body of our people must have its own professional leaders who shall be able to measure up with others in all forms of intellectual life. It is well to remember, however, that our teachers, ministers, lawyers and doctors will prosper just in proportion as they have about them an intelligent and skillful producing class."[68] Washington's articulated affirmation of college and professional schools' utility represents a shift from his earlier and almost exclusive advocacy of the industrial model of education he voiced in the 1880s and 1890s. This apparent shift, however, represents not only a response to Du Boisian ideological arguments in support of classical education for Blacks, but also a response to a critique within the black community beyond Du Bois. For instance, in 1890, Harry Smith (black), editor of the *Cleveland Gazette*, was critical of the fact that Tuskegee and Hampton graduates were landing jobs as porters and waiters. In a balanced critique, Smith affirmed the efficacy of industrial education, but argued for "the fullest development of the [Negro] mind" through classical liberal arts education.[69] Calvin Chase (black), editor of the *Washington Bee*, took his

---

[67] Booker T. Washington, "Industrial Education," *Gospel Plea* 8/42 (28 October 1903): 6.

[68] Quoted in Louis R. Harlan, *Booker T. Washington: The Wizard of Tuskegee, 1901–1915* (New York: Oxford University Press, 1983) 174–75.

[69] Smith quote in Anderson, *The Education of Blacks in the South*, 65.

preference for classical education a step further. Chase, according to James Anderson, "relegated industrial education to a secondary role and to place top priority on the training of lawyers, doctors, and scientists, and other professional persons."[70] Washington's "conversion," if you will, to recognizing the utility of a classical education in furthering the socioeconomic and political concerns of black people seems to have been complete by 1910. Commenting on this point, Harlan writes, "Neither Washington's private letters nor his magazine article revealed much understanding of the nature of higher education, but he so clearly supported it that he was embarrassed that the editors of the *Independent* felt it necessary to preface his article with a note declaring 'how mistaken is the idea that he is concerned only in the industrial training which will fit the race to support themselves in a humble station of life.'"[71]

Du Bois's alleged preference was for African Americans to have classical/higher or liberal arts education. In truth, Du Bois never took a position that encouraged Blacks to avoid industrial education altogether. He did believe, however, that the most intellectually "talented tenth" should be exposed to the most rigorous forms of classical or liberal arts education available to them. It was this group who would serve as the black intelligentsia, providing the necessary leadership that would allow black people to become a socially, economically, and politically self-determined people. His was a both/and approach for black education and not an either/or. In an address Du Bois delivered at Hampton in 1906, he stated,

> The aim of the Higher Training of the college is the development of power, the training of a self whose balanced assertion will mean as much as possible for the great ends of civilization. The aim of Technical [industrial] Training on the other hand is to enable the student to master the present methods of earning a living in some particular way.... It is no criticism of the college to say that its graduates are not technically

---

[70] Ibid.
[71] Harlan, *The Wizard of Tuskegee, 1901–1915*, 184.

efficient, just as the industrial school cannot justly be criticized for not turning out men of culture.[72]

I believe in [industrial education], but not as a complete program. [In 1900] I believed that we should seek to educate a mass of ignorant sons of slaves in the three R's and the technique of work in a sense of the necessity and duty of good work. But beyond this, I also believed that such schools must have teachers, and such a race must have thinkers and leaders, and for the education of these folk we need good and thorough Negro Colleges.[73]

Black response to what many believed to be a conciliatory posture to Whites by Washington was national in scope. In 1905 at a meeting in Niagara Falls, Du Bois was a central figure among leaders from across the country in what would become known as the Niagara Movement. The movement focused on developing a racially cooperative plan to respond to the socioeconomic and political injustices experienced by Blacks and to strengthen the Southern economy in a way that would be beneficial to Blacks and Whites. In 1910, out of this movement was born the National Association for the Advancement of Colored People (NAACP).

Both Du Bois and Washington had a deep concern for their people. Each clearly desired to impact the ideological perspective that black leaders and educators would embrace. As for a so-called debate between Du Bois and Washington, the quantitative social scope of those embracing the opposing philosophical views was much broader than that of a debate between two men. The potential socioeconomic implications for a people, a church, and a nation associated with each educational model were indeed quite profound. What was at stake was for a people to decide whether or not they would challenge a racist system aimed at their destruction or if they were going to accommodate it. Anderson puts it this way:

---

[72] William E. B. Du Bois, "The Hampton Idea," speech delivered at Hampton Institute, 1906, quoted in Herbert Aptheker, ed., *The Education of Black People: Ten Critiques, 1906–1960* (New York: Monthly Review Press, 1973) 13–14.
[73] Ibid., 5.

This dogmatic determination to spread the Hampton model throughout the Afro-American South set the stage for the early twentieth-century struggle over the proper education of black people. Though many historians would come to view this struggle mainly as the Washington-Du Bois debate, it is well to remember that the Hampton model was launched in 1868, the year Du Bois was born. The Washington-Du Bois controversy merely represented one of the last great battles in the long war to determine whether black people would be educated to challenge or accommodate the oppressive Southern political economy.[74]

During the last quarter of the nineteenth century and into the next, black and white Disciples were confronted with choices regarding schooling for African Americans. The choices centered on either challenging or accommodating the racist policies, practices, and structures in the US that undermined efforts to improve the social, economic, and political conditions of African Americans. The choices for black Disciples have been outlined above. As for white Disciples leaders, they too had choices. Their choices concerning black education would be dictated by what they deemed to be of greatest import— holding together the white membership of their communion in an effort to restore New Testament Christianity, and crafting a system of education that would serve to solidify further the prevailing power relations of the Southern social order.

---

[74] Anderson, *The Education of Blacks in the South*, 77.

6

BLACK LITERACY DEVELOPMENT AND SCHOOLING WITHIN THE CHRISTIAN CHURCH

So persistently did black Southerners seek a voice in their own education in the late nineteenth century that it is possible to speak of an African American agenda in education, though in fact, the most consistent black demand was that their education should be similar to everyone else's. Whenever white educators argued that Negroes were "not yet ready" for some role, or advocated curricular experiments not standard in white schools, they could count on clear and steadily increasing black resistance. The most bitter arguments between Blacks and Whites involved issues of practical control, not educational philosophy.[1]

Little wonder that when the [Disciples of Christ] of that day looked over the world for a fertile mission field, they saw the enslaved Black person in the United States not so much as a child of God to be [supported] but too often as an object of mission to be secured like cattle in order to raise the material value of the Christian estate.[2]

---

[1] Eric Anderson and Alfred A. Moss, Jr., *Dangerous Donations: Northern Philanthropy and Southern Black Education, 1902–1930* (Columbia: University of Missouri Press, 1999) 13–14.

[2] Brenda M. Caldwell and William K. Fox, Sr., *Journey Towards Wholeness: A History of Black Disciples of Christ in the Mission of the Christian Church*, vol. 1 (Indianapolis: National Convocation of the Christian Church [Disciples of Christ], 1990) 2.

In the process of establishing schools for African Americans, I
have argued that scholars of Disciples of Christ historiography have,
with some exceptions, relegated the role of black participation in this
process to that of passive recipients of white benevolence and largesse.
In challenging this interpretation, I have argued that African-American
Disciples were proactive participants in this process, demonstrating
great courage, sacrifice, and ingenuity in their struggle to provide
schooling for their communities. Examination of the historical record in
support of these arguments is the focus of this chapter.

Intra-church Debate among Whites and Initial Efforts

Unlike most of the larger Protestant organizations of their day, the
educational mission of the Christian Church with and among Blacks
prior to the Civil War is largely nonexistent. I have already illustrated
how the major Protestant movements demonstrated great interest in
religious instruction (evangelizing) and literacy development among
Blacks during the antebellum period. Regrettably, white leadership
within the Disciples of Christ demonstrated little interest in any type
of work among Blacks until after the Civil War. "As the Civil War was
concluding," writes Lyda, "the American Christian Missionary Society
took measures to carry out its desire to support evangelical work among
the freedmen; its second concern was education."[3]

When the Christian Church did finally generate any semblance of
interest in the form of mission activity among Blacks, it was largely a
reaction to the activities of other Protestant churches; a sign of an
evolving sense of self-interest; and, to a lesser extent, a reaction to
internal pressure to respond to the needs of more than five million
Freedpeople in the South. An 1863 report of the Home Mission
Committee of the GCMC gives expression to a concern that "other
denominations have already seen the importance of labor."[4]

---

[3] Hap Lyda, "A History of Black Christian Churches (Disciples of Christ) in the
United States Through 1899," Ph.D. diss., Vanderbilt University, 1972, 114.
[4] Quoted in David E. Harrell, Jr., *The Social Sources of Division in the Disciples of
Christ, 1865–1900* (Atlanta: Publishing Systems, Inc. 1973) 160.

Commenting on the Disciples' slow response, McAllister and Tucker write,

> After the Civil War, concern for the evangelization of the Southern Negro grew in both North and South. Some Northern white Disciples considered carrying the gospel to the freedmen a missionary cause. Disciples saw other denominations evangelizing Blacks and felt that they should do as much…. Early efforts by Disciples to evangelize the Negro were marked by the enthusiasm of a few leaders with little financial backing or organized efforts. In the 1870s as much evangelistic work was carried on outside the [American Christian Missionary Society] as had been done through it.[5]

Some of the concerns expressed about what other religious groups were doing among Blacks could be interpreted as anti-Catholic. Responding to Catholic mission efforts in the South, Charles L. Loos, an outspoken advocate for Disciples evangelism among Blacks, expressed his concern about the Catholic Church. In an article titled "The Catholic Scheme for Freedmen," he wrote, "We trust that this movement on the part of the Catholics will awaken us to our duties in the case. It would be a grand triumph of Rome if in the heart of the great nation, to which it has always looked with anxious and eager eyes, it could build up so great a power for itself as the bringing of the negro race into its fold."[6] It is possible that Loos was trying to use anti-Catholic sentiments, which were widespread at the time, as a motivational tool to stimulate a Disciples movement to engage in mission among Blacks. Again he wrote, "We cannot win and convert the negro, or any other people from a distance…. To raise the cry of alarm at what the Catholics are doing, and denounce them for it, and

---

[5] Lester G McAllister and William E. Tucker, *Journey of Faith: A History of the Christian Church (Disciples of Christ)* (St. Louis: Chalice Press, 1995 [1975]) 294.

[6] Charles L. Loos, "The Catholic Scheme for Freedmen," *Millennial Harbinger* 37/10 (October 1866): 473.

call this time doing nothing worthy of the hour ourselves, is a zeal so poor as to deserve not a moment's regard of the attention of a word."[7]

The initial Disciples of Christ efforts concerning Blacks were clearly focused on evangelism and religious education as opposed to normal or industrial education. This approach was taken because of intense opposition to the education of Blacks voiced by influential Disciples of Christ leaders in the North and the South. William K. Pendleton, who succeeded Alexander Campbell as editor of the *Millennial Harbinger*, was adamant in his opposition to church involvement in anything other than religious instruction: "Shall [the church] undertake to teach the Negro geography, grammar, arithmetic, science, or nature, or of government? She must know her business better.... Today the Sunday-school, if practicable, may be made an everyday school, but let the lessons be religious not secular. If reading be taught, let the lessons be Bible lessons, and the teachers, preachers of the Cross.... Southerners tend to be opposed to secular education [which is] the duty of the state.[8]" C. Bulland of Clear Fork Christian Church in Tazewell County, Virginia, agreed with Pendleton: "How shall the religious instruction and care of the negro be provided for? It is a common and easy answer to say, '*educate them.*' This is a means, but it is vague and indirect. By what means shall we educate them, and what shall the instruction be? These, however, are questions for the state, not for the church.... But as things have gone for the last half century, education, such as is *common*, has not always led to Christianity."[9] Bulland's comments reveal the belief of many Disciples that the sole purpose of education, at least for Blacks, was to lead them to an acceptance of the Christian faith. John W. McGarvey, a vocal neutralist on the war and slavery, voiced a similar view on education. He claimed what Blacks wanted most: "With the small amount of means in the hand of our missionary boards, it appears in the light of these

---

[7] Charles L. Loos, "The Catholic Church and the Freedmen," *Millennial Harbinger* 40/9 (October 1869): 573.

[8] William. K. Pendleton, "The Great Want of the Colored People," *Millennial Harbinger* 40/3 (March 1869): 172, quoted in Harrell, *Sources of Division*, 180–81.

[9] C. Bullan, "The Great Want of the Colored People," *Millennial Harbinger* 40/3 (March 1869): 170.

facts, nothing less than a waste of money and opportunity to send any of it in providing a common school, or even a normal school, for colored children....What the colored brethren want most is to have the true and complete gospel preached among them by an army of preachers almost as numerous as their present army of teachers."[10]

Once the Disciples of Christ through the ACMS made a commitment, albeit modest, to the evangelization of the Freedpeople, white evangelists were found to be ineffective. McAllister and Tucker state, "Viewed in terms of measurable results, efforts to evangelize among [Blacks] met with little success, so Disciples placed emphasis upon the improvement of educational opportunities for Black Americans."[11] The need to train a cadre of black ministers, who proved to be far more effective evangelists among black people, became evident. The decision to train black men for the purpose of evangelizing black people served as the initial motivating factor for white Disciples of Christ to support an educational effort by the ACMS. Tied to this training was an interest in sending Blacks to Africa as part of an African colonization agenda both to repatriate Blacks and to evangelize Africa. James L. Thornberry, a Disciples of Christ minister from El Paso, Illinois, is representative of this concern:

> Now, I suggest to our well-informed colored brethren to look to Africa as a quiet home for the children of Ham among us. You who are informed in Bible history know that Africa was settled by Ham whose descendents you are.... Now would it not be a grand move in religion, morals and science for some of our colored brethren of talent to make a move towards Africa, and thus take the poor colored people to their fathers land, and take with them their experience and civilization.... My present thoughts are, God will never let the conflict between the races end until this movement is made. It cannot be that the God of Abraham suffered the colored race to be brought here and then freed

---

[10] John W. McGarvey, "What Shall We Do for the Freedmen," *Apostolic Guide* 19 (11 November 1887): 584, quoted in Harrell, *Sources of Division*, 181.

[11] McAllister and Tucker, *Journey of Faith*, 324.

without some great design. My reason says it was to educate our colored brethren among us to civilize and Christianize Africa."[12]

Thornberry's sentiments were held by many leaders in and out of the Disciples of Christ, some of whom were black, well into the twentieth century. For others, African colonization was impractical. At the 1894 General Convention held at Dallas, Texas, E. L. Powell reflected the latter position on African colonization during a keynote address. Note also the anthropological and ontological assumptions about African Americans that are revealed in his comments:

We might as well hold a meeting, and pass resolutions and devise schemes to induce the English sparrow to go back to England. The colored man and the bird have both become Americanized and both have built their nests in this country. A new generation of Afro-Americans has been born to freedom. They are natives. The Negro's morality is at such a low ebb that unfortunately his immorality is regarded as almost innocent by his white employer.... It is a people—this Negro race—wanting in any worthy ambition, having no ideal, dominated for the most part by present enjoyment and physical satisfaction and comfort.[13]

Powell's use of the term "Afro-American" is uncommon for this period in general and among Disciples in particular. His views, however, concerning Blacks are, as I will demonstrate, quite common among those who would shape the Disciples' educational policy for black people.

The ACMS required that black evangelists under their employ be literate and be supervised by a white preacher in the area. Most notable among early black evangelists were Levin [sic] Wood of Mississippi, William Brookes and H. Jackson Brayboy of Alabama (who played a

---

[12] James L. Thornberry, "A Suggestion to Colored Christians of the South," *Apostolic Times* 4 (21 January 1875): 1. For an in-depth examination of African-American missionary activities in Africa during the period addressed in this study, see Walter L. Williams, *Black Americans and the Evangelization of Africa, 1877–1900* (Madison: University of Wisconsin Press, 1982).

[13] Proceedings of the General Christian Missionary Convention, 1894 (Cincinnati: Standard, 1894) 8.

central role in founding a school for Blacks as addressed below), and S. W. Womack of Nashville. The preaching and teaching of these men and others proved to be instrumental in the conversion of thousands of African Americans into the Christian faith and membership in the Christian Church.[14]

A sustained effort and commitment by the Disciples of Christ to provide schooling for Blacks was slow in coming. "Until 1873," writes Lyda, "the Disciples had done nothing in ecclesiastical education, and Black churchmen longed for training before their churches left them behind."[15] He also observes that "White agencies never had available in their missionary coffers the amounts of money needed to provide first-class education and support for their home mission enterprises; they were unable to raise significant amounts at the national level."[16] Lyda is correct in his observation concerning ACMS finances, but he fails to explain why the Disciples were unable to raise funds while other Protestant organizations poured funds into their mission agencies for the purpose of black education and evangelism.

Several factors contributed to the ACMS's weak fundraising efforts that hindered response to black education and evangelization. First of all, the Disciples leadership, as I have stated, was primarily concerned with maintaining union within the church. Deep scars remained between churches in the North and South resulting from the ACMS's 1863 resolution that affirmed its commitment to the Union. Second, the ACMS continued to feel the impact resulting from opposition concerning the formation of a national organization that for many was contrary to their understanding of biblical truth. Third, influential leaders were present within the church, North and South, who held conservative views concerning African Americans. Adding to these tensions were conflicting views surrounding the education of black people and the role of the church, if any, in this process.

---

[14] McAllister and Tucker, *Journey of Faith*, 295. Lyda refers to Levin Wood as "Eleven" Woods ("A History of Black Christian Churches," 97).

[15] Lyda, "A History of Black Christian Churches," 112.

[16] Ibid., 176.

For the sake of healing the wounds among white Disciples, national leaders, many of whom were Northern moderates, did not press the issue of black education one way or the other. The predominant motivating factor that informed decisions affecting schooling for Blacks supported by Disciples mission agencies was whether it was useful to the interests of Whites in general, and whether it accommodated to the Southern church and their concerns. Harrell agrees with this point: "The moderate spirit of patience grew into acquiescence to Southern demands for control of the Negro problem. There was truth in the charges...that [the] moderate church leaders had adopted the same spirit of compromise that Campbell had taken in the slavery controversy. Reform fervor was sacrificed on the altar of church unity and peace."[17]

Representing a distinct minority in number and influence, some white Disciples were strong advocates for literacy development and schooling for African Americans. Among these reformers were John Shackelford and Lewis Pinkerton, both of Kentucky, and James Butler of Alabama. Shackelford, who served as the ACMS secretary in 1866, made what is probably the most progressive proposal of his time concerning black education. He advocated for Blacks to be admitted into Disciples colleges such as Hiram and Bethany. Ironically, at least on the surface, his proposal was met with intense opposition from Northern Disciples who were outspoken abolitionists. According to Harrell, Shackelford "could find little support, even among the antislavery preachers of the North. Burke Hinsdale, president of Hiram College, argued that 'the practical difficulty of co-education' of Negroes and Whites was simply too great."[18]

An outspoken advocate for black evangelism and education, Lewis L. Pinkerton became a Freedmen's Bureau agent in January 1866. His decision to work in this capacity was met with intense opposition, which resulted in his being ostracized by the Disciples of Christ in Kentucky. Those opposing his association with the bureau tried to secure an appointment for him to work as a missionary for the ACMS,

---

[17] Harrell, *Sources of Division*, 172.
[18] Ibid., 184.

but Pinkerton was much too controversial for that group. "I have as yet," wrote Pinkerton, "seen but few evidences of concern for the welfare of the freedmen, on the part of their late owners.... There are a majority of the late slave-holders of Kentucky, well pleased to hear of the failures that overtake the negro."[19] In a letter to James Garfield, Pinkerton wrote, "For the present I am 'apostle' to the poor negroes— lecturing them on life, and duty, and destiny; aiding them in establishing schools, etc. Incidentally, I am knocking at the foundations of our Ku-klux Christianity, and, unless I am mistaken, I am doing more for the white people than for the freedmen."[20] Among Disciples, Pinkerton can be considered a radical liberal. He did not hesitate to articulate his scathing critique of white Disciples' response to the needs of the Freedpeople of his state. While not being opposed to religious training, he was clear about the utility of secular or normal school education for Blacks. He wrote,

> There are two hundred thousand negroes in Kentucky, much needing instruction in everything pertaining to this life and the life to come, and the Disciples of Christ, many of whom are enjoying the wealth earned by these negroes ought now to labor and pray for their enlightenment and salvation.... I have hope in schools chiefly, and if we could have a normal school in which fifty or more lads or girls could be prepared for teaching, and inspired with reverence for holiness of life, and pride of character, it would do more in a few years than a score of ordinary preaching, brawling about doctrines and ordinances could accomplish in many.[21]

Harrell describes James Butler as "an ardent antislavery Mississippian...[who] reported in 1866 that he had donated eighty acres

---

[19] Lewis Pinkerton, "Kentucky," *Christian Standard* 1/7 (19 May 1866): 53, quoted in Harrell, *Sources of Division*, 169.

[20] John Shackleford, Jr., *Life, Letters and Addresses of Dr. L. L. Pinkerton* (Cincinnati: Chase and Hall, 1876) 86–87, quoted in Harrell, *Sources of Division*, 170.

[21] Lewis Pinkerton, "Miscellaneous," *Independent Monthly* 1/10 (October 1869): 343–44, quoted in Harrell, *Sources of Division*, 170.

for the establishment of a Negro school [non-Disciple] in Arkansas." Butler added, "The most ebony schools in the South are the most flourishing and progressive we have. The teachers are superior as to scholarship and discipline."[22]

At Hiram College in Ohio, G. W. Neely gave a stirring message concerning the needs of Freedpeople in the South. Following Neely's appeal, there was a series of lectures by Charles Loos, Robert Milligan, and Isaac Errett. These appeals focused on the adverse impact on the U.S. that would result if Blacks had suffrage without education. A small group of students were moved by what they heard and formed the Freedmen's Missionary Society. In November 1867, two students, Orrin Gates and Mary Atwater, traveled to Lowndes County, Alabama, as missionaries to the Freedpeople of that area. Mary Atwater was joined by Laura Brown in 1869. Each of these missionaries was met with intense opposition from within the Disciples of Christ as well as hostility by Southern Whites. The society was unable to raise adequate funding to sustain their effort. They received little support from Disciples around the country. Atwater and Brown's work was discontinued in 1869, and Neely's in 1870. Harrell refers to the effort of these students as "the most important early project to send Northern Disciples evangelists to work..." in the South among Blacks during the period.[23]

Southern churches were not universally opposed to schooling for Blacks. A central issue for Southern white Disciples was that of control of schooling for Blacks. David Lipscomb, as I previously mentioned, was a powerful and influential Disciples Tennessee preacher and editor of the *Gospel Advocate*. His comments are reflective of the sentiments held by many of his Southern contemporaries. In 1869, responding to Isaac Errett's influential role in instigating the work of the Freedmen's Missionary Society, Lipscomb advised the Hiram preachers and students to "attend to the Dutch at Cleveland and leave the Southern

---

[22] James Butler, "A Voice from the South," *Christian Standard* 1/5 (5 May 1866) 34, quoted in Harrell, *Sources of Division*, 182.
[23] Harrell, *Sources of Division*, 165–66.

people to mind their own business."[24] Advocating for some form of
schooling for Blacks, Lipscomb said later in 1883, "It was certainly a
suicidal policy for Southern people to refuse to teach the negro, and so
throw away this effective means of influencing him. It was, and is, a
foolish and wicked prejudice.... Providence has in a special manner
committed the welfare of the negro to the care of the Southern people.
It was and is, their religious duty to do all in their power to instruct and
elevate him."[25]

The questions of what type of schooling, whose, and what purpose
would it serve; who would have voice in decisions concerning schools
for Blacks; and who would teach in and ultimately control these
institutions would be at the center of tensions between Disciples in the
North and the South as well as between Blacks and Whites for decades
to come.

Protestant Parallels on Race and Control: The Baptists

I think it is important and instructive to locate the racially-oriented
tensions surrounding schooling for Blacks among white and black
Disciples within the larger context of African-American education
history in general and church-related education in particular. In doing
this, I call attention to these tensions and the questions that
precipitated them—issues that were not unique to the Christian
Church. Protestant organizations that were much more aggressive in
providing schools for Blacks throughout the South experienced similar
struggles that were directly related to race and institutional control.
Tensions between black Baptists and the white-controlled American
Baptist Home Missionary Society (ABHMS) serve as a good example.

By the last decade of the nineteenth century, the ABHMS had
established several schools for Blacks throughout the South. Most
notable among these institutions were Spelman College for young
women and the Atlanta Bible College (later renamed Morehouse
College) for young men. These schools were under the control of

---

[24] Ibid., 172.
[25] David Lipscomb, "Our Relation to the Negro," *Gospel Advocate* 25 (12
September 1883): 580, quoted in Harrell, *Sources of Division*, 181.

ABHMS. Thomas Morgan, the corresponding secretary for the ABHMS in the late 1890s, had long voiced his support of the idea that Blacks would and should "eventually" control their own institutions. Dissatisfied with the ABHMS's reluctance to transfer control of the Atlanta schools to black leadership, in 1892 black clergy organized the National Baptist Educational Convention (NBEC) in Washington, D.C.[26] Despite heavy opposition from the ABHMS, and pulling together the collective resources of black Baptists in Georgia, the NBEC opened Central City College (CCC) in Macon, Georgia, on 3 October 1899.[27] The inspiration and concerns undergirding the education reform initiatives of black Baptists in Georgia are revealed by Rev. Emmanual K. Love, who served as the host pastor for NBEC's first and only national convention.

> All civilized nations have colleges or institutions of learning of their own.... The more cultured and refined a people become, the more racial pride they will have, the more independent manhood they will possess and the more earnestly will they desire and struggle to have something of their own and seek to manage their own affairs.... I believe that it is just as reasonable to hold that Negroes can best teach Negroes as it is to hold that Negroes can best preach to Negroes.... I don't believe any white man is color blind.... I believe in a color line just a firmly as I believe in a racial line. I believe every race should recognize its racial distinction. I believe in race schools and I believe in Negro ownership of these schools.[28]
>
> Our people have been taught that God is white, the devil is black; whereas God is spirit.... And to think of [God] as simply white is a relic of degrading slavery. How can all this be straightened out? To my mind, only by putting before our

[26] Journal of the First National Meeting of the National Baptist Educational Convention, September 1892, p. 5, on file at the American Baptist Historical Society, Valley Forge PA.

[27] Announcement in the *Baptist Truth* (26 October 1899): 1.

[28] Minutes of the Missionary Baptist Convention of Georgia, June 1897, pp. 38–39.

children Negro ideals. Every race teaches its own ideal.... Our school will be one built, born in the tears of a struggling race, our own hand helping our own children! And whether it is perfect or not, if we did it ourselves, there will come to us a pride that otherwise we could not feel. But when we depend all the time upon others to head our institutions, we cannot, as leaders, get the full respect of our own race, much less the respect of others.[29]

The ABHMS's corresponding secretary, Thomas Morgan, the man who voiced affirmation for black self-reliance and independence, was the most vocal opponent of the CCC initiative. In response to these efforts by Blacks to realize self-reliance in education, Morgan responded, "Judging by the past, it would require your people two centuries to build such institutions as we have built up for them in the city of Atlanta, Spelman and Atlanta Baptist College....To attempt to establish another college in Georgia, therefore, for your people, is not only foolish but well nigh criminal, as it involves necessarily a division of interests, a waste of funds, and an engendering of antagonism that cannot be otherwise than hurtful to your people."[30]

These tensions within the Baptist church did not manifest themselves structurally or organizationally until nearly forty years after ABHMS educational missions with and among Blacks began. The actual break to form a separate school represents a form of ideological maturation and a movement from rhetorical to structural/organizational expression and actualization.

Given white Disciples' comparatively late arrival to support a sustained educational mission with and among Blacks, ideological differences held by Blacks, as we will see below, did find institutional expression, albeit short-lived, at various points. For those Blacks who continued to identify with the "Disciples of Christ," tensions never led to a formal schism resulting in an independent and fully autonomous

---

[29] Emmanual K. Love, "Center City College" *Baptist Truth* (26 October 1899): 1.

[30] The *Baptist Truth* (16 November 1899): 2.

movement. However, attempts to develop internal organizations did occur at least three times during the period covered in this study. The most "successful" effort would not occur until 1917 when black Disciples formed the National Convention of the Churches of Christ, later called the National Christian Missionary Convention. Late as it may have been, when comparing the black institutional formation of other Protestant organizations, this initiative by Blacks was rooted in concerns similar to those of the black Baptists. I do not mean to suggest that these tensions and the issues that caused them were not present among the Baptists, Disciples of Christ, and other groups from the beginning of their joint efforts to establish schooling for Blacks—they clearly were. I merely want to highlight the existence of tensions in Protestant organizations that have demonstrated more progressive missiological activity regarding African-American education. I will return to the National Christian Missionary Convention and examine the motivation for its formation in chapter 8.

Early Schools and the Emergence of Mission Agencies

Six years after the Civil War ended, five million-plus Freedpeople were struggling to overcome the deeply ingrained socioeconomic and political vestiges of nearly 300 years of enslavement. By this time, literally thousands of Protestant church-supported schools of all types— from Sunday schools to colleges—dotted the Southern landscape. In the meantime, the ACMS of the Christian Church had not yet established one school for the education of African Americans. The Disciples continued to study the situation and discussed the issue in committees. R. H. Peoples comments on the state of the Disciples of Christ's response to the educational needs of Blacks during this period: "In 1871, a committee on work among the Freed-men reported in part that: 1. The Convention should recognize as a pressing duty the evangelization of the colored people. 2. Education is considered the best possible method.... The following year another committee studying the same problem recommended: 'The surest way to elevate the negroes would be to establish schools, preferably the normal and theological schools.'"[31]

During the 1871 convention, the following resolution was passed: "That all colored ministers employed by the society be required to frequently call the attention of their people to the subject of education and to urge upon their people the paramount duty of providing schools for their children."[32] After more than twenty years of debate, study, and committee work, white Disciples had now passed a resolution reflecting what black people, and many Whites for that matter, knew more than fifty years before "freedom come."

Beginning in 1872, several significant developments occurred concerning the education of Blacks by schools supported by Disciples of Christ mission agencies. In 1872, the ACMS established the Committee on the Education of a Colored Ministry during the General Christian Missionary Convention (GCMC) in Louisville, Kentucky. Thomas Munnell, who served as the secretary of ACMS, made this report to those gathered in Louisville: "We present also for consideration by the Convention, the question of arranging for the education of a colored ministry. A careful correspondence with the brethren of the church, especially in the South, convinces us of the practicability of the movement, the propriety and necessity of which cannot be doubted."[33] An agent was appointed by the convention to raise funds for the effort.

Responding to the demands of black preachers and white concerns for an educated black clergy, the Christian Church moved to establish the first school for Blacks to be supported by a white Disciples agency. In 1872, Thomas M. Harris appealed to the GCMC to secure funds for a theological school to train black ministers. In 1873, the Louisville Bible School (LBS) opened its doors. The school's primary purpose was to train black ministers for evangelism and leadership for local

---

[31] R. H. Peoples, "The Disciples of Christ Negro Churches" (Indianapolis: United Christian Missionary Society, ca. 1943).

[32] Quoted in Harrell, *Sources of Division*, 180.

[33] Report of Proceedings of the Twenty-fourth Anniversary Meeting of the General Christian Missionary Convention, 1872 (Cincinnati: Bosworth, Chase and Hall, 1872) 17–18, quoted in Harrell, *Sources of Division*, 182.

congregations. The curriculum included geography, grammar, arithmetic, and study of the Old and New Testaments. A Louisville physician by the name of Winthrop H. Hopson, "along with Blacks" in the area, was central in the founding of LBS. An all-white board was formed to oversee the school, and Pitt H. Holmes (white) was appointed as its first principal. LBS was established in the 1870s during the years of the depression, which compounded funding shortages already being experienced by the Disciples' mission activities. A lack of funding caused LBS to close on 12 June 1877.[34]

The effort to sustain a school in Louisville marked the beginning of increased effort and expenditure of human and financial resources by the Disciples of Christ mission agency for black education. At the 1877 General Convention, a report of the Committee on the Evangelization of the Freedmen presented by W. A. Belding concluded, "It is impossible to Christianize them [Blacks] without educating them." He submitted a resolution that a "very laudable effort be made to establish the school in Mississippi already under contemplation for the education of men to preach to them."[35] It is important to note here that as late as 1877, Disciples continued to emphasize "evangelization" of African Americans and not "education." Even when the need to "educate them" was acknowledged, it was to be provided only within the framework of educating for the purpose of achieving the outcome of "Christianizing" them with no articulated concern for the socioeconomic and political development of black people.[36]

The school in Mississippi being "contemplated" is what would become known as the Southern Christian Institute (SCI) in Edwards, Mississippi. The founding of SCI was the fruit of a collaborative effort between Northern and Southern white Disciples. William T. Withers of Mississippi, at the encouragement of James Garfield, donated 160 acres of farmland for the school. Ovid Butler of Indianapolis drew up a

---

[34] Elmer C. Lewis, "A History of Secondary and Higher Education in Negro Schools Related to the Disciples of Christ," Ph.D. diss., University of Pittsburgh, 1957, 47; Lyda, "A History of Black Christian Churches," 46.

[35] Quoted in Harrell, *Sources of Division*, 180.

[36] D. Duane Cummins, *Disciples Colleges* (St. Louis: Christian Board of Publications, 1976) 89.

charter for SCI that became "a capital stock company organized to raise money for a Black Junior College with an emphasis on preparation for Teachers." SCI secured its charter on 8 April 1875. Its board of commissioners for the stock company was comprised of eight Northerners and eight Southerners—all white. A second board was elected in December 1877. This board was made up of six white men, five from Mississippi and one from Indiana, and one African American, Levin Woods of Mississippi. After years of raising funds, the school did not open its doors for instruction until October 1882. Prior to this, according to Lewis, two educational efforts were launched under the SCI charter. One was opened by William Irelan (white) in 1881 at Hemmingway, Mississippi. The other was "conducted" by a black man named A. I. Williams in that same year in Jackson. "The school at Hemmingway," writes Lewis, "was begun through the efforts and suggestion of Thomas Munnell. It is reported that white pressure forced Irelan to close the school and leave Hemmingway. The second school, near Jackson, was under the supervision of Randal and Letitia Faurot (white). Faurot was a chaplain in the Tennessee army during the Civil War and he had started teaching Negroes in his camp before the end of the war."[37] Each of these schools was absorbed by SCI when it opened in 1882. In 1954 SCI was merged with Tougaloo College near Jackson.

SCI was the flagship institution for black education initiated by Disciples of Christ. According to its charter, the purpose of the school was "to train common school teachers for country colored schools and to educate students in Christian faith and morality according to the Scriptures."[38] Thirty students were enrolled the first year of SCI, and the first Disciples student did not attend until 1887. In 1883, Jephthan Hobbs (white) was named president of SCI and directed the institution until 1891 during a time when it came under the control of the Christian Women's Board of Missions. SCI came under the leadership of its next president, Joel B. Lehman, in 1891. It was at this point that

---

[37] Lewis, "A History of Secondary and Higher Education in Negro Schools," 44.

[38] Southern Christian Institute Catalog on file at the Disciples of Christ Historical Society, Nashville.

industrial education became entrenched as the primary—if not
exclusive—method of black education supported by Disciples of Christ
mission agencies. Lehman, who in 1912 became the national
superintendent of Negro work for the CWBM, was clear concerning
his philosophy of education for black people and why it was important.

> We ascribe our present success to a definite policy of work
> that we adopted the first day we began. This is stated about as
> follows: 1. We determined that we would do the work so it would
> do no injustice to the Christian white people. 2. We determined
> that we would do the work in such a way that our students would
> be humble and deferential, and would have an intense desire to
> do their part in the worlds of work, and that they would see the
> great problems from the standpoint of the white people as well as
> from their own.[39]

> The first step in this larger work confronting the church is to
> make preparation for the proper care of those within our gates,
> those who are more or less alien in character, the most important
> of whom are the negroes of the Southland.... If we do not take
> care to discharge our Christian duty towards them, their
> degeneration will rapidly undermine our society.... With the
> Christian Industrial School we can prepare leaders who can go
> and have an influence on the minds of a generation.[40]

We can get a glimpse of the kind of black leader Lehman and
other white Disciples leaders hoped SCI and other institutions would
produce. President W. H. Council of Normal Alabama Institute was
one of the black men Lehman presented as an exemplary and "wise
leader." In an address given in Birmingham, Alabama, on 25 July 1903
titled "What the Negro Owes to the South," we get a clear sense of
why Lehman considered him such a "wise leader": "We are so prone to
say unkind things of the South because of slavery that it is hard to look

---

[39] Joel B. Lehman, "The Work Among Negroes," *Missionary Tidings* 27/8
(December 1909): 365.

[40] Joel B. Lehman, "The Work of the CWMB Among the Negroes," *Missionary
Tidings* 28/7 (November 1910): 232.

with favor upon anything the South has done. In my opinion the black man owes more to the South and to the Southern people than to any other section in the world. For three hundred years, the South has been a great missionary tent, in which thousand of barbarians have been transformed into millions of industrious citizens."[41]

Given this example of what Lehman considers to be an exemplary black leader, we can grasp the resolute conservatism of the educational philosophy that shaped schools for Blacks supported by Disciples mission agencies. The desired educational outcome of these schools was intended to produce docile men and women who would accommodate a social order characterized by a dominant white supremist ideology. This reality precipitated both an exodus of large numbers of Blacks from the Disciples of Christ toward the end of the nineteenth century and protest from many of the black leaders who chose to remain.

Clara Schell (white) ran a school for black children in Washington, D.C. Concerning this effort Schell wrote, "Our missionary work here, though fraught with many difficulties, is not without great promise. The school was opened 9 April 1882, with an attendance of twenty-seven students and twelve officers and teachers." Schell reported that within a year the school's average attendance was ninety-eight students with eighteen teachers.[42]

A second effort to provide theological education for Blacks, the Louisville Christian Bible School (LCBS), opened its doors on 11 October 1892 under the direction of the Board of Negro Education and Evangelism (discussed below). LCBS was the result of a Disciples mission agency effort that allowed for some black participation in its development. Adoniram J. Thompson (white) served as principal of the school during the entire twenty-two years of its existence. The purpose of the school, as stated in the school's 1892–1895 catalog, reflects the Disciples' primary concern for black education: "Its chief purpose is to be instrumental in bringing about such teaching acquaintance with the Word of God as shall fit colored students of that Word for teaching it to

---

[41] W. H. Council, "Wise Black Leader," *Gospel Plea* 8/35 (12 September 1903): 1.
[42] Clara Schell, "A Sketch of the Colored People of Washington, D.C.," *Christian Messenger* 21 (October 1882): 471.

the multitudes of their own race, both by precept and example.... It does not undertake to accomplish this purpose by teaching its young men the dead language, the higher mathematics, or the various curricula of sciences, language and literatures."[43]

This statement of purpose is commensurate with the predominant Disciples of Christ educational philosophy for Blacks, which was to develop persons who were controllable, virtuous, skilled and semi-skilled industrial workers who would not seek to challenge the position of power and privilege enjoyed by Whites. The goal was to "train," not educate, black preachers and evangelists. Once trained, black preachers would then articulate a depoliticized gospel—"as shall fit colored students"—fixed on reward in the life to come as opposed to giving critical attention to making substantive transformation of their socioeconomic and political condition in this life.

Up to this point, the processes of policy-making and decision-making regarding missionary activity in the Disciples of Christ were dominated by white men. White women were understandably frustrated with the overall reticent response of the Christian Church in the area of home and overseas missions. Particularly annoying for women was an awareness of the intense level of activity being waged by mission agencies of other Protestant movements under the leadership of women. As early as 1870, James Challen commented on the success experienced by women leading other missionary organizations. In a report he gave at the Louisville Convention, he stated, "We feel assured that there is an element of power here, almost unknown to us, and unemployed, which needs to be called into active labor."[44]

In 1874, under the leadership of Caroline Neville Pearce, who spoke of a vision she had to organize women to provide leadership in the church's missionary enterprise, and others, the Christian Women's Board of Missions (CWBM) was born. The CWBM was the only Disciples organization administered and controlled by women. In

---

[43] Catalog of the Louisville Christian Bible School on file at the Disciples of Christ Historical Society in Nashville.

[44] Frances Craddock, *In the Fullness of Time: A History of Women in the Christian Church (Disciples of Christ)* (St. Louis: Chalice Press, 1999) 3.

addition to overseas missions, a chief function of the CWBM home mission's focus was to give attention to education. Lewis states, "The Board's first educational effort was in 1893, with the establishment of a chair for the teaching of English Bible in connection with the University of Michigan at Ann Arbor. Later, lecture courses were offered at the Universities of Virginia, Pennsylvania, Georgia, Texas, and Kansas. The courses at the Universities of Pennsylvania and Georgia were soon discontinued. The courses at the Universities of Virginia, Kansas, and Texas resulted in the establishment of Bible Chairs at these schools."[45]

The zeal and commitment to black education that the CWBM would come to embrace in the years ahead are reflected by Virginia Hearne, who served as the statewide secretary for CWBM in Texas during the early 1900s:

> I want to arouse sympathy for the men and women of the South and North, but most of all I want to deepen conviction of responsibility for the black man. I want my class to want to help. They will then be led to recall times when they dealt unjustly, even when they meant only the best.... I would close by telling of the missionary woman who objected to missions among the negroes, and was silenced by the reply of another, who said: "Yes, you are right, Jesus did say, 'go into all the world and preach the gospel,' to the whole creation—except negroes." I would ask the class to consider very earnestly, in their own hearts, whether they had tampered with the commission, either by adding to it or by ignoring it altogether. [I ask your prayers for] the dark skinned children of God in Africa and America.[46]

On 21 October 1875, at the Louisville Convention, men responded to the establishment of the CWBM by forming the Foreign Christian Missionary Society (FCMS). According to Toulouse, the FCMS focused its energies to spread "the word of restoration/unity and to win converts" to Christianity: "In the 1880s, members of these two

---

[45] Lewis, "A History of Secondary and Higher Education in Negro Schools," 30.
[46] Virginia Hearne, *Missionary Tidings* 27/11 (March 1910): 457.

organizations decided to become more intentional about communicating the gospel to those who had never heard it before. In 1882, the CWBM and the FCMS combined their resources and sent missionaries to India. Within the next few years, they sent missionaries to Japan, China, Panama, the Belgian Congo, and Cuba."[47]

In 1889, the GCMC appointed John W. Jenkins as Superintendent of Missions and Schools among the Colored People. Responding to a recommendation made by Jenkins, the Board of Negro Education and Evangelism (BNEE) was formed at the General Convention in Des Moines, Iowa. Headquartered in Louisville, Kentucky, the BNEE became the lead organization for the Disciples of Christ's mission with and among African Americans. The makeup of the board's membership solidified Southern dominance of the educational mission of the Disciples of Christ among Blacks. M. F. Robinson, pastor of Hancock Christian Church in Louisville, Kentucky, was the only black member of the board. His appointment was offered only when a white invitee refused his appointment. Commenting on the Southern domination of the board, Harrell writes, "The makeup of the board constituted a triumph for Southern Disciples. Of course, by 1890, there were few remnants in the church of the postwar bitterness, but the Southern domination of the Negro work was somewhat unexpected."[48]

Jenkins recognized the need for a greater effort by the movement and urged the convention to appoint a full-time field secretary to coordinate the educational work among black people. The decision that the secretary should be white is not surprising, but the board's reasoning was that the person should be white "since negro religious hucksters had caused Blacks not to trust their own."[49] In January 1892, the GCMC appointed C. C. Smith to serve as corresponding secretary

---

[47] Mark G. Toulouse, *Joined in Discipleship: The Maturing of an American Religious Movement* (St. Louis: Chalice Press, 1992) 193.

[48] Harrell, *Sources of Division*, 178.

[49] General Christian Missionary Convention, "Work Among Negroes in the United States, 1864–1892," (unpublished) 33–38, quoted in Lyda, "A History of Black Christian Churches," 117.

of the BNEE.[50] The formation of the BNEE and the subsequent appointment of Smith represent a defining period for Disciples' educational mission with and among African Americans. Commenting on Smith, McAllister and Tucker write,

> Smith brought considerable experience, a capacity for organization and a sense of dedication to his task. Within a few years, the Disciples Negro program enjoyed a measure of success for the first time. The financial support of the Negro work improved steadily under his leadership. A special Sunday offering for Negro work was established in 1891. The Board of Negro Education and Evangelization was dissolved in 1900 when the Kansas City convention asked the Christian Women's Board of Missions to assume responsibility for the work among black Disciples.[51]

There is no questioning of the commitment of C. C. Smith and others regarding their dedication to the mission to provide schooling for African Americans. He and others who engaged in this work were faced with numerous challenges including the hostility, often expressed violently, of white Southerners. Smith, Lehman, and others had their lives threatened and were often ostracized by peers, family, and friends for their work with and among black people. Acknowledging their courage, however, does not preclude the necessity to examine the attitudes and assumptions that shaped the schooling they provided for Blacks. Additionally, the courage of Northern and Southern white education reformers does not place them beyond the bounds of

---

[50] There seems to be some uncertainty about Smith's first name. Lewis ("A History of Secondary and Higher Education in Negro Schools," 1957) refers to him as "Charles C. Smith." McAllister and Tucker (*Journey of Faith*, 1975) refer to him as "Clayton C. Smith," and Harrell refers only to "C. C. Smith" (*Sources of Division*). John C. Long ("The Disciples of Christ and Negro Education," Ph.D. diss., University of Southern California, 1960) refers to "Clayton Chaney Smith, an article in *The Encyclopedia of the Stone-Campbell Movement* (2004) refers to "Clayton Cheney Smith, and Effie Cunningham (1922) refers to him as "Charles C. Smith." My examination of documents such as board minutes, pamphlets, and field reports consistently refer only to "C. C. Smith."

[51] McAllister and Tucker, *Journey of Faith*, 299.

historical scrutiny. They refused to allow Blacks to have a place at the table where decisions were being made concerning the form and function of the schools intended for black men, women, and children.

From the 1890s forward, black education would be shaped by concerns Whites had for themselves and the attitudes they held about Blacks. Concerning the need to provide schools for Blacks, Smith stated, "The Negro is a valuable laborer; let us improve him and make his labor more intelligent, more skilled, more productive...unless the white people, the superior, the cultivated race, lift up the lower both will be inevitably dragged down."[52] Lehman echoed the motive of self-interest in providing church-supported schooling for Blacks, stating, "It has been becoming clear to many that we must give the negro the element of Christianity for he will, his helplessness and sin, drag us down. Already in those neighborhoods where nothing is done, he has dragged the sons from the best Virginia stock down to a plane lower than the negro himself."[53] Here Lehman seems to reference the degraded social conditions of the Appalachians, suggesting that they are the result of Whites' exposure to black people who somehow "dragged them down" to an inferior social position. It is possible that these rhetorical tactics may have been aimed at affecting financial support to this work, but it also reflects the ideology of Disciples leaders who influenced the form and function of schooling for Blacks.

Addressing the concern of the national interest in educating Blacks, Frederick D. Power, a Disciples minister from Washington, D.C., wrote: "Nothing can be more hostile to our prosperity as a nation than illiteracy. All our boasted arts and industries, and liberties, would be speedily lost if the interest of mankind were given over to men and women who could neither read nor write. What must be the peril of our institutions, if the polls, for example, should be controlled by ignorant voters? Yet more than a million negroes with the ballot nearly 70 percent are unable to spell out their names on their ballots."[54] "If the

---

[52] C. C. Smith, "The Principle Underlying Training of the Negro," *Christian Standard* 40/44 (29 October 1904): 1519.

[53] Joel B. Lehman, "Is It Worth While?" *Missionary Tidings* 28/1 (May 1910): 9

[54] Frederick D. Powell, "Ethiopia's Hands," *Christian-Evangelist* 30/43 (26 October 1893): 675.

negro is not educated," wrote a Disciples clergyman named K. R. Brown, "no race will suffer more than the white man, for the negro is here and here to stay, and is capable of attaining any kind of education, and some will acquire the highest education if for no other purpose than to be contrary to the wishes of someone, although a plain, practical education is the one that is needed."[55]

In 1900, faced with ongoing financial problems, C. C. Smith appealed to the CWBM to take control of all work currently being done in the area of African-American education and evangelization. Shortly after Smith's recommendation, the CWBM took control of all mission work among African Americans. At the time CWBM took control, the Disciples of Christ were supporting four educational institutions for Blacks. These included Southern Christian Institute and the Louisville Christian Bible School mentioned above, the Lum Alabama Graded School, and the Piedmont Christian Institute in Virginia, both of which will be introduced in chapter 7.

---

[55] Quoted in "The Negro as I See Him," which was a tract published by K. R. Brown and printed in the *Gospel Plea* 11 (22 March 1905): 3.

7

AFRICAN-AMERICAN AGENCY

> Those of us who are working out the various problems in our school believe that the student should be given an elementary education from the textbooks, and that he must be a skilled workman.... But we feel that if his education goes no farther, his work in the world will be greatly hampered.... The training of the intellect and of manual powers progresses faster than soul-growth; and yet this soul development is most important. What plans have we made to assist in this?[1]

The above quote was written at the turn of the nineteenth century by T. M. Burgess, a black Disciples clergyman. His articulation of the purpose and scope of education reflects the tripartite approach to schooling embraced by many Blacks: an education that included religious instruction (of the heart), industrial training (of the hand), and classical/intellectual or liberal arts college education (of the head). Religious instruction and spiritual formation was foundational and would direct how a student would use whatever skills he or she would learn. Religious education was needed for moral development and had implications for both this life and the next. Industrial education was economically pragmatic and allowed for students who lived in a predominantly agrarian society that was increasingly becoming industrialized to meet the immediate needs of their families and communities. Beyond this, for the individual and the community to "go farther," the opportunity for higher education should be available and even encouraged.

---

[1] T. M. Burgess, "Head, Hand, and Heart," *Missionary Tidings* 27/3 (July 1909): 99.

African-American Disciples were by no means a monolithic group in their approach to education. There were some who embraced Lehman's philosophy of education for black people. Others were adamant in their demand for schools to provide an education for the "head, hand, and the heart." Both groups desired either to have complete control of their schools or, at the very least, to have equal voice with their white brothers and sisters at the table where decisions were being made about their schools. Contrary to the impressions given by some historians of the Christian Church, from the beginning, Blacks were active and involved in establishing all types of schools for their people.

Schooling for Blacks supported by the Christian Church (Disciples of Christ) had diverse beginnings in terms of those responsible for their establishment. Like Tennessee Manual Labor University, the first Disciples-supported school for Blacks mentioned earlier, some were established exclusively as a result of African-American initiative and resources. Some were started by individual white Disciples while others were established by Disciples mission agencies. Schools that were able to sustain an operational life beyond three years were eventually controlled by the Christian Women's Board of Missions. As I have mentioned, after 1900, this board became the primary Disciples agency with oversight of black education. Regardless of how they were founded or who founded them, central to the story of the sustenance of each school is a struggle of resistance, black and white control, and educational philosophy.

Over the years through their mission agencies, the Disciples of Christ established and/or supported three types of schools—industrial, general or normal, and theological. It was, however, the industrial model that garnered the most support by the white leadership. Commenting on this preference for industrial education, Lyda writes,

Industrial education came to be viewed as the best educational means for molding persons recently released from bondage into Christian citizens. Many Negroes came to hope in the efficacy of industrial education and believed Booker T. Washington.... Industrial education helped to equip persons to compete in the utilitarian-oriented American society, but it did not prove to be the blessing for which Lehman and others hoped. The primitive technological training presented by the schools could not keep pace with the rapidly changing technology in industry.[2]

It is arguable whether or not white Disciples of Christ leaders "could not" or simply chose not to keep the curriculum and training at their schools in concert with technological advances. There is no evidence to support that CWBM or their predecessors were committed to providing the best education that would facilitate black self-determination and empowerment. The brand of education supported by agencies controlled by white Disciples was always dictated first by what best reinforced the dominant social norms of the South. Disciples of Christ mission agencies demonstrated little, if any, interest in maintaining schools for Blacks whose curriculum was responsive to trends in the industrial labor markets. Making the necessary curricular revisions demanded by technological advances in industry to maximize the employability and marketability of black graduates was a secondary issue to supporting the sociopolitical concerns of white Southerners. Schools supported by Disciples mission agencies during the Progressive Era offer classic examples of oppressive and market-driven schools as defined by William Watkins, who writes, "The education of Black Americans has always been inextricably connected to state politics and the labor market.... [E]ducation, that is schoolin [Watkins's spelling], in the modern corporate industrial society has emerged as central to state political and ideological management. Political and ideological management involves ideation, which in this context means the imparting and reinforcement of ideas and values that support the current economic and social order."[3]

---

[2] Hap Lyda, "A History of Black Christian Churches (Disciples of Christ) in the United States Through 1899," Ph.D. diss., Vanderbilt University, 1972, 135.

[3] William H. Watkins, *The White Architects of Black Education: Ideology and Power in America, 1865–1954* (New York: Teachers College Press, 2001) 1, 9.

An Overview of the Schools

D. Duane Cummins identifies eleven schools founded between 1865 and 1913 by "the restoration movement" known today as the Christian Church (Disciples of Christ). The schools are listed here:

Year	Institution	Location
1868	Tennessee Manual Labor University	Nashville, Tennessee
1873	Louisville Bible School	Louisville, Kentucky
1875	Southern Christian School	Edwards, Mississippi
1882	Clara Schell's School	Washington, DC
1884	Christian Bible College	New Castle, Kentucky
1884	National Colored Christian College	Dallas, Texas
1892	Louisville Christian Bible School	Louisville, Kentucky
1900	Goldsboro Christian Institute	Goldsboro, North Carolina
1900	Alabama Christian Institute	Lum, Alabama
1900	Piedmont Christian Institute	Martinsville, Virginia
1913	Jarvis Christian College	Hawkins, Texas[4]

During my research, I identified references to Disciples-related schools for African Americans not mentioned by Cummins. Lewis names three schools started by the CWBM after it became the primary agency responsible for black education in 1900. Lewis also mentions a school located in Shepherdsville, Kentucky. "These new schools," writes Lewis, "were Tennessee Christian Institute at Jonesboro, Tennessee; Jarvis Christian College at Hawkins, Texas [listed by Cummins]; and Central Christian Institute at Shepherdsville, Kentucky." Central Christian Institute was the last school exclusively for Blacks founded by the Disciples of Christ. Holding its first classes in fall 1923, the school was forced to suspend operations at the close of the 1926–1927 school year due to lack of funding. [5]

---

[4] D. Duane Cummins, *Disciples Colleges* (St. Louis: Christian Board of Publications, 1976) 90.

[5] Lewis, "A History of Secondary and Higher Education in Negro Schools Related to the Disciples of Christ," 71.

Another school not listed by Cummins is the "Christian Institute" at Winston-Salem. Lewis credits an African-American preacher named R. L. Peters with starting this school. Apparently, it was considered the "predecessor" of the Winston-Salem Bible College that according to Lewis opened in 1945. Lewis quotes Leland Tyrrell, president of Winston-Salem, who spoke at the funeral of R. L. Peters (died circa 1951): "There was not always a Winston-Salem Bible College or its predecessor the Christian Institute but for almost fifty years in Winston-Salem there was R. L. Peters who was a one-man Bible College training young preacher after preacher in his church office until it can truthfully be said that the whole town has been affected religiously directly or indirectly by his thinking."[6] I've noted that the Winston-Salem Bible College was founded by the Christian Churches/Churches of Christ. According to Tyrrell's comments, however, it seems that R. L. Peters started this "Institute" prior to the 1906 schism within the Stone-Campbell movement, thus making the Christian Institute, arguably, a "Disciples" institution at its inception though not one supported by a Disciples of Christ mission agency.

Jarvis Christian College is the only institution founded exclusively for African Americans by the Disciples of Christ remaining in operation today. It's worth noting that four other schools for Blacks were established by churches associated with the Stone-Campbell movement after 1914. They are Nashville Christian Institute (Churches of Christ in 1920), Nashville, Tennessee; College of the Scriptures (Christian Churches/Churches of Christ in 1945), Louisville, Kentucky; Winston-Salem Bible College (Christian Churches/Churches of Christ in 1945), Winston-Salem, North Carolina; and Southwestern Christian College (Churches of Christ in 1950), Terrell, Texas.[7]

Brenda Cardwell and William Fox, Sr., identify three black Disciples-related institutions not mentioned by either Cummins or Lewis. A 1988 manuscript of a book that was later published in 1990

---

    [6] Quoted in Ibid., 155.
    [7] Foster, Blowers, Dunnavant, and Williams, eds., *The Encyclopedia of the Stone-Campbell Movement*, 227, 552, 695, 776.

mentions the South Carolina Christian Institute at Allendale. The book also mentions the South Carolina Bible Institute at Fairfax. Dates of operation or whether or not these schools are in some way related to one another is unclear. Caldwell and Fox's book also mentions the Tennessee Central Christian Institute at Jonesboro. Maybe this is the same school that was previously mentioned with a slightly different name, but I cannot confirm it. The Central Christian Institute of Tennessee at Rogersville is mentioned in the 1988 unpublished manuscript of Caldwell and Fox's book. Founding dates or persons involved in the establishment of these schools are not identified by Fox and Caldwell.[8]

It is not clear if Cummins's founding dates are based on when the schools opened their doors for instruction or when they received their charters. The date a school was "founded" can reflect the perspective of the writer or person making the report. For instance, C. C. Smith has Alabama Christian Institute starting in 1904. Note that Cummins has it opening in 1900. The school, under black control, opened its doors in 1894 under the name Lum, Alabama, Graded School. In 1904 it came under the control of CWBM and even then continued to operate under its original name. The Lum Graded School's name was changed to Alabama Christian Institute in 1914. More will be said about the founding of Lum below, but for now, the point I want to make is that the dates historians identify as "founding dates" of institutions sometimes fail to list the actual dates when formal instruction at the school began under black leadership.

Black Agency

Any discussion concerning the involvement of African-American Disciples in the establishment of schools must begin with their participation in the Sunday school and state convention movements. Sunday schools, as I have stated, were critical venues of formal instruction that more often than not performed the dual function of

---

[8] Brenda M. Caldwell and William K. Fox, Sr., *Journey Towards Wholeness: A History of Black Disciples of Christ in the Mission of the Christian Church* (Indianapolis: Unpublished manuscript, 1988) 4.

religious education and literacy development. Some of these schools evolved to become normal schools.[9] Additionally, Sunday schools served as a catalyst for broader state and regional organizational structures for black Disciples. These organizational developments often occurred under the leadership of women whose votes were disregarded by male-dominated conventions.

Some Sunday schools were started prior to the Civil War when an owner of enslaved persons allowed them to establish a Sunday school separate from the white congregation. One such example is Bartley Dickerson, who was enslaved on the plantation of Mrs. John Hedrick (formerly Ms. Julia Ann Stratford of Giles County) in Tazewell County, Virginia. It is believed that the Sunday school Dickerson established was the foundation of what became the Colored Christian Church at Bluefield.[10]

Soon after hostilities ceased between the North and South in 1865, African-American Disciples, like other Blacks throughout the South, immediately embraced opportunities that church membership and their newfound freedom afforded them. The creation of many black Disciples Sunday schools resulted from the desire of both Whites and Blacks to have separate places to teach and worship. In 1867, the General Cooperation of Christian Churches in Virginia passed a resolution calling for "all congregations to organize separate Sunday schools for their Black members."[11] Many of these Sunday schools laid the foundation for what would eventually become congregations.

Early on, it was clear that within the Christian Church, Sunday schools and organizational configurations beyond the local church had as their priority both religious and secular education. An excellent illustration of the role of Sunday schools in education reform is this notice sent to all churches: "An earnest request, therefore, is hereby sent out to all state [Sunday school] Boards, or Boards having the

---

[9] An example of this type of transition is the case of Second Christian Church in Indianapolis, Indiana. In cooperation with the city's school board, Second's Sunday school was transformed into "Public School #23" (Foster et al., eds., *The Encyclopedia of the Stone-Campbell Movement*, 12).

[10] Lyda, "A History of Black Christian Churches," 58.

[11] Quoted in ibid., 59.

management of Sunday-school work, to appoint a Normal committee, say three persons, to take charge of this phase of our Sunday-school work to co-operate with similar committees of other states, in arranging a suitable course of Normal study, plan a uniform system of normal examinations, graduation, classes and study in its own state."[12]

The establishment of congregations and separate Sunday schools was a normative pattern among black Disciples. In Mississippi, for example, a General Convention report written in 1873 reported the existence of twenty churches and seven Sunday schools. In 1893, Alabama reported "thirty-eight churches with 2,485 members, [and] fifteen Sunday Schools with 650 members."[13] In Kentucky, the State Missionary Convention of the Colored Christian Church met for the first time in 1873. This Kentucky effort illustrates the concerns for education, the role of using Sunday schools in response to this concern, and the leadership of women. Lyda comments on the Kentucky assembly and its aftermath:

> The first assembly was held in 1873 under the presidency of H. Malcolm Ayers of Lexington. The men monopolized this convention, so the women formed the Kentucky Christian Women's Board of Missions Convention in 1880. Mrs. Mary L. Mead led the women's organization, assisted by Mrs. Amanda Hathaway of Little Rock, Mrs. Susie M. Brown of Mt. Sterling, and Miss Maggie Freeman. Church school workers formed their own Sunday School Convention of the Christian Churches in Kentucky to give that state three separate conventions. The annual meetings were held in conjunction: the men and women met on day one for the Sunday school portion; the men met on days two and three, and four for the church portion; and the women met on day five for the missionary portion. No one was barred from any of the three conventions, but only those to

---

[12] "State Report for Illinois," *Christian-Evangelist* 30/43 (26 October 1893): 45.
[13] Lyda, "A History of Black Christian Churches," 99.

whom the convention "belonged" had a voice in the proceedings.[14]

The developments in Kentucky were indicative of organizational developmental patterns among black Disciples throughout the South. African-American Disciples in Tennessee formed a statewide convention in 1880, followed by those in Mississippi in 1887, and in Georgia in 1891. African-American Disciples in North Carolina developed a convention structure that was arguably the best structured and strict in terms of the requirements placed on its clergy. They were the first among all Disciples, black or white, to establish specific educational requirements for the ordination of clergy. According to Toulouse, black Disciples in North Carolina, along with Texas, developed "an organized and systematic method of examining and evaluating candidates for ordination." Lyda adds, "Ministers were expected to have at least a 'normal' education, an equivalent of twelve grades of schooling, available to most persons in North Carolina through the public schools."[15] Describing the development of the North Carolina assembly, McAllister and Tucker write,[16]

> Discipline and organization gave strength to the program. Each local congregation held a Quarterly Conference at which the business of the church was considered, the foot-washing ceremony observed, and Holy Communion was held. On the weekend of every fifth Sunday, the churches of one or more counties would gather for three days of fellowship and worship. Out of these gatherings grew the council of seven elders or "chiefs." Since these assemblies were controlled by the men of the church, the women formed their own "Sisters Union" in 1892.

---

[14] Ibid., 107.

[15] Mark G. Toulouse, *Joined in Discipleship: The Maturing of an American Religious Movement* (St. Louis: Chalice Press, 1992) 149; Lyda, "A History of Black Christian Churches," 158.

[16] Lester G. McAllister and William E. Tucker, *Journey of Faith: A History of the Christian Church (Disciples of Christ)* (St. Louis: Chalice Press, 1995 [1975]), 301.

According to Lyda, the North Carolina Assembly discussed starting a school and established an education fund as early as 1898.[17]

Given what we know about the dualistic function of Sunday schools in the context of black churches throughout the nineteenth century, these schools must be considered as examples of African-American agency in education reform within the Christian Church. At times, Sunday schools would evolve into a church that would, in turn, give birth to a separate non-Sunday-school educational institution. The work of Peter Lowery serves as an example of such a process. In 1859 Peter Lowery of Nashville, Tennessee, organized a Sunday school with more than 200 pupils. Lowery is described by Herman Norton as "an aggressive individual. He had purchased his freedom and also that of his mother and three brothers and two sisters about twenty-five years [prior to starting the Sunday school]. He had accumulated real estate holdings valued at forty-thousand dollars and had the admiration, respect, and support of the white business and religious community. He was easily the most outstanding negro religious leader in Nashville, and probably the south."[18]

Lowery used his considerable business acumen to benefit his people. On 10 December 1867, he secured a charter to establish the Tennessee Manual Labor University (TMLU). After purchasing 300 acres of farmland near Ebenezer, Tennessee, TMLU opened in 1868. It became the first school for African Americans to be established by a member of the Disciples of Christ. The 1868 founding of TMLU makes Lewis's claim, "The earliest Negro school to be started among Disciples of Christ was the first Louisville Christian Bible School," incorrect. According to the charter, "the purpose of this school was 'for the elevation of the Freedmen…[for the promotion of] Education, Industry, and Pure Christianity.'" Even though the school claimed to

---

[17] Lyda, "A History of Black Christian Churches," 81.
[18] Herman A. Norton, *A History of the Christian Church (Disciples of Chris) in Tennessee* (Nashville: Reed & Co., 1971) 130.

offer "Literature, and Science, and the Mechanical Arts," it apparently was primarily an industrial school.[19]

Initially there was a measure of support for TMLU by some influential white Disciples. William Pendleton, the editor of the *Millennial Harbinger*, put out a call to the wider church to support Lowery's effort: "We have received from Bro. Peter Lowery, of Nashville, Tenn., a circular setting forth the objects and claims of this Institution. It is designed, especially, for the benefit of the colored race, and appeals to the friends of humanity everywhere for contributions to carry out its benevolent aims.... The true direction for the elevation of the colored man...should heartily be encouraged."[20]

Articles calling for support of TMLU were published in the *Christian Standard* and the *Christian Advocate*, both influential Disciples periodicals. The schools also received support from more sixty businessmen in the Nashville area. TMLU seemed to be a school of great promise until it was ruined by scandal. According to Norton, Lowery's son, Samuel, moved north several years prior to the opening of TMLU. At some point, the younger Lowery faced financial difficulty. His services were later secured by the ACMS to serve as an evangelist and fundraising agent for the school. It seems that Samuel's misappropriation of church funds led to the school's demise. In an article printed in the *Christian Standard*, a Disciples minister from Chicago, J. C. Power, wrote this assessment of TMLU resulting from his investigation: "The whole thing is a deliberate swindle against the colored race by colored men. The Manual Labor farm is a humbug, having few huts to shelter some very indolent negroes and make a den of prostitution for both black and white. The money, provisions and clothing are appropriated for private use, and agricultural implements,

---

[19] Ibid., 132. See also David E. Harrell, Jr., *The Social Sources of Division in the Disciples of Christ, 1865–1900* (Atlanta: Publishing Systems, Inc. 1973) 182,; and McAllister and Tucker, *Journey of Faith*, 299.
[20] William K. Pendleton, "Tennessee Manual Labor University," *Millennial Harbinger* 39/4 (April 1868): 227–28.

seeds, nursery stock, etc., are wasted without doing the slightest good."[21]

According to Norton, the *Christian Standard* conducted an independent investigation of these charges and found the allegations to be true. With 180 students enrolled, the school closed within months of the article's printing. Resisting the temptation to engage in anachronism, I can only wonder how the culturally based social and behavioral norms of Blacks in the South - just a few years after centuries of enslavement—may have looked or have been judged through the lens of a white Northerner. Also, given the intense opposition to black education within the Christian Church—a church that up to this point had done virtually nothing to establish schools for Blacks and was predisposed to acquiesce to the demands of white Southerners—I am led to question the objectivity of Powers's assessment or merits of the "independent investigation." Commenting on TMLU's demise, McAllister and Tucker state only that "the school came to a quick end in the midst of a financial scandal."[22] Harrell simply states that the TMLU effort "was commended by the editors of the church, but the short-lived venture, plagued by financial scandal, had little practical impact on the Disciples nationally."[23] Harrell does, however, question the ACMS's support of Samuel Lowery.

> The work among the Negroes of Nashville revealed the typical pitfalls of the early efforts by Disciples. The society was ill informed about the character of Lowery, whose father was a respected minister, and supported him simply because he was an available black. Lowery was reportedly both a "good preacher" and "possessed considerable wealth." The society continued to support him for two years, but the society's reports were vague and its support was probably very limited. Eventually, Lowery was exposed as a fraud.[24]

---

[21] J. C. Power, no title, *Christian Standard* 5/44 (27 October 1870), quoted in Norton, *A History of the Christian Church*, 139.

[22] McAllister and Tucker, *Journey of Faith*, 299.

[23] Harrell, *Sources of Division*, 182.

[24] Ibid., 163.

A successful example in terms of a sustained effort of a Sunday school evolving into a normal school is the Martinsville Christian Institute, which I will discuss below.

There were several early efforts by Blacks to establish an organizational structure beyond the local church. In May 1867, under the leadership of Rufus Conrad, a group of black Disciples ministers in Nashville, Tennessee, organized the American Christian Evangelizing and Education Association (ACEEA). The very name of this organization speaks volumes to the dialectic relationship that schooling and religious education had among African-American Disciples. As a church-based organization, ACEEA stated that it was "dedicated to the establishment of both secular and Sunday schools among negroes." According to Lyda, who refers to Conrad as "Robert," the ACEEA appealed to the ACMS for support.[25] Black preachers sought to use cooperative means to achieve their goals and objectives.

The work of the ACEEA resulted in the establishment of several congregations in the eastern part of Tennessee. There is no record of the ACEEA establishing a school, but given its location and date of existence, it is quite probable that ACEEA had some involvement, for good or bad, with Tennessee Manual Labor University. There is no record, however, to substantiate such involvement. The existence of the ACEEA was also short-lived. Lyda dates the conclusion of its existence to be in the early 1870s. McAllister and Tucker state that ACEEA received "little support from either Whites or Blacks in the depressed post-Civil War economy; the effort failed."[26]

The Colored Christian Convention and the Colored General Christian Missionary Convention were both organized in the mid-1880s. Records indicate these groups held annual gatherings until the end of the century. There is no evidence that suggests either of these groups had any impact on schooling for Blacks. According to Harrell, for most of its organizational life the Colored Christian Convention

---

[25] Lyda, "A History of Black Christian Churches," 92; Foster et al., eds., *The Encyclopedia of the Stone-Campbell Movement*, 12.
[26] McAllister and Tucker, *Journey of Faith*, 300.

was "financially bankrupt and did little more than issue appeals to the white convention for support of the Negro work."[27]

Another annual gathering of African-American Disciples, beyond the local congregation, was the Workers' Conference that met at the end of each school year on the campus of Southern Christian Institute. C. C. Smith reported on the national scope of this gathering. In 1907 he wrote, "Wednesday forenoon was given to the Workers' Conference. This was a conference of representatives of the Church (negro) from the different states. There were present twenty-two delegates from Alabama, Arkansas, Texas, and Mississippi. The exercise took on something of the character of a national convention for the negro church." The origin of the Workers' Conference was articulated by William Alphin of Texas in 1905:

> Since the closing of SCI this year, I have thought it would be a wise and helpful effort if the colored ministers of all the states would have a regular annual meeting at the opening or closing of the SCI Perhaps the closing would be better…. We must have a better understanding among ourselves and organize our forces and systematize our evangelical and educational work in the church. I don't know a better time or place for this meeting. Surely the situation and the condition of our work in all states demand such a meeting on our part.[28]

It is possible that Alphin's proposal was an attempt to replicate the "Workers' Conference" that was established at Tuskegee Normal and Industrial Institute in 1892. The Tuskegee conference was organized in response to the dire economic conditions and challenges facing black farmers and workers in the South.

Perhaps the most progressive black Disciples organization—in terms of education—was the National Convention of the Churches of Christ (NCCC). This group was initially organized in 1873 by Preston Taylor, pastor of the Colored Christian Church of Mt. Sterling, Kentucky, and H. Malcolm Ayers of Lexington, Kentucky. The

---

[27] Harrell, *Sources of Division*, 202.
[28] William Alphin, "Shall We Do It?" *Gospel Plea* 10/24 (28 June 1905): 3.

NCCC pressed for a stronger role in the Disciples' mission among Blacks. They formed an advisory committee to work with the ACMS, and later BNEE, on black-related issues. In 1879, during an address to the General Convention, Taylor asked for shared leadership on matters related to black evangelism and education. It was the desire of black leaders associated with NCCC to work cooperatively with the GCMC to avoid separation from the movement. According to Lyda, "The General Convention received the committee at least once in 1883, but when it formed the Board of Negro Evangelism and Education in 1890 it appears to have ignored the National Convention and the advisory committee."[29]

The apparent exclusion of the NCCC by the General Convention comes as no surprise given the NCCC educational agenda. The primary spokesperson for NCCC was Preston Taylor. Taylor, an extraordinary Nashville entrepreneur, was one who pushed the GCMC concerning its educational mission among Blacks in the South. He was a mortician who owned the largest cemetery in the South. Taylor also served as national evangelist for the GCMC from 1883 to 1886. Prior to accepting a call to serve as pastor of Gay Lea Christian Church in 1886, Taylor spearheaded an effort to establish a school at New Castle, Kentucky, which is discussed below. Taylor became a major force after 1900. He called for Disciples mission agencies to support higher education and a higher quality of theological education for African Americans.

In 1883, during his brief tenure as national evangelist for GCMC, Preston Taylor launched an effort in Mt. Sterling, Kentucky, to establish a school for ministerial training. After providing the leadership to raise an initial $1,000, Taylor, along with H. Malcolm Ayers and T. Augustus Reid, approached the State Missionary Convention of the Colored Christian Church in Kentucky with a proposal for a school. Their proposal was endorsed. Funds were raised to purchase buildings that belonged to the defunct Brinker College in New Castle. The cost of the property was $2,500. Taylor raised the balance. A board was formed that consisted of five Blacks and six

---

[29] Lyda, "A History of Black Christian Churches," 110.

Whites. The Christian Bible College (CBC) opened its doors in September 1886.

Harrell names T. Augustus Reed (black) as CBC's first principal. However, an article written by C. C. Smith in the *American Home Missionary* names Dr. (Joel) M. Manwaring as the first principal. Reed, nevertheless, began his tenure in fall 1888. Reed is described as "a scholarly man," one who "ranks high as an educator among his people" and who "resigned a paying and certain position in the public schools" in order to serve as CBC's principal.[30] Smith's article affirms the agency of Blacks in this enterprise of education reform within the Disciples of Christ: "This institution is an outcome of an effort made by the colored brethren of the Christian Church during the sessions of the Eleventh Annual Convention held at Richmond, Kentucky, in 1883, to have a school for the education of the ministry of the church.... The committee raised the money principally among the colored churches, paid for the property and passed it to the board of eleven persons—six white and five colored—J. W. McGarvey, president."[31]

Due to financial problems, the board decided to cease operations at the school during the 1887–1888 academic year, and turned to GCMC for assistance. The General Convention agreed to help under the condition that the property be placed under the General Convention's control. In its initial evaluation of CBC, the General Convention discovered that it was operating as a coeducational institution. In his report to the GCMC, John Jenkins, Superintendent of Missions and Schools Among the Colored People, declared that the "negro race has not yet reached the plane of civilization that will admit of co-education when the college is in charge of one of their own color."[32] The GCMC took control of the school and closed it in 1892. The proceeds

---

[30] R. B. Neal, "The Colored Bible School," *Gospel Advocate* 30 (10 October 1888): 1, quoted in Harrell, *Sources of Division*, 194.

[31] C. C. Smith, "History of Our Mission Work Among the Negroes," *American Home Missionary* 6/3 (March 1900): 17.

[32] John W. Jenkins, "Colored Schools and Missions," report presented to the Board of the General Christian Missionary Convention, 1889, quoted in Lyda, "A History of Black Christian Churches," 125.

from the sale were used to reopen the Louisville Bible School as the Louisville Christian Bible School.[33]

Around 1880, black Disciples in Texas began serious discussions concerning their desire to establish a school in their state. They too were interested primarily in a school for ministers. In 1893, after a period of meetings and fundraisers, a minister by the name of M. T. Brown proposed that the school be located at Waco. A committee selected H. S. Howell (black) to head up a fundraising effort to establish the National Colored Christian College. Howell traveled extensively to rally support for the Texas school. The promoters of the project eagerly began construction on a building. In the meantime, Howell was reported to have secured donations of land and $800 before he absconded with the money. This failed effort would prove to affect adversely a second effort to establish a school in Texas less than fifteen years later.[34]

The first sustained Disciples of Christ effort to provide schooling for African Americans started by Blacks was the Lum Graded School in Lowndes County, Alabama, which is about 28 miles south of Montgomery. As I mentioned previously, the dating of Lum, whose name would later be changed to Alabama Christian Institute, by historians and others is itself indicative of the failure to acknowledge African-American agency in education reform within the Disciples of Christ. Perhaps the best way to comment on Lum's beginnings and the role of black people in this process is simply to share how the story has been told over the years. C. C. Smith, the corresponding secretary of the BNEE and later CWBM, shared these comments affirming African-American agency, but also conflicting in terms of dating its founding:

---

[33] Lyda, "A History of Black Christian Churches," 124–25. Also see Harrell, *Sources of Division*, 193–94; Lewis, "A History of Secondary and Higher Education in Negro Schools," 49; and John C. Long, "The Disciples of Christ and Negro Education," Ph.D. diss., University of Southern California, 1960, 145–47.

[34] "National Colored Christian College," *Christian Standard* 23/2 (14 January 1888): 29. Also see Cummins, *Disciples Colleges*, 90; Harrell, *Sources of Division*, 193; and Lyda, "A History of Black Christian Churches," 166.

The Lum Graded School, at Lum, Alabama, was opened in
October of 1894.[35] ...It is impossible for one to realize what this
means unless he could know of their poverty. We of the North
can hardly realize this, and of the sacrifice they made in "quitting
an hour earlier in chopping out the cotton" to work on the new
school building.... The school has three grades: the primary, the
intermediate, and the normal, and last year [1899] 128 pupils.[36]
...All of the work at Lum has been accomplished by the negroes
themselves with the little guidance I've been able to give.[37][

After acknowledging the year of Lum's opening as 1894, Smith
later wrote,

The story of the Lum Graded School is the story of what
those trained in our schools have been instrumental in doing for
their own race.... So, when the Lum school opened in 1904,
many of the patrons were owners of small tracts of land and were
freed from the curse of the mortgage. This made a stable
community in which to found a school.... In 1893 [local Blacks]
discussed the advisability of starting a school in their midst....
These consulted with white people and talked with the best
negroes of the community, and finally they decided to start a
school.... These men drew up plans for a school building and
bought the lumber for it on the mortgage system, one of them
mortgaging all he owned to do this.[38]

According to Lewis, Lyda, Harrell, and a report written by Effie
Cunningham around 1922, Lum opened its doors on 15 October 1894,
under the direction of H. Jackson Brayboy and Robert Brooks. They

---

[35] C. C. Smith, "Negro Education and Evangelism," (Indianapolis: Christian
Women's Board of Missions, ca. 1901) 4, undated pamphlet on file at the Disciples of
Christ Historical Society, Nashville.
[36] C. C. Smith, "History of Our Mission Work Among the Negroes," *American
Home Missionary* 6/3 (March 1900): 22.
[37] C. C. Smith, "Secretary's Report," *Missionary Tidings* 27/2 (June 1909): 62.
[38] C. C. Smith, "The Lum Alabama Graded School" (Indianapolis: Christian
Women's Board of Missions, ca. 1905) 4–5, undated pamphlet on file at the Disciples
of Christ Historical Society, Nashville.

were both graduates of Southern Christian Institute. Upon returning home from SCI, Brooks, a native of Lowndes County, took the Alabama teachers examination and secured the highest certification available at that time. Brooks started the school in an old building that was secured with the assistance of David Mercer of Bowling Green, Ohio, who provided a donation of $100. The first board consisted of members of the black churches of Lowndes County. The board's first president was a minister who was a graduate of Louisville Christian Bible School. A local white landowner donated 5 acres, and the BNEE would later purchase and donate another 60 acres.[39]

While under the guidance of the BNEE, Lum's board was unable to raise the amount of funding to sustain their effort to run the school. At a time when it was difficult to secure financial support from church sources, a 1907 report in the *Missionary Tidings* reveals how weather played a role in undermining revenue gained from tuition. The report read in part, "The school opened amid unfavorable conditions. On account of a disastrous storm which occurred about the first of October, cotton picking was late, and the children were kept at their homes to pick cotton. This was the cause of some children entering very late and others not entering at all."[40] The following year the CWBM agreed to assist Lum in getting out of the financial difficulties it was experiencing. A CWBM report states that it would provide "$1,000" for "Lum, Alabama school with the privilege of naming the school."[41] The Lum Graded School officially became known as the Alabama Christian Institute (ACI) in October 1914.[42]

---

[39] Effie Cunningham, "Work of Disciples of Christ with Negro American" (St. Louis: United Christian Missionary Society, ca. 1922) 10–11, and Robert G. Sherer, *Black Education in Alabama, 1865–1901* (Tuscaloosa: University of Alabama Press, 1997) 90. See also Harrell, *Sources of Division*, 195, Robert Jordan, *Two Races in One Fellowship* (Detroit: United Christian Church, 1944) 54, Lewis, "A History of Secondary and Higher Education in Negro Schools," 67, and Lyda, "A History of Black Christian Churches," 134.

[40] "Lum Graded School," *Missionary Tidings* 25/7 (November 1907): 273.

[41] "CWBM Report," *Missionary Tidings* 26/6 (October 1908): 237.

[42] The name was changed at the "annual convention." It's not clear if this was a state convention or the CWBM convention. Notice appeared in *Missionary Tidings* 32/7 (November 1914): 306.

Up to this point, Lum, for all intent and purposes, was an elementary school. Under the CWBM, it offered junior high courses. In both situations, the school's curricular emphasis was industrial education. ACI closed in 1923 supposedly because "the public schools of Alabama are now improved so as to take care of this work."[43] I use the word "supposedly" because the Alabama public school curriculum did not offer the religious instruction that the Disciples of Christ affirmed to be central to their educational philosophy. Even if it did, nothing less than the strict teaching of restorationism would be an acceptable form of religious instruction to the Disciples of Christ. Since public education was suddenly considered sufficient, it suggests an abandonment of church-related education for Blacks in Lowndes County by the CWBM.

Perhaps the best interpretation of the Lum's beginning is from the school itself. This excerpt from a 1908 catalog was written at a time when the school, now ACI, was under the control of CWBM.

> [ACI had its] origin in the mind of a few disciples who decided that something could, and must be done to raise the educational standard in this section…. Before a building was erected, sheets were used to cordon off classroom space on the property of "the old church" which stood on the property where Lum would be located. They initially employed 3 teachers…. In the meantime, men were in the woods felling trees and hewing timbers for the erection of the school building. But the necessary material could not be obtained from the woods…. Having no funds to complete work, Elder Brayboy used "one of his plantations" to secure funds.[44]

Of interest here is that the catalog refers to the school as entering its "9th annum," which suggests the school was founded in 1900. This may explain why Cummins uses 1900 on his list. As I mentioned earlier, 1900 is the year CWBM took over all Disciples mission work

---

[43] "Alabama Christian Institute Closing," *World Call* 5/12 (December 1923): 37.

[44] 1908–1909 catalog of the Lum Alabama Graded School on file at the Disciples of Christ Historical Society, Nashville.

among African Americans. The language used in the catalog provides the reader with no clue of explicit African-American agency in the founding of the school other than naming H. Jackson Brayboy as a benefactor. Regarding those who operated the school—a school that had been in operation for at least six years prior to 1900—it seems their efforts and sacrifices were not worthy of mention. Another example of what appears to be a dismissal of black achievement at Lum is reflected in a comment made by the 1912 commencement speaker, O. P. Speagal [sic]. In his address, he noted that with the class of 1912, Lum had "reached the highest enrollment in its history this year, when 106 were enrolled."[45] Prior to CWBM control, C. C. Smith wrote that the class of 1899 totaled 111 students.

Clearly, some wanted to diminish the accomplishments of black leadership at Lum prior to it being taken over by CWBM in 1900. While it is plausible to conclude that racism lies at the core of these omissions of black agency, I will allow for another possible explanation for this omission in the 1908 catalog. Historically, the BNEE was tied to the ACMS, an organization that was never successful in raising funds for home mission among Blacks. I believe part of the reason for this ineffective fundraising, other than a lackluster effort by male leadership, was that Southern churches never forgave them for the 1863 resolution that openly sided with the Union. The CWBM was much more successful in its overall mission operation, including fundraising. It is reasonable to consider the possibility that CWBM, in order to maximize financial support throughout the church, needed to distance themselves from the ACMS and its legacy at all costs. Additionally, in 1906, the Disciples of Christ experienced a formal schism ostensibly over the issues of the use of instruments in worship and the existence of national organization. The geographic lines represented by the churches that broke away from the Disciples of Christ over these issues, becoming the Churches of Christ, are strikingly similar to the lines that represent the Southern churches that embraced the Confederate cause. Again, distancing themselves from this ACMS-related past because of financial reasons could be viewed as

---

[45] "Lum Alabama Graded School," *Missionary Tidings* 30/3 (July 1912): 94.

prudent for the CWBM. It would be in their best interest to garner financial support from both sides of the schism to advance their mission efforts. Whatever the reasons for CWBM's apparent omissions, it is neither prudent nor justified to eliminate the many contributions made by African Americans in the history of ACI and the Lum Graded School. Such a decision relegates the role of African Americans to virtual nonexistence beyond being passive recipients of white benevolence and largesse.

Another example of the role and function of black Disciples of Christ Sunday schools and their utility in education reform is seen in the events that led to the founding of the Piedmont School of Industry (later called Piedmont Christian Institute and Martinsville Christian Institute). On 26 June 1907, the Sunday schools of the Piedmont District gathered at Martinsville, Virginia, for their annual meeting. The keynote speaker for the opening session was "Professor J. L. Hill," who served as principal of Martinsville graded schools. His address focused on "some very helpful suggestions in regards to the influence that might be exerted by pastors and leaders in filling the Martinsville Christian Institute with students if they would but interest themselves in the work."[46] Having such a speaker to deliver the opening address at its annual meeting speaks volumes of the primacy black Disciples in the Piedmont District placed on normal education in relation to the religious instruction of their Sunday schools. It also serves as an example of agency in education reform by the planners of this meeting.

Under the leadership of W. H. Cole and a group of black Disciples in the Piedmont sections of Virginia and North Carolina, these reformers acted upon their desire to have a Disciples-related school in their area. A corporation called the Piedmont Disciples of Christ was formed to sponsor the endeavor. In a one-room church named Fayette Street Christian Church of Martinsville, the Piedmont School of

---

[46] Justin Spencer, *Century of Disciples' Progress in the Piedmont District: A Synoptic History* (Roanoke: Roanoke Tribune, 1959) 9.

Industry (PSI) opened 8 October 1900.[47] Alice Liverett describes the agency and commitment of these black Disciples and how they made the most out of what little they had. She writes, "Mr. Thomas opened the Martinsville school of seven pupils with the sole equipment of a short stretch of slated canvas, blackboard, a box of chalk, and two erasers. The story of that school is one of heroic struggle against seemingly insurmountable odds."[48] James H. Thomas (black) served as PSI's only principal. He served from 1900 until its closing in 1932.

The 1923 Piedmont bulletin provides a self-portrait of the school's beginnings. In it, we get a glimpse of this school's birth. This was a school born out of black resistance to the predominant educational philosophy that shaped schools for African Americans supported by the GCMC and CWBM. "The school had its inception in the minds of certain devoted, public spirited Negro men of the Piedmont section of Virginia and North Carolina, who felt that their religious communion, the Disciples of Christ, was not supplying its full share of Christian education for the Negro youth of the country.... [Thomas was promised a salary of $30.00 per month] but it soon developed that only a total of $10 was available from the expected source."[49]

The deed to purchase land from J. B. Lavinder for $700 was secured in January 1901. Blacks raised $200 and the Christian Women's Board of Missions provided a loan for $600. The land consisted of "a couple of ramshackle, four-room tenant-houses in a beautiful oak grove of less than three acres." One building was in such

---

[47] My dating here is based on James H. Thomas's report "The Piedmont School of Industry," *Gospel Plea* 6/42 (30 October 1901): 7. Lewis dates the opening on 1 October 1900 ("A History of Secondary and Higher Education in Negro Schools Related to the Disciples of Christ," 1957, 69); and Long cites a published report by W. A. Cole where he states "we made preliminary arrangements for the final opening of the Piedmont School of Industry on Friday, October 4, 1900" (W. A. Cole, *American Home Missionary* 6 [November 1900]: 79, quoted in Long, "The Disciples of Christ and Negro Education," 180).

[48] Alice Liverett, *Biographical Sketches of Leaders of Negro Work of the Disciples of Christ* (Indianapolis: Department of Missionary Education, United Christian Missionary Society, 1936) 4.

[49] "1923 Piedmont Christian Institute Bulletin," on file at the Disciples of Christ Historical Society, Nashville.

bad condition "that nothing remained but to raze it."[50] It is important to note that the school began operations prior to any assistance from the CWBM. Long writes:

> The first mention of the school by the Christian Women's Board of Missions is in the minutes of the Executive Committee for November 21, 1900, where "C. C. Smith wrote a detailed report of his visit to Martinsville, Virginia." Next month, December 19, 1900, another report was made by him. He had found that the school was being successfully carried on in the church and the work was then self-supporting, but the people had located a piece of property which they could purchase for $800.00. They had $200.00 in hand and desired that an advance of $600.00 be made them. It was taken by consent that this loan be made and "that Bro. Smith secure the property and try to raise the money this year."[51]

Through the agency of African-American Disciples, the loan from CWBM was paid off by February 1902. "They also paid for repairs and 'for all the running expenses at the school'; furthermore they were 'not in debt for anything.'"[52]

Concerning PSI's purpose, Lewis quotes Thomas from a 1930 publication. According to Thomas, "The purpose of Piedmont Christian Institute is to gather these young people to herself, to deepen their religious convictions, and thus solidify their loyalty to the church."[53] This statement of purpose is a far cry from the vision of purpose Thomas articulated one year after the school opened its doors. In a published article Thomas wrote,

---

[50] Ibid.

[51] Long, "The Disciples of Christ and Negro Education," 181.

[52] "The Piedmont School of Industry," *Missionary Tidings* 18 (February 1901): 249, quoted in Long, "The Disciples of Christ and Negro Education," 181.

[53] J. H. Mohorter, *Survey of Piedmont Christian Institute* (Indianapolis: Department of Religious Education, United Christian Missionary Society, 1930) 58, quoted in Lewis, "A History of Secondary and Higher Education in Negro Schools," 69.

The name would imply that the principal feature of this school is intended to be industrial; but we wish to correct this. We realize that no man, however thrifty and industrious, is any credit to God unless he is a moral and intelligent man. Nor is he yet a full-fledged man until he fully realizes and appreciate his obligations, responsibilities and duties as a citizen. Consequently, while we are training our pupils in industry and thrift, we shall lay equally as much stress upon Bible and moral and intellectual training, and shall endeavor to give them a practical training for citizenship. We believe, by this means we shall be able to come nearer to preparing our boys and girls to meet the demands and requirements which the 20th century, undoubtedly, [will] require of them.[54]

In 1901, Thomas articulated an educational purpose for PSI that reflects a commitment to provide an education that would nurture and stimulate the head (intellectual), the hand (industrial), and the heart (spiritual). In 1901, Thomas spoke of preparing black men and women to meet the demands of the twentieth century. Some years later in 1930, Thomas spoke almost exclusively of an educational purpose that focused on the heart, of "deepening religious convictions" and "loyalty to the church." What happened to cause such a radical shift in Thomas's educational philosophy? Did Thomas experience an ideological transformation that moved him to embrace an educational philosophy more congruent with those in charge of Disciples mission agencies? I seriously doubt this to be the case. It must be kept in mind that Thomas was leading a black school in a climate of immense white opposition to black-controlled schooling. Additionally, his financial support and ecclesial membership were tied to a church whose leadership opposed—or who did not support—higher education for Blacks at a time when the country was digging its way out of the Great Depression. Also, Blacks in the region had other options for schooling that kept PSI's enrollment down. Thomas reported that "there are several schools for higher training in the state, offering all those

---

[54] James H. Thomas, "The Piedmont School of Industry," *Gospel Plea* 6/42 (30 October 1901): 7.

facilities and advantages of which we can not boast, and to which every student with any degree of pride in his alma mater justly delights to point, and that there is a good public school here employing four teachers, not to mention a Presbyterian parochial school."[55]

Each of these factors is likely to have played an influential role in the development of a watered-down and depoliticized 1930 statement of purpose as compared to the more progressive philosophy held by Thomas in 1901. Diminished enrollment resulting from institutional competition in the area, noted by Thomas, no doubt created additional financial strain for PSI. By 1930, Thomas's articulated shift in PSI's statement of purpose serves as a classic and sad example of how progressive black education reformers were forced to capitulate to the demands of white church leaders. These white church leaders had the financial wherewithal to keep the schools solvent—under the condition that institutional control was handed over to them.

There seems to be some conflict concerning the name of PSI at its inception. Citing a 1946 dissertation written by Rolla James Bennett, Lewis writes, "The school was first thought of in terms of a Piedmont School of Industry, but when it was opened Monday, October 1, 1900, in the little one-room Fayette Street Christian Church (Negro) of Martinsville, the name of Martinsville Christian Institute was used. The report of the school published in the 1908 *Year Book of the Disciples of Christ* calls it Piedmont Christian Institute, by which name it was commonly known through the years."[56]

I believe Lewis and Bennett are incorrect regarding the initial name of this school. The 1901 article by Thomas that I have cited uses PSI. In 1902, a published report on the school also uses the name Piedmont School of Industry. The Thomas report previously cited was published in the *Missionary Tidings* in 1904 under the heading "The Martinsville Christian Institute." Cummins uses "Piedmont" on his

---

[55] James H. Thomas, "The Martinsville Christian Institute," *Missionary Tidings* 22/7 (November 1904): 261.

[56] Lewis, "A History of Secondary and Higher Education in Negro Schools," 69, cites Rolla James Bennett, "History of the Founding of Educational Institutions by the Disciples of Christ in Virginia and West Virginia," Ph.D. diss., University of Pittsburgh, 1946, 20.

aforementioned list of schools.[57] The Piedmont School of Industry is the name black Disciples reformers, responding to the educational needs of their community, gave their school. Undoubtedly, the name change to the Martinsville Christian Institute is related to the transition of institutional control from the founders to the CWBM. This is a pattern, as I have demonstrated, the CWBM used with the Lum Graded School in Alabama when they agreed to provide financial support with the condition that they had "the privilege of naming the school." Again, as I have mentioned, Lum then became known as the Alabama Christian Institute.

In 1908 a published report announced the opening of a school in Jonesboro, Tennessee, called Warner Institute. According to Lewis, Warner was named after Englishman Yardly Warner, who started the school as early as 1875 under the auspices of the Society of Friends. Warner Institute was later operated by the Congregational Church and sold to black Disciples in East Tennessee. The purchase price for Warner was $1,500, of which Blacks had raised only $400. The balance was secured through a loan from CWBM. The physical plant of the school consisted of two buildings that sat on 1 1/4 acres of land. With James E. Baker (black) serving as principal, and two teachers who were graduates of the Martinsville Institute Normal School, Tennessee Christian Institute (TCI) opened its doors on 26 October 1908. Gertrude Smith submitted the following proposition to the CWBM concerning Warner: "That [CWBM] purchase the property and obligate themselves to pay for it; that they deed it to CWBM and make payments through it; that with the help of the county and city funds they conduct a school jointly with CWBM, asking them that they secure the principal of the school and pay his salary and give their guidance and oversight of the work. All the rest of the expense besides salary of the principal to be taken care of by the local (negro) board."[58]

---

[57] Mrs. O. B. Sears, "The Piedmont School of Industry," *Missionary Tidings* 20/3 (July 1902): 80; and Thomas, "The Martinsville Christian Institute," 260.

[58] "Jonesboro, Tennessee School," *Missionary Tidings* 26/8 (December 1908): 368.

In an article titled "Negro Work," there is a reference to Warner Institute, whose name was changed to "Tennessee Christian Institute in 1913." The principal of this school was H. D. Griffin, who was black.[59] In an undated handwritten year-end report to CWBM, Griffin stated that enrollment was "just past 71." He also wrote, "We sent out two young persons, a boy and a girl, of whom we are proud. One is a minister in the Methodist Church, and the other is teaching in the county." It appears that TCI closed in 1914. A 1914 *Missionary Tidings* article references the school's purpose in the past tense: "The aim of the school was to provide religious, moral, intellectual, and industrial training."[60] The use of the word "intellectual" here likely points to the desire of black Disciples in East Tennessee to provide more than industrial education.

A sustained effort for Disciples-related schooling for Blacks in North Carolina appears to be the only example of African-American agency in education totally void of any assistance from a white-controlled mission agency throughout the life of the institution. According to Lewis, the Goldsboro Christian Institute (GCI) began its work in 1910 and was owned and operated by the Goldsboro-Raleigh Assembly of Christians who called themselves "Churches of Christ composed of Disciples."[61] A published article provides a brief summary of the school's history. GCI sat on a 16-acre tract of land purchased by the Goldsboro-Raleigh District in 1910. "Elder E. S. L. Whitfield was chosen to head the movement." He supervised the clearing of the swampy area, carried the logs to a sawmill, and built "a 17 room two-story building and followed with formal opening of the Training Center." Whitfield contracted pneumonia during the construction of the building and died shortly after its opening. "The Elder died an untimely death working to make real the vision which moved his Forefathers to launch the Assembly on a program of training for Church leadership." A succession of four principals was unable to keep the school going. It closed in 1936 because "the assembly found itself

---

[59] "Negro Work," *Missionary Tidings* 32/7 (November 1914): 306.
[60] Ibid..
[61] Lyda, "A History of Black Christian Churches," 156.

unable to maintain the operating budget and since no help was coming from sources outside the District, the project closed and remained so for about thirty years."[62]

The Jarvis Story

On 15 January 1913, Jarvis Christian Institute (later renamed Jarvis Christian College) opened its doors in Hawkins, Texas. The story of the conceptualization, planning, and founding of Jarvis Christian Institute (JCI) provides the most revealing example of African-American agency in education reform within the Disciples of Christ. The story of Jarvis is indeed a story of collaboration among black and white Disciples. The vision, sacrifice, and commitment, however, of black Disciples of East Texas in securing quality education for their community is a story that Disciples historians have not adequately told.

It is worth reiterating an interpretation of the founding of JCI to which students of Disciples history are often exposed. In his widely read book on the history of Disciples of Christ colleges, Cummins writes,

Ja[r]vis Christian College is the only Black higher education institution in covenant with the Christian Church (Disciples of Christ) in our own day. It was founded as Jarvis Christian Institute through the encouragement of the Christian Women's Board of Missions (CWBM) and with a donation of 465 acres of land near Hawkins, Texas, by Mrs. Ida V. Jarvis in 1910. Thomas B. Frost, a graduate of Southern Christian Institute, was appointed by the CWBM in 1911 to develop the school. With the help of Charles A. Berry, Sr., he cleared and fenced the land, built a dormitory-dining hall-classroom building, and designed the course of study by patterning the new institute

---

[62] "Goldsboro Christian Institute," *The North Carolina Christian* 37/11 (December 1956): 11.

along the same format as J. B. Lehman's Southern Christian Institute and Booker T. Washington's Tuskegee Institute.[63]

Cummins's brief summary of JCI's origins gives the reader the impression that African-American agency did not appear in the process of establishing Jarvis until after the CWBM "encouraged" its founding and land was secured by a generous benefactor. Blacks enter the story only when they are "appointed" to "develop the school." Here are additional interpretations of JCI's beginnings that present African Americans as actors in founding of Jarvis long before CWMB became involved. Colby Hall writes,

> This excellent college is the expression of the desire for education of their people on the part of Colored Disciples in Texas.... The idea [of Jarvis] grew up in the heart of Mrs. Mary Alphin, state organizer among Negro women, and other leaders in that work. The concept was encouraged by CWBM which believed in education and understood the Negro problem.... The one unbroken string on which the pearls of progress of the Negro Texas Disciples can be strong was the continuous, persistent, unremitting effort to establish a college for education of their children; especially preachers.[64]

An article in the *Missionary Tidings* states, "Among the Negro churches of Texas, there had been a silently growing fund for a Negro College. This came to the attention of some white friends in Texas; it was between 4 and 5 hundred dollars...a large sum to have been secured almost noiselessly and without effort."[65]

In an article published in the *Gladewater Mirror* near Hawkins, Texas, Dana Dickson writes,

> In fact, the dream that became Jarvis Christian College was born in 1904 when the Negro Disciples in Texas, led by state organizer Mary Alphin, in conjunction with the Christian

---

[63] Cummins, *Disciples Colleges*, 90.

[64] Colby Hall, *Texas Disciples* (Ft. Worth: Texas Christian University Press, 1953) 330–32.

[65] "Jarvis Christian Institute," *Missionary Tidings* 31/1 (May 1913).

Women's Board of Missions, began to plan for a school to meet
the needs of black youth. Financial goals were set and the Negro
Disciples were to raise $1,000.00, while the CWBM committed
$10,000.00 to the cause. [Virginia Hearne, state head of CWMB,
convinced] Ida VanZandt Jarvis of the need for a school for
Blacks.[66]

Perhaps the most insightful glimpse into JCI's beginnings can be
gleaned from the reflections of the men who "cleared and fenced the
land"—Charles Berry, Sr., who would later serve as JCI's first
superintendent and instructor, and Thomas B. Frost. The following
words are taken from an undated handwritten manuscript by Berry
sometime prior to 6 September 1962, the date of his death.

Many long years ago, before there even was a Jarvis
Christian Institute, somebody saw the great need of such an
Institution that could train our own boys and girls for Christian
leadership in our own particular Brotherhood. The vision of
Jarvis was born in the hearts and minds of a few pioneers, souls
among whom were Bro. and Sister Haley, Elders M. Knight,
M. J. Brown, G. W. Rodgers, William Alphin, Mrs. Alphin
and Prof. J. W. [maybe T. M.] Pratt and a few others.

[Those who had the vision] went about to create a desire
and sentiment in that direction [of building a school]. They
began saving and giving nickels and dimes long before the idea
was sold to the state Brotherhood. At least the idea was brought
to the State Convention and a few of the wide awake men and
women of God, with a great vision championed the cause the
most of whom have passed on, and their labors and names
almost forgotten, but their work "do follower them." After many
years of struggle; prayers, tears, and anxiety (Seems like there
was a struggle within the church to get support for the school) a
school was started at Hawkins, Texas, and Prof. T. B. Frost was
sent from Edwards to a virtual "wilderness" and "jungle" to start

---

[66] Dana Dickson, "Jarvis Christian College Celebrated," *The Gladewater Times*,
28 February 1991.

the school. In the year of 1912 while I was at my printers case in the office of Elder W. A. Scott in Jackson, Mississippi, one bright day morning the call came to me saying, "Go to Texas and join Prof. T. B. Frost for the Christian Brotherhood, in order that the Old Jerusalem Gospel may spread more rapidly among Negroe [sic] peoples doubting nothing." It took every fiber of courage within me to resign an excellent paying position, as a printer in Jackson, Mississippi to accept the call from the late President J. B. Lehman under the auspices of the C.W.B.M. in August 1912 to come to Hawkins, Texas, and work with Bro. T. B. Frost and wife in a vast wilderness with the hope of establishing a Christian Institution, where boys and girls could receive a Christian Education. Yes it took more than mere courage; for it was a challenge to every inkling of faith I possessed to visualize an Institution of learning towering in such a remote jungle.[67]

Thomas B. Frost arrived in Hawkins early on a Sunday in mid-December 1911. In a letter to Joel Lehman he wrote, "I reached Big Sandy Sunday morning at six o'clock. I found a Christian Church house in town; but it belonged to the other side.[68] I went out to the land Sunday evening and found a place to stay on the land with some old people that lived in one of the old shacks."[69] In a report on the progress made during the first year of clearing the land, Frost wrote,

In the period from January 1, 1912 to September 1, 1912, when Mrs. Frost and I were in the work alone, a ten-acre field south of the railroad was cleared and planted in corn and garden, and a campus north of the railroad was fenced up, and the cabins

---

[67] Charles Berry, Sr., undated handwritten manuscript written sometime prior to 6 September 1962, on file at the Olin Library and Communications Center, Jarvis Christian College, Hawkins TX.

[68] In Frost's reference to "the other side," it's not clear if he meant a white church that was inhospitable or one of the churches that took part in the 1906 schism or both.

[69] Thomas B. Frost to Joel Lehman, 12 December 1911, on file at the Olin Library and Communications Center at Jarvis Christian College, Hawkins TX.

were fixed up and a barn was built. On September 1, 1912, we were joined by C. A. Berry and we at once began to build the first new building which was to serve as a residence for me, a home for the girls, and room in which to open the school. This was finished and dedicated by January 15, 1913, and Professor Berry conducted the school till May, enrolling fourteen pupils.[70]

The point that I want to underscore here is that African-American Disciples in Texas did not respond to an initiative taken by CWMB and the Jarvis family to establish JCI. I argue that the reverse is true. Black Disciples had the desire, vision, and initiative to raise funds. CWBM later responded with their assistance, which resulted in the founding of JCI. In fact, it can be argued that Jarvis's origins are indirectly, if not directly, associated with at least two other efforts by black Disciples in Texas to establish a school. This process would span a period of nearly thirty years.

The first attempt by black Disciples in Texas to establish a school was the aforementioned attempt to establish a school in Waco. Regrettably, this ended in a scandal when the preacher, H. S. Howell, absconded with the funds. This incident was not soon forgotten by black Disciples in Texas as it would make subsequent school fundraising efforts extremely difficult. The extraordinary leadership of Mary Alphin, wife of the aforementioned William Alphin, was vital in making the vision of JCI become a reality for African Americans. Reflecting on the difficulty to raise money among black Disciples in East Texas, she was no doubt making reference to the Howell incident and its impact when she wrote, "Our people have too often been the victim of grafters. Twenty years ago, the Negro Disciples of Texas raised money for a Christian School and were ready to build when one of the leaders took the money and ran off. For these reasons it has been hard to reestablish confidence in the hearts of those who had

---

[70] Thomas B. Frost, "Twentieth Annual Report of Negro Work," *Missionary Tidings* 31/7 (November 1913): 269.

given, and as workers pleaded for gifts for the school they were often told what had happened years before."[71]

It appears that black Disciples in Texas made a second attempt at starting a school. The secondary sources I have referenced, however, do not mention it. Two documents published in 1902, a report and a letter, reveal an effort to establish a school in Dixon, Texas, in 1902. Because this effort does not show up in other secondary sources that I have examined below, I am providing a rather lengthy quotation of the letter. The report is from A. E. Colbert, who writes of progress made toward the establishment of a school. "We are striving to build Christian Institute in Dixon, Texas, the place for location of the institute in N. E. Texas.... The second Lord's day in March is our rally day for the college."[72] Even more revealing is a letter from A. J. Hurdle of Dixon, Texas. Hurdle's letter reveals a number of his concerns, and probably those of others who were involved in this effort. Further, it includes an apparent reference to the Howell incident and an awareness of the damage created by it—a break from the state convention to gain autonomy and control of the plan to establish a school; some disagreement as to where the school would be located; some success in raising funds; and an openness to receive assistance from the CWBM, avoiding a posture of dependence on this group and at the same time maintaining a sense of responsibility and self-determination.

I am in receipt of a circular from Bro. M. T. Brown of Waco, stating that he has located a college site in Waco consisting of 5 acres of land and building on it at a cost of $8,000.00. This makes no account of the N. E. District, especially Center Point location, which was agitated and agreed upon in the Pine Hill Convention, November 19, 1901. Remember we have labored under [the] auspices of the state for 15 years, and have tried to restore the confidence the brethren had lost in our previous leader. So in January 1901, we drew off from state and formed

---

[71] Mary Alphin, "The Opening of Jarvis Christian Institute," *Missionary Tidings* 31/1 (May 1913): 13.

[72] A. E. Colbert, "The Work in Texas," *Gospel Pleas* 7/10 (March 1902): 2.

ourselves into a N. E. District Convention.... We have more money already on hand for college purposes than the state convention raised in fifteen years, clear of expenses. We hope to be able to see Bro. C. C. Smith if he comes to Texas in March and have his advice concerning our work, but let us not depend entirely upon our white brethren to do all our planning, and our thinking and our work; but let them advise and instruct and help us to help ourselves.[73]

I have been unable to determine what became of the effort to establish a school in Dixon, Texas. Nevertheless, what is made clear is that JCI was the culmination of African-American agency; with BNEE's and later CWBM's assistance, black members of the Disciples of Christ in Texas desired to establish a school there.

Not surprisingly, tension existed between black Disciples in Texas and the CWMB over the issue of who would control the funds being raised for the school. Bertha Fuller states, "The CWBM promised financial help and supervision, but in turn required all funds and property to pass through their hands for accounting.... To this, the Negroes demurred. They had been deceived by one of their leaders. They did not know the white folk too intimately and they stiffly withheld their approval of assets and funds being sent to Indianapolis."[74] The record seems to indicate the CWBM dispatched Sarah Lou Bostick to reconcile the two sides on this issue. Concerning Bostick, Craddock writes,

Mrs. Bostick's great vision for education opportunities for her race led her to accept the invitation from Bertha Masson, CWBM field worker in Texas, to spend some time there among the Black congregations, organizing missionary societies for women and promoting the much-talked of school for Black young people in East Texas.... Mrs. Bostick was National President of Negro CWBM, and her presence in Texas, to coordinate the

[73] A. J. Hurdle, "The Work in Texas," *Gospel Plea* 12/7 (12 February 1902). This is a copy of a letter that was dated 30 January 1902.

[74] Bertha M. Fuller, *Sarah Lou Bostick: Minister and Missionary* (private printing, 1949) 8, on file at the Disciples of Christ Historical Society, Nashville.

efforts of both boards, helped greatly in realizing their mutual goal.[75]

Apparently Sarah Lou Bostick's efforts paid off as the project to establish a school in East Texas moved forward.

Mary Alphin worked tirelessly to raise funds for the school project in East Texas. She apparently found it difficult to convince some black Disciples to give sacrificially in support of the project. A report on a two-week fundraising trip that was published in 1910 reveals this struggle but also reveals her intention for the school to offer more than an industrial education.

> How much our work suffers among our people for lack of leaders.... We are trying to impress on people to give in a way so they show that they want a school in Texas.... We tried to impress the splendid opportunity CWBM was offering the young people by preparing them for their life work by training the head, hand, and heart. There are many anxious to go to school, but their parents are not able to send them. For this reason we begged them to make great sacrifices so as to bring a school near, where boys and girls may be trained.[76]

Mary Alphin's reference to an education for "the head, hand, and heart" in the above quote is a coded, if not clear, reference to Alphin's desire for the Texas school to include higher education. In the early 1900s, the so-called Washington-Du Bois debate, which I addressed in chapter 5, was elevated by continued national media attention.[77] As was the case among the Baptists, the issues of institutional control and access to higher education were being debated among and between

---

[75] Frances Craddock, *In the Fullness of Time: A History of Women in the Christian Church (Disciples of Christ)* (St. Louis: Chalice Press, 1999) 50.

[76] Mary Alphin, "Report to the Board," *Gospel Plea* 28/2 (June 1910): 35.

[77] Louis Harlan, *Booker T. Washington: The Making of a Black Leader, 1865–1901* (New York: Oxford University Press, 1972) 265–68. Also see David L. Lewis, *W. E. B. Du Bois: Biography of a Race, 1868–1919* (New York: Henry Holt and Co., 1993) 302–303; and Louis R. Harlan, *Booker T. Washington: The Wizard of Tuskegee, 1901–1915* (New York: Oxford University Press, 1983) 85–86.

Blacks and Whites throughout Protestantism in the U.S. The
Disciples, in this instance, were no different.

Undoubtedly, Joel Lehman was well aware of the growing demand
among black Disciples for the infusion of college degree-earning
curricula at Disciples-related schools for Blacks. This point is supported
by Lehman's apparent need to try to convince Blacks of the futility of
higher education. Such an attempt is made evident in a letter Lehman
wrote to James Nelson Ervin as Ervin began his twenty-four year
tenure as Jarvis's first president. Lehman, in addition to being SCI's
president, replaced C. C. Smith in overseeing CWBM's work among
Blacks in 1913. He wrote,

> Now a word about the nature of your courses. This is not in
> the nature of instructions, but simply suggestion. It would be
> neither wise nor possible for us to think of making a school that
> would devote itself exclusively to collegiate work.... Your greatest
> success will come by your studying things your people actually
> need and fitting them for it.... I do not say that you should not
> work towards college courses, but you should not feel unhappy if
> the majority of your supported students will be from the fifth to
> the tenth grade. In fact, you would not do the community much
> good if it were not so for a while.[78]

Ervin was a college-educated man who had graduated from
Morristown College. He also had a year of study at Columbia. Thus,
Lehman was aware of his probable proclivity toward higher education.
It seems that Lehman wanted to cut off or limit possibilities of future
exposure by Ervin to higher education institutions for Blacks even to
the extent of trying to prevent Ervin from sending his sons to attend a
university. In the same letter, Lehman responded to Ervin's concerns
that JCI course work might not be appropriate for his sons whom Ervin
wanted to send to Howard or Lincoln universities. Lehman wrote, "I
have felt that our course was not such as you would care to recommend
your boys or your graduates to.... If your boys would come here and will

---

[78] Joel Lehman to James Ervin, 13 April 1914, on file at the Olin Library and
Communications Center at Jarvis Christian College, Hawkins TX.

enter into the spirit of our work, we will fit them better for the work they will have to do than they would be if they should go thru some of the universities."[79]

Lehman's comments in this letter to Ervin illustrates his, and by extension the leadership of the Disciples of Christ mission agency's, ongoing determination to lock black men and women into a fixed class of labor by limiting their formal schooling to an industrial model. More than thirty-five years had gone by since the Disciples of Christ mission agencies began evangelizing and educating African Americans, and much had not changed. Black schools supported by the GCMC and CWBM continued to embrace educational objectives and calculated outcomes designed to reproduce a fixed socioeconomic and political status for Blacks in the U.S. in general, and the South in particular.

Ervin, who was recruited from outside the Disciples of Christ to lead Jarvis, had a different vision. For him, moving to Hawkins, Texas, to lead Jarvis was a response to a sense of duty. He wanted to uplift his people. This sense of duty is reflected in Ervin's acceptance letter addressed to Lehman, where he wrote, "It is my belief that all men should do their level best to work where they can be of the greatest service to the most people. As I stated to you, I have a fine position here in Johnson City [Tennessee], and can remain here as long as I desire, but the idea of working for the church directly has, for a long time lingered on my mind."[80] In terms of his vision for Jarvis and the education it would provide for black people, Ervin made clear his intention to build an institution whose curriculum would offer not only industrial and religious education, but much more.

> What our people need is tradesmen of their own kind—Negro grocers, merchants, lawyers, doctors, nurses, educated farmers, teachers—not because your people do not offer us professional service; they do but because by launching out the "odd job" and "potato patch" class our people will do these things for themselves to their great individual and class development.

[79] Ibid.,

[80] James N. Ervin to Joel B. Lehman, 20 March 1914, on file at the Olin Library and Communications Center at Jarvis Christian College, Hawkins TX.

Shiftless! It is taboo. We will have none of it. Everyone must work here. Study, launder their clothes, sew a straight seam, saw logs, master chemistry experiments, get that math, or learn that shorthand; and in the meantime keep their rooms tidy, and if one does not care to work one is sent home. A disciplined mind and energy are big steps on the way to success.[81]

According to Charles Sherman, Lehman desired that JCI would replicate the SCI and required Ervin to consult with him on all matters. Describing the escalation in tension between Lehman and Ervin, Sherman writes,

> President Ervin had to consult President J. B. Lehman on all major issues. This arrangement presented Ervin with one of his first major problems.... Jarvis became almost a carbon copy of SCI in Mississippi. Mrs. Jarvis wanted Jarvis not only to duplicate SCI but do more. President Ervin also wanted more and he was presented with his first organizational problem.... President Lehman and the Disciples Brotherhood were against higher education for Negroes. Ervin had other thoughts of higher education for his people. This caused friction. When the state of Texas began to require higher standards for teacher certification, standards not met by SCI grads [who were supplying Jarvis with teachers up to that point], Ervin refused to allow them to teach at Jarvis. This created further tension.[82]

Before JCI opened in 1913, black Disciples viewed it as an opportunity to develop the type of school they had sought to establish. By 1912, the demand for higher education was being voiced much more intensely from black Disciples. R. H. Peoples describes black concerns about education during this period in his 1943 report on work among Blacks: "Certain of the Negro leaders began to question the way Mr. Lehman was administering the Negro program. One of the main

---

[81] James N. Ervin, quote from an undated statement on file at the Olin Library and Communications Center, Jarvis Christian College, Hawkins TX.

[82] Charles Sherman, "J. N. Ervin in Action," in *The J. N. Jarvis Lectures: a Trilogy, 1977–1978–1979* (Hawkins TX: Jarvis Christian College Publishers, 1979) 14–15.

criticisms was at the point of training leaders for the church. The leaders thought that we should have a real Bible college to develop ministers. It was this dissatisfaction in making the policies that would guide the work that gave rise to the organization of the National Convention [National Christian Missionary Convention, 1917]."

Preston Taylor was a central figure of the NCMC when it was finally organized in 1917. It was organized as a formal and structured expression of resistance to the conservative method of educating Blacks that was supported by Whites. Speaking before the NCMC at their inaugural convention in September 1917, Taylor echoed the deeply held concerns and growing demands of African-American Disciples concerning Disciples of Christ-supported schools for black people: "It is to be remembered that it is extremely difficult, if not quite impossible, to make first class leaders by third rate methods. We are in dire need of at least one school of standard college curriculum where our leaders, especially those entering the ministry may be adequately equipped for their work; where the boys and girls of the church may have a liberal education in the church; where they may be won [sic] for Christian Leadership."[83]

Jarvis Christian Institute achieved high school status in 1914 and secured state accreditation in 1921. In 1928, Jarvis received accreditation as a junior college and became an accredited four-year college in 1938. The story of Jarvis's founding and the intra-church struggles that surrounded the school during its early years is indicative of white resistance. Since 1872, this white resistance sought to place limitations on black socioeconomic and political upward mobility through the educational institutions it supported. It is also a story of the agency and resistance on the part of black men and women who struggled to carve out institutions of church-related schooling for their children. Theirs was an effort in education reform aimed at responsibly providing for the needs of their children and their communities, as they understood them to be within the theological, biblical, and

---

[83] R. H. Peoples, "The Disciples of Christ Negro Churches" (Indianapolis: United Christian Missionary Society, ca. 1943), quoted in Caldwell and Fox, *Journey Towards Wholeness*, 9.

doctrinal traditions embraced by the Christian Church (Disciples of
Christ).

8

UNITY, EDUCATION, AND THE NIHILISTIC THREAT

How did African Americans within the Disciples of Christ interpret the principle of unity? How did this interpretation inform their decision to remain in this movement in the face of oppressive policies and practice within the Disciples of Christ? These questions were posed by colleagues familiar with my thesis during its dissertation phase. I have argued that the primary motivations for African Americans to remain in fellowship with white Disciples were their attraction to the restorationist doctrine, which called for a rejection of all creeds, and the Disciples of Christ polity that emphasized local church autonomy. I reiterate here a point previously made that the opportunity to control their own churches made Disciples membership, particularly for preachers, quite attractive to black people. My argument on this point was challenged by one of my former professors and mentor, Dr. Rufus Burrow, Jr. In a letter dated 9 July 2006, Burrow wrote,

> [W]hat if Blacks interpreted the unity emphasis of Campbell and others in the group more broadly than Whites? ...What if Blacks also gave it a more ethical interpretation to mean not only unity of the church, but unity along racial lines? Something like this, it seems to me, could account significantly for why they stayed despite White practice. I can tell you that the Church of God (Reformation Movement) was founded on the principles of unity and holiness, and that Blacks gravitated toward the group

shortly after its founding by D. S. Warner in 1880, because they interpreted the unity emphasis to also mean racial unity.[1]

It is quite conceivable black Disciples' understanding of God's call for unity within the Body of Christ transcended dominant white interpretive limitations to include racial unity as well as socioeconomic and political equity.

It must be stated that the attraction to the Christian Church and the opportunities presented by the polity of local church autonomy partially explains the initial attraction, but does not explain why Blacks would stay after decades of experiencing the consequences of racist policies and practice within the church. To understand why Blacks maintained affiliation with the Disciples under extreme conditions of racial bias and inequity requires us to examine not only black identification with Disciples of Christ polity, but their theology. Here, I believe a complete and passionate buy-in by Blacks of the theology of the restorationist movement as articulated by Disciples of Christ leadership should not be underestimated. Taken to its limit, the decision to leave the movement or stay could be analogous to deciding to be in right relationship with God or not. This point, however, does not preclude the possibility of a desire for racial unity by Blacks. Nor does it deny the existence of a biblical interpretative tradition among black Disciples that informed a broader understanding of unity, thus serving as a motivating factor for Blacks to remain. The problem is that I have not uncovered any primary source material to support this notion during the period addressed by the study. Beyond 1914, however, is another story. There is clear evidence that African-American Disciples were motivated by both traditional restorationist concerns regarding Christian unity and the recovery of the primitive church as well as racial unity in deciding to remain in fellowship with the church.

As early as 1915, there is clear evidence that African-American Disciples understood the Scriptures as containing a mandate to condemn racist policies and practice or any notion of the superiority of one race over another. Samuel R. Cassius was an outspoken black

---

[1] Dr. Rufus Burrow, Jr. to author, 9 July 2006. Burrow is the Indiana Professor of Christian Thought at Christian Theological Seminary in Indianapolis.

Disciples minister who left the Disciples of Christ branch of the Stone-Campbell movement as a direct result of his experience with racism within the church. Cassius sighted Acts 17:29 as biblical evidence that the gospel mandate required not only church unity, but racial unity as well. In circa 1915, Cassius proclaimed, "That one verse ought to serve every purpose of a Christian's mind and cause him not to think more highly of himself than he ought to think, because it teaches there is no superiority in color and no difference in race."[2] Cassius went on to unite with the Churches of Christ, who separated from the Disciples of Christ in 1906. Interestingly, the Churches of Christ were viewed as more theologically conservative, but Cassius believed they offered a more equitable fellowship for Blacks, stating that "The great uplift of the ten million of American Negroes is now up to the Church of Christ." He held this position largely because of his understanding of the Church of Christ's approach to biblical interpretation, citing, "We teach that the word of God means just what it says and is not subject to any man's private interpretation."[3]

African Americans who remained in the Christian Church (Disciples of Christ) beyond 1914 were committed to both church unity and racial justice. In fact, it is probably accurate to say that church unity and racial justice could not be properly understood apart from each other. Tensions created by what often seemed to be polarized rather than dialectic realities convinced many Disciples leaders of the need to empower themselves by developing separate institutional structures that would be under their control while remaining in fellowship with the Disciples of Christ. This of course was not a new concept among black Disciples. I have already noted several attempts by black Disciples to establish fully autonomous state conventions, schools, and other organizational structures beyond the local congregation to address their spiritual, socioeconomic, and political concerns as they defined them.

---

[2] Quoted in "Race Relations," in Douglas A. Foster, Paul Blowers, Anthony L Dunnavant, and D. Newell Williams, eds., *The Encyclopedia of the Stone-Campbell Movement* (Grand Rapids: William Eerdmans Publishing Co., 2004) 620.
[3] Ibid.

Until 1917, Blacks were unable to sustain many of these efforts, but this
was about to change.

Black discontent with the refusal of white Disciples to support
higher education for their constituencies found substantive and
sustained organizational expression with the formation of the National
Christian Missionary Convention (NCMC) in 1917. Under the
leadership of Preston Taylor, African-American Disciples gathered in
Nashville, Tennessee, on 5–9 September 1917 to organize the
NCMC. The organization of the NCMC was perhaps the most
decisive, proactive, and widely embraced organizational reaction by
black Disciples in the nearly 100 years of enduring the consequences of
racist policies and practice within the Christian Church. The
organization of NCMC was aimed at addressing the unique needs of
African Americans within the church and society. Chief among these
needs was the provision of Disciples-related schools that offered
higher-education curricula and the development of educated Christian
leadership.

A careful examination of Taylor's speech to the plenary gathered
in Nashville provides fascinating insights into black Disciples'
assessment of their historical and contemporary treatment by white
Disciples; a clear sense of the priority black Disciples placed on
cultivating empowerment for their communities; and a glimpse of a
broader understanding of the type of "Christian unity" demanded by
the New Testament. Due to the tremendous importance of Taylor's
speech relative to my thesis, and the significance of this historic event,
it is instructive here to offer a rather lengthy quotation of a portion of
this historic address.

> For the past twenty-five years, [the ACMS] has been charged
> with practically all of the work done by the Disciples of Christ
> among the colored people. The responsibility was thrust upon
> the Christian Woman's Board of Missions, rather than having
> been chosen by it. Up to the time of acceptance of the colored
> work by the C.W.B.M., the church had maintained what was
> then known as the Board of Negro Education and Evangelization.
> For reasons which will shame some of our leaders at the

judgment bar of God, this Board was dissolved and its black wards rendered homeless. The C.W.B.M. took them in and deserves to be credited with whatever gains they have made during these years.... We have had, for most of the time involved, no medium of exchange of opinion or way of comparing methods and results and thereby obtaining the possible encouragement from one another. We had no newspaper nor have we one now of national import.... The attitude of our white brotherhood on the race question accounts largely for our smallness. Without intentional wrong or neglect, the relation of the white to the colored brotherhood has been little more than trifling. It is only within comparative recent years that any conscious plan and purpose, however meager, have actuated our white brotherhood with regard to their colored brethren. He was in most cases simply let alone, separated by an ever increasing and corroding class spirit which denied him the help, inspiration, and encouragement so much needed. Indeed in some striking instances, the Disciples of Christ have set the pace in heartless, unnecessary and silly racial discrimination.... Too often our white brethren have reasoned that almost anything is good enough for the Negro. At all events he is different from anybody else, in that he is regarded as about the last of descending human ratios. Perhaps this fact is most clearly shown by the church's educational ideal for colored men. More than thirty years ago it was held that a knowledge of the English language and the English Bible was all that was necessary for the colored minister. We have not changed that standard. In the training of leaders generally the church has felt that the higher culture is not only unnecessary for the colored race, but detrimental. So we have among us the same spirit which threatened the great white brotherhood twenty years ago—the spirit of suspicion and doubt concerning the really educated man.... This policy has resulted in either sending the majority of our liberally trained men into other professions than Christian leadership or into other communions for service and in putting a premium on a type of leadership that is incompetent to meet the problems of our day.... Back of all I have said, running through

all and overlooking all are two striking features. One of them is
the almost pathetic loyalty of the embattled and straggling colored
Disciple of the Christianity of the New Testament as presented
by the Disciples of Christ and the other is the great, warm,
sympathetic, but ignorant, busy and therefore indifferent heart of
the Disciples of Christ toward the colored brotherhood.... There
is no doubt that the ten million colored people in the United
States need the Disciples of Christ and their message, perhaps as
no other. There is simplicity and rationality about it that fits in
healthfully with the heartful makeup of the colored man, thus
tempering him in the interest of normal, strong Christian
manhood.... The Disciples of Christ, strange as it may seem,
need the colored people, if for no other reasons, as the acid test
of Christian orthodoxy and willingness to follow the Christ all of
the way in His program of human redemption. For if the white
brother can include in his religious theory and practice the
colored people as real brothers, he will have avoided the heresy
of all heresies.[4]

Taylor's address provides verification that at least some African-
American Disciples were indeed compelled to remain in fellowship
with the Christian Church for reasons beyond an acceptance of
traditional Stone-Campbell conceptions of Christian unity and
restoration of the New Testament church. Many black Disciples
remained because they not only affirmed mainstream Disciples' notions
of Christian unity, but they also expanded white restorationist biblical
interpretation and theology asserting that Christian unity and living out
the biblical mandate to restore the primitive church must include racial
equality in every social, economic, and political sphere. In a real sense,
Taylor implies a rejection of white Disciples theology due to the wide
gap between the rhetoric of Christian unity and the love of Christ and
their dehumanizing treatment of Blacks. If Taylor's perspective is
reflective of the broader black Disciples membership, and there's

---

[4] Preston Taylor, "The Status and Outlook of the Colored Brotherhood," as
printed in the *Report of the First General Convention of Christian (colored) Churches in
the U.S.A.*, September 1917, pp. 21–24.

reason to conclude that it was given his position of leadership, it can be argued that black Disciples viewed their struggle to achieve improved socioeconomic status, political justice, and full acceptance into the "whole church" as their mission to realize the true New Testament church. Furthermore, it could be argued, based on Taylor's comments, that white Disciples represented a "mission field" for those Blacks who remained in the Christian Church. Their mission: to help white Disciples "avoid the heresy of all heresies."

I've given a great deal of attention in this book to examining the form and function of schools for Blacks supported by the Disciples of Christ between 1865 and 1914. I've argued that African Americans within the Christian Church played an active role, both in cooperating with Disciples' mission agencies and in acting independently of these agencies in the conceptualization and founding of schools for their communities. In addition, contrary to Disciples reformers' claim of being motivated by their desire to "elevate the Negro race," they nearly exclusively applied the industrial model of education in the schools they established for African Americans. This reflects an intentional effort by Whites within this movement to encumber African-American efforts to achieve socioeconomic and political advancement, autonomy, and self-determination. Finally, the conservative approach to schooling for African Americans was largely the result of Northern Disciples' acquiescence to the demands of Southern members of the church for the sake of maintaining unity within the national church.

The period examined in this book was a time when African-American people as well as many Whites made enormous sacrifices, often risking and losing their lives, to obtain an education for millions of Blacks who were denied such access. Schooling was viewed as the key to socioeconomic and political advancement and the only means to take full advantage of the opportunities made available through the Thirteenth and Fifteenth Amendments of the U.S. Constitution. Churches and schoolhouses throughout the Southern states, and large school buildings in Northern cities, overflowed with children and adults who sought to secure the promises of normal, industrial, and classical forms of education.

The need for ongoing revisionist scholarship and examination of the black experience within the Christian Church (Disciples of Christ) as well as the racist ideology and practice of white Disciples leaders that shaped and informed the type of schooling made available to Blacks cannot be overstated. Romanticized Disciples historiographies of the period examined here as well as the distortions, omissions, and/or neglect by many white Disciples historians of African, and later African-American, agency in the founding of schools has gone virtually unchallenged by serious scholarly research and analysis. Honor must be given to those who have labored to tell "our story" despite not having formal training in historical research and analysis.

Today, however, African-American Disciples and black people in general need to raise a different question. Now is a time to engage in serious self-examination in addressing our role and complicity in the state of black education both within and beyond the Christian Church. How is it that we've gone from considering the building, funding, supporting, and attending of schools as some of the highest priorities of our communities to a time when our children are dropping out of schools in urban America at alarming and unprecedented rates? As black Disciples, we've gone from a period of actively seeking collaborative methods of founding, controlling, and sustaining black Disciples schools that reflect our values and vision of a quality education to giving only meager support to Jarvis Christian College, the only remaining historically black college affiliated with the Christian Church (Disciples of Christ). How black Disciples moved from placing great emphasis on the need for a black-controlled Disciples-related institution of higher education for the development of black leadership to the largely marginal national attention given to the institutional viability of Jarvis Christian College by black Disciples requires an examination of the journey of black Disciples from 1917 to today. What has happened?

Achieving sustainable racial equity and inclusion in the "whole church," and gaining access to higher or classical forms of education at Disciples-supported institutions, served as perhaps the primary catalyst for the organization of the NCMC. The articulation of these demands and the appearance of organized efforts to secure this form of education are not new among black Disciples. The 1917 initiative by black

Disciples—which linked Christian unity with racial justice, education, and leadership—stands firmly in the legacy of prior education reform efforts dating back to 1867 with the organization of the American Christian Evangelizing and Education Association in Nashville. The 1917 gathering also laid a foundation for future efforts by the next generation of black Disciples leaders to attain quality church-related education for their people.

Seeking to prove their value and worthiness for full access to the rights and privileges of all U.S. citizens, African Americans served gallantly in a segregated military during the First and Second World Wars. During each of these conflicts, black civilians provided sacrificial support, along with other U.S. citizens, to the war effort back home. After experiencing the ongoing vestiges of Jim Crow segregation, lynching, and other forms of racist policies and practice in the North and South, the demands of African Americans for full protection of the Constitution and full access to jobs, housing, and quality education took on an unprecedented level of energy and organization. After making great sacrifices to protect the ideals of democratic republicanism, black expectation and demand for access to the benefits it offered—and that were enjoyed by Whites—grew exponentially, and conversely so did white repression and resistance in order to maintain the structures of dominant racial, class, and gender power relations of the period. Thus, in the years immediately following the end of the Second World War, the civil rights movement was born.

Linking the same sociopolitical elements that were addressed in 1917, Charles Berry, Jr., and E. W. Rand conducted a study titled "Negro Education in the Disciple Brotherhood" in 1948. In the study, Berry and Rand raised this question: "To what extent does the Disciple Brotherhood perpetuate the ideals of freedom, justice and dignity of the individual by offering to its Negro youth an educational program comparable to that of its white youth?" Recognizing the role of education in achieving the equity and access black Disciples and other African Americans struggled to secure, Berry and Rand went on to say that it was "the responsibility of the college, and particularly the church related college, to assume the role of leadership in resolving the conflicts, if we are to attain the maximum adjustments in peace, goodwill and fraternity, before the time limits."[5]

By 1948, options for Blacks who desired a college education had increased significantly. Both church-related as well as land grant institutions of higher education were available for those who sought them. But for black Disciples, the push for quality college education at an institution related to and supported by the Disciples of Christ remained a priority. This need was in part due to the injustices black Disciples experienced in predominantly white Disciples colleges that allowed Blacks to enroll. The experience of Emmit J. Dickson, who served as a distinguished Disciples of Christ minister and administrator in virtually every setting of the Christian Church, is illustrative.

Upon receiving the equivalent of an associate degree from Southern Christian Institute in 1931, Emmit Dickson was accepted to attend and play football at Culver-Stockton College (white), a Disciples of Christ college in Canton, Missouri. In an interview I conducted with Dickson, he shared the following story concerning his experience:

> I left Southern Christian Institute—now that's a real journey. I left [SCI] with the idea that I was going to Culver-Stockton College in Canton, Missouri as a football player, registered and everything.... I left [SCI] with my band on my arm so that the coach would know me when I got to St. Louis.... Well, when I arrived in St. Louis, the coach had his arm band on. Both arm bands matched. He [the coach] told me he couldn't use me. I asked why. I told him to let me pull out my papers. He said that I know why. I told him, no that I didn't know why. The coach said

---

[5] Charles Berry, Jr., and E. W. Rand, "An Abstract of Negro Education in the Disciple Brotherhood, a Comparative Study" (Bloomington: Bureau of Educational Research, Indiana University, 1949) 29, quoted in Brenda Cardwell and William K. Fox, *Objects Of to Partners in the Mission: From Convention to Convocation* (Indianapolis: National Convocation of the Christian Church [Disciples of Christ], 1988) 7.

"Well, I can't use you. You can get on the train and go back home."[6]

The coach left Dickson at the station with no money. He remembered that while touring the country with the SCI quartet, he had visited the Union Avenue Christian Church (white) in St. Louis. At the station that evening, Dickson was able to contact an Abbott Book who served as director of Christian education at Union Avenue. Book arranged for a taxi to bring Dickson to the church. He first considered sending Dickson on to Drake University, a Disciples college that Abbott, according to Dickson, said "didn't have any race problems." Because Abbott had recently sent a black student from St. Louis to Drake, he decided to make arrangements to have Dickson attend Butler University, which is a predominantly white Disciples of Christ-related college in Indianapolis. Abbott contacted the pastor of Second Christian Church (black) in Indianapolis and then called Butler. Dickson recalled, "Well, he called Butler University and they told him to send me on. I was sitting there near the phone and heard them. The voice said, 'Yeah, send him on. Send him on.'" All of this took place the evening Dickson arrived in St. Louis. That very night he was on a bus headed to Indianapolis.

Upon arriving at Butler, Dickson found his troubles were not over. First he found that he could not play football because "the association would only permit one black to make the varsity. They already had one." Then he found out that Butler had a policy to allow a maximum of twelve Blacks to attend the college at one time. Initially, said Dickson, "They wouldn't let me in. They wanted me, but they couldn't do it because I was thirteen." Finally, after the school decided to waive the quota, Dickson's credits were initially not accepted because the registrar

---

[6] Lawrence Burnley, "Pearls of Wisdom: Reflections of [a] Senior Black Disciple Leader," vol. 1 (Indianapolis: National Convocation of the Christian Church [Disciples of Christ] 1996) 8. This booklet is a transcription of an interview I conducted with Rev. Dr. Emmit J. Dickson on 21 February 1990, at Christian Theological Seminary, Indianapolis. The NCCC(DC) printed and distributed the interview in memory in Dr. Dickson.

questioned SCI's accreditation. As it turned out, it was determined that SCI was accredited "even before Butler University."[7]

Once Dickson began his coursework at Butler, he ran into yet another problem. A Religion and Biblical Studies major, Dickson was told by his Greek professor that he was unable to comprehend Greek. Dickson recalled this experience, saying, "We had a teacher here in Greek and we had to take Greek. The teacher said, 'A Negro man cannot get Greek.'" Dickson said black women's ability to learn Greek was not called into question.

> Oh, yeah, 'cause we had several women who were making straight A's. She knew that. She loved that. She loved that. I could recall her name if you want it on tape. Miss McDonald.... I had a [friend] that got mad and told her off, [and] then he left Butler and went on to the University of Chicago. He was going to show her that he could get Greek and understood it. He almost burst in his brain. He went on his way and he died. I switched over to Hebrew. I didn't argue with her...but I didn't accept the fact that I couldn't.[8]

After graduating from Butler in 1933, Dickson took a teaching position at Jarvis Christian College. While teaching at Jarvis, Dickson made an interesting discovery concerning the Greek language and black males—one that he would surely want to share with Miss McDonald.

> After I was out of school, I was teaching down at Jarvis College. I found out that the textbook [Miss McDonald] was using to teach Greek here at Butler University was written by a black professor over at Wilberforce. I couldn't wait to get back to tell Miss McDonald.... I caught the train as soon as school closed.... I just caught the train and came back. She was here. She was very cordial. She wasn't mean. I said "Oh, Miss McDonald, you still teaching that Greek?" She said, "Oh yes, yes." "Well, what textbook are you using? [showing her a copy] It's just like this one, isn't it?" She said, "Oh yes, Dr. so and so."

---

[7] Burnley, "Pearls of Wisdom," 10–11.
[8] Ibid., 12–13.

I said, "Did you know that he was a Negro?" She said, "No, he's not, no, no, no." I said, "Yes, yes, yes." [nodding his head and smiling] ...Before the end of the term she had gone to the committee to change the textbook.... They didn't do it and she still had to use it at least three years.[9]

These types of experiences by Blacks at predominantly white Disciples institutions served to fuel black Disciples' struggle to improve the quality of education at black Disciples-related schools.

Black Disciples' determination to achieve justice—and what that meant for them regarding education, leadership, and access to and equal participation in the "whole church"—was informed by their conviction to maintain unity within the church at all costs. Over the next two decades following the war, several developments demonstrate this point. In 1960, the NCMC entered into a Merger of Program and Agreement with the UCMS. According to William Fox, the merger was the culmination of "a generation of gradual movement from separateness toward racial integration and wholeness in the church...."[10] In 1969, a second merger agreement was consummated. This time the merger was between NCMC, UCMS, and the International Convention of the International Convention of the Disciples of Christ, which was organized as a result of denominational restructuring. With this merger the NCMC ceased to exist as a staffed organization with an annual assembly and became "primarily an investment-holding corporation." The merger also gave birth to the National Convocation of the Christian Church (Disciples of Christ) (NCCC[DC]), a body that is embedded in the national structure of the church. The creation of the NCCC(DC) was intended to exemplify racial equity and inclusiveness as well as a model of Christian unity more in line with what was mandated by Scripture. The administrative secretary of the NCCC(DC) became a member of the Christian Church's general minister and president's staff and had the responsibility of monitoring the delivery of services of the general

---

[9] Ibid., 14–15.

[10] William K. Fox, Sr., "National Christian Missionary Convention," in Foster et al., eds., *Encyclopedia of the Stone-Campbell Movement*, 555.

church to predominantly black, Hispanic, and Asian Disciples of Christ. The primary goal of the second merger agreement and the creation of the NCCC(DC), according to Fox, was to move "toward racial inclusiveness and unity within the whole church."[11]

Until this day, black Disciples' efforts to achieve racial justice and integration within the church have never waned, but it is a goal that has not been achieved. The term "integration" is often misused in describing the socioeconomic and political outcomes of the Civil Rights Movement and other struggles to secure racial justice in the United States. More than simply coming together or having a seat at the proverbial "table," racial "integration" suggests equal access for Blacks to services such as quality education, healthcare, housing, employment, equity in the distribution of available resources, and shared power at the highest levels of government and private industry. "Integration," when understood in this manner, has never been achieved by African Americans within the Christian Church or the broader U.S. society. Within the Disciples of Christ and the wider society, the term "integration" continues to be used to describe the achievement of some level of "presence" of persons of color in communities, schools, or places of employment that were previously exclusively white. A closer analysis of the socioeconomic and political landscape will reveal that "integration," as the term is popularly understood and used, has not significantly altered traditional structures of power and privilege in the Christian Church or in the wider society. I return to a more in-depth discussion on integration in the next chapter.

Conversely, the commitment of black Disciples to achieving and sustaining a fully funded institution of higher education of the highest quality for the development of African-American leaders has diminished significantly. Why is this? Many detractors of Historically Black Colleges and Universities (HBCUs) have argued that "access" to colleges and universities that were previously inaccessible to African Americans diminishes the need for schools such as Jarvis Christian College. It's important to note that the term "access" is relative. The ongoing realities of socioeconomic disparities between people of color

---

[11] Ibid., 555.

(particularly Native Americans, Blacks, and Hispanics) and white Americans; the proliferation of poverty and the manner in which it informs low academic achievement, undermining student learning outcomes; and the presence of individual and institutionalized racism that continues to pervade predominantly white colleges and universities, making for hostile learning environments for Blacks and other persons of color all support the argument that the day Jarvis and other HBCUs are no longer needed has not arrived. The continuing vital mission of the United Negro College Fund and the leaders being produced by institutions such as Jarvis, Morehouse College, Spelman College, Howard University, Bennett College, Dillard University, and Fisk University, just to name a few, demonstrates significant ongoing support of these institutions by African Americans and others. At the same time, black Disciples' leadership is void of any coordinated national effort to provide much-needed support to Jarvis Christian College.

There are a number of senior Disciples of Christ leaders and a network of Jarvis alumni who continue to give active support to Jarvis Christian College. However, after my twenty-five years of giving leadership in the Christian Church (Disciples of Christ) in local, regional, national, and international settings, and through my close and active association with African-American clergy and lay leaders throughout the country, it is apparent to me that a strong commitment to Jarvis Christian College among black clergy is absent. The "love" for Jarvis expressed by many black Disciples leaders is characterized more by passive nostalgia than active support. Many of them remain uninformed by what is actually being accomplished at this institution. For instance, Jarvis Christian College operates with a balanced budget in spite of its meager resources; completed its reaffirmation for accreditation without any difficulty; is constructing a new three-story living and learning complex; received accreditation of its business administration curriculum; promotes annual research and scholarly presentations through the National Science Foundation; supports students as they serve key internships with corporate and governmental agencies, including Congressional offices; has its highest enrollment in twenty years; was recognized as College of the Month by the Tom

Joyner Foundation; and has consistently been recognized as one of *U.S. News & World Report's* best colleges, to name a few of its accomplishments. With the exception of a committed faculty, staff, and administration led by Dr. Sebetha Jenkins, an active alumni base, and some black Disciples leaders across the country, a national, strategic, and coordinated effort in support of Jarvis to develop and sustain a reputation of distinction within the church and the academy does not exist among black Disciples leaders as a whole.

To close a keynote address I delivered at the Jarvis Christian College luncheon during the 2003 General Assembly of the Christian Church (Disciples of Christ) in Charlotte, North Carolina, I made the following challenge:

> In a little over ten years Jarvis will celebrate its centennial. What do we envision for Jarvis's future? Do we envision growth, prosperity, and the ongoing education and empowerment of young black men and women who are being nurtured and prepared for effective leadership in a global community by a dynamic black Disciples college? Or do we see something less promising? Whatever the outcome, as black Disciples, we need not look beyond ourselves to either claim or blame. I believe that at a time such as this, the God of Creation is calling us to embrace Jarvis anew, but just as it was for Noah, Ezekiel, Mary Alphin, Charles Berry, Sr., and yes, even Jesus, we serve a God who gives us options. Life or death? Blessing or curse? The choice is ours. Let's choose blessing. Let's choose life. Let's choose God. Let's choose Jarvis. Amen.[12]

One can't help wondering if many among black Disciples leadership privately question the need for Jarvis Christian College. The black community in general is in dire need of effective black leadership whose primary motivation is not to maximize individual investment portfolios and the accumulation of material wealth for

---

[12] Keynote speech, "Options," delivered at the Jarvis Christian College Luncheon of the General Assembly of the Christian Church (Disciples of Christ), 23 October 2003, in Charlotte NC.

strictly self-centered out-comes. Leaders are needed who are motivated by a desire to serve and to utilize their time, talents, and treasures to dismantle the conditions within black communities across the United States that are impacted by the rapidly increasing economic disparities and the destructive conditions that are given birth by such disparities. Colleges such as Jarvis are needed to give access to students who otherwise could not afford to go to college or who, due to a myriad of socioeconomic conditions, were not afforded a quality education but who would, with proper nurturing, challenge, standards of excellence, and expectations of greatness—when greatness is linked with service to humanity—soar to unlimited heights, making unimaginable contributions to a suffering world.

It is important to point out here that there are numerous black Disciples lay and ordained leaders, some of national and international renown, giving vital leadership to addressing the educational crisis in the black community through various initiatives and organizations that are local, statewide, international in scope. However, a vital and organized national effort by black Disciples ministers or through the NCCC(DC) simply does not exist today. While black Disciples leaders pressed on to achieve racial justice, equity, and access to participation in the "whole church," the period between 1948 and 1969 saw the closing of three of the remaining four black schools/colleges supported by the Christian Church. The last closure was that of Southern Christian Institute in 1954.

At a time of unprecedented access to education at every level, black youth are experiencing a rapid and bewildering decline in achieving optimal educational outcomes. African Americans currently represent roughly 12.3 percent of the U.S. population, yet African-American men represent more than 43.9 percent of the prison population. This figure represents a 900 percent increase from 1954 when the number of black men in prison totaled 98,000, to today when there are 910,000 black men in prison out of a total incarcerated population of 2.1 million men in the United States. One out of every five black males between the ages of eighteen and thirty years are formally connected with the criminal justice system through parole, probation, or incarceration. According the "Sentencing Project," "For Black males in their twenties,

1 in every 8 is in prison or jail on any given day. These trends have been intensified by the disproportionate impact of the 'war on drugs,' in which three-fourths of all persons in prison for drug offenses are people of color." The high school dropout rate for black males ranges between 40 and 60 percent in most urban school districts in the United States. Due to their lack of basic math skills, black males are categorically rendered noncompetitive in the job market by the time they reach age seventeen in what is rapidly becoming a highly technocratic society. The number-one cause of death for black males between the ages of sixteen and twenty-five is violence at the hand of other black males.[13]

Today in the U.S., there is what Cornel West has referred to as a "nihilistic threat" within the black community. According to West, this "threat" is characterized by a sense of hopelessness, lovelessness, and meaninglessness among African-American youth at an unprecedented level in our experience in the United States. The insidious nihilistic state is informed by a growing "spiritual impoverishment." West writes,

> And a pervasive spiritual impoverishment grows. The collapse of meaning in life—the eclipse of hope and absence of love of self and others, the breakdown of family and neighborhood bonds—leads to the social deracination and cultural denudement of urban dwellers, especially children. We have created rootless, dangling people with little link to the supportive networks—family, friends, school—that sustain some sense of purpose in life. We have witnessed the collapse of the spiritual communities that in the past helped Americans face despair, disease, and death and that transmit through the generation's dignity and decency, excellence and elegance.[14]

The loss of hope is of greatest concern, for it shapes and informs a sense of self-hatred that manifests itself in the relentless violence and black-on-black crime seen in urban America today. According to West,

---

[13] Statistical sources: Tavis Smily et al., *The Covenant with Black America* (Chicago: Third World Press, 2006) and "Racial Disparity," report summary of *The Sentencing Project*, http://www.sentencingproject.org/IssueAreaHome.aspx?IssueID=3.

[14] Cornel West, *Race Matters* (Boston: Beacon Press, 1993) 5.

the primary concern for African Americans today is not systemic forms of oppression and discrimination, "but rather the nihilistic threat—that is, loss of hope and absence of meaning. For as long as hope remains and meaning is preserved, the possibility of overcoming oppression stays alive."[15]

A national, coordinated, and focused response to the educational crisis now facing black youth in general, and black males in particular, is nonexistent in the Christian Church. It is a sad commentary that the provision of substantive attention and support to the only remaining Disciples-related predominantly black college is far from being the priority for black Disciples leaders today. In describing black Disciples' overall support of Jarvis, Dr. Jenkins lamented that "even though I have addressed the needs to our national leadership, the church body remains mute on the support and existence of Jarvis."[16]

A member of the United Negro College Fund, Jarvis Christian College provides students from diverse socioeconomic backgrounds the opportunity to receive a college education. Many of these students, often young men and women who exemplify the proverbial "diamond in the rough," are instructed by a committed faculty and administration in a nurturing and challenging academic environment. Jarvis currently enrolls 675 students, of which 94 percent are African American and 4 percent Hispanic. Currently, 0.1 percent of the student population is international, representing 1 country. In 2006, 398 students applied to Jarvis with 236 being admitted and 113 enrolling. The average high school grade point average for the class of 2010 is 2.4. Failure to bring to bear the collective expertise and financial resources of African Americans within the Disciples of Christ, and failing to provide the type of sacrificial commitment to education exemplified by our forefathers and mothers whose vision and genius laid the foundation for black Disciples-related schools are symptomatic of the diminished concern for black-controlled Disciples-related higher education. Such failure also demonstrates the church's unwillingness to understand its

---

[15] Ibid., 15.

[16] E-mail conversation with Dr. Sebetha Jenkins, president of Jarvis Christian College, dated 8 October 2007.

prophetic role and responsibility to launch a national effort in addressing the educational crisis now facing black youth and the broader nihilistic threat to our communities across the nation.

What has happened? How did African-American Disciples move from a people who made incredible sacrifices to build schools to a people who are dropping out of them in alarming rates in little more than 125 years? While we can justifiably point to institutionally and well-entrenched systemic forms of oppression that inform our contemporary reality, the time has come for African Americans in general, and black Disciples in particular, to critically examine the ways in which we perpetuate our own oppression. How do we, without coercion, participate in modes of oppression rooted in constructions of class, race, sex, age, and other forms of discrimination? How do we contribute to the nihilistic threat so pervasive in our communities?

The need for African-American Disciples to create and control their own organizations, publications, schools, and other structures of support is as great today as it was when Preston Taylor and others gathered in Nashville, Tennessee, in 1917. Without question strides have been made in the area of race relations, but fundamental shifts in power and privilege have not changed much. By power, I'm not simply speaking of access to wealth—African Americans generate more than 300 billion dollars annually, which is proportionately diminutive relative to the aggregate wealth of this country. I'm speaking of the manner in which we strategically utilize financial wealth and other resources to effect substantive and sustained transformation of the conditions that trap black people and others in a vicious cycle of poverty.

In 1917, Preston Taylor stood before black Disciples and lamented, "We had no newspaper nor have we one now of national import." Taylor addressed the issue of white control of the one publication in which Blacks often published articles, *The Gospel Plea*, published by Southern Christian Institute. "The Gospel Plea," said Taylor, "will always be a Southern Christian Institute paper, dominated by local interests." Today African-American Disciples continue to be without any national publication of any "import" they control. White leadership within the church continues to control national mediums of communication today as they did in 1917. Demonstrative of this control by Whites is the response of Chalice Press, the primary publisher of the Christian Church (Disciples of Christ), to a manuscript submitted by an African-American historian. This black Disciples of Christ scholar sought to have his manuscript that focused on an aspect of black Disciples historiography published. For at least the past twenty-five years, Chalice Press has expressed a desire to publish a book that examined some aspect of African-American Disciples history. The rationale for having not published such a book to date was that "no serious scholarship had been produced in this area." According to this scholar, the submission of a dissertation—which met the requirements to earn a Ph.D. at an Ivy League institution—to Chalice Press for publication received the following response from a senior editor of Chalice Press: "I did speak about your project with my co-workers. We agree that the scope of your dissertation is just too narrow for a mass market book."[17]

The sacrificial and unyielding commitment to institutions like Jarvis Christian College that existed nearly 100 years ago no longer exist among black Disciples leaders as a collective effort national in scope. In the midst the pervasive nihilistic threat, expanding poverty, and rising mortality in the black community, the Ministers Fellowship of the NCCC(DC) recently proposed and seriously considered expending untold amounts of money to convene an upcoming national Black Ministers Retreat on a cruise to the Caribbean. While not unique to this communion, the consideration of expending resources by leaders at a time such as this is demonstrative of the crisis in black leadership within the Disciples of Christ. West is instructive in articulating this dilemma when he writes,

> One reason quality leadership is on the wane in black America is the gross deterioration of personal, familial, and communal relations among African Americans. These relations— though always fragile and difficult to sustain—constitute a crucial basis for the development of a collective and critical

---

[17] Email communication from Chalice Press dated,18 July 2006.

consciousness and a moral commitment to and courageous engagement with causes beyond that of one's self and family. Presently, black communities are in shambles, black families are in decline, and black men and women are in conflict (and sometimes combat). In this way, the new class divisions produced by black inclusion (and exclusion) from the economic boom and the consumerism and hedonism promoted by mass culture have resulted in new kinds of personal turmoil and existential meaninglessness in black America. There are few, if any, communal resources to help black people cope with this situation.[18]

What will it take for African-American Disciples of today to have the prophetic vision and wherewithal of a Preston Taylor and his contemporaries to reclaim a demonstrated commitment to the prophetic tradition of the church? What must be done to foster the prerequisite healing and empowerment to severe their dependency on the white Disciples' dominance and, at the same time, launch a credible and effective battle against the nihilistic threat facing our communities?

---

[18] West, *Race Matters*, 36–37.

9

FOR THE SAKE OF UNITY:
A TIME TO INTEGRATE AND
A TIME TO SEPARATE

What we may call "white Christianity" in Europe and North America has made a deep and lasting impression upon Blacks everywhere, including Africa. But Blacks have used Christianity not so much as it was delivered to them by racist white churches, but as its truth was authenticated to them in the experience of suffering and struggle, to reinforce an enculturated religious orientation and to produce an indigenous faith that emphasized dignity, freedom, and human welfare…. Most sociologists of religion agree that religion does much of the same thing for all sorts and conditions of peoples. But it is a matter of serious debate whether a specific religion belonging to a specific people can be transmitted *in toto* to another people—even in the same geographical location—without certain substantive changes due to ethnicity, custom, social structure, and many other factors. Especially is this true when one people is free and another is enslaved.[1]

The story of African-American education in the South from 1865 to 1914 is one of determination, control, and resistance. Whites were determined to control the newly freed black population through fear and through monitoring the process of schooling that would shape and inform how African Americans would view themselves, the world around them, and their place in it. The control of black education was

---

[1] Gayraud Wilmore, *Black Religion and Black Radicalism: An Interpretation of the Religious History of African Americans* (Maryknoll NY: Orbis Books, 1998) 4.

essential for Whites who were committed to undermining black efforts to achieve socioeconomic and political power. Religion, in this case Christianity, was a primary and powerful instrument used by Whites determined to control and resist African-American advancement.

Conversely, African-American men and women were unceasing in their determination to resist white oppression. Continuing what many had begun during the antebellum period, African Americans immediately took steps to gain control of their churches during and after the Civil War. With unprecedented intensity, Blacks throughout the South also acted to establish schools and to attain a more influential role in, if not control of, schools already in operation. Through their schools and their churches, they challenged the pedagogical methods, assumptions, and conclusions reflected in the normal and Sunday school materials. Also challenged in black-controlled institutions were the theological presuppositions and interpretive approaches to Scripture imposed upon them by Whites that were aimed at achieving specific and dehumanizing sociopolitical outcomes for their race. As reflected in the above quote from Gayraud Wilmore, white efforts to control Blacks by getting them to accept wholesale their brand of Christianity, and the methods of schooling to perpetuate and reproduce these views, were met with great resistance in the struggle for freedom and dignity.

From the genesis of the Stone-Campbell movement to the present-day Christian Church (Disciples of Christ), the call for Christian unity and church union has been constant. Equally constant during this period has been an unwillingness on the part of the majority of its leaders to radically disrupt the structure of power relations and distribution of resources in a manner that reflects socioeconomic and political equity for all persons. While the call to ecumenism and Christian unity persists, destructive class distinctions and other forms of dehumanizing power relations have and continue to flourish.

Throughout this "journey of faith," Africans and African Americans have also embraced a commitment to achieving Christian unity and church union. Blacks, however, perhaps from the beginning of this movement, brought with them a broader interpretation of "unity"—one that included a Divine demand for racial equality and justice. Like the vision of a unified "New Testament" church, the dream of Disciples integrationists to achieve racial justice with full access and equity of the resources of the church has not been realized.

Over the years, I've never ceased to be amazed to hear some of my colleagues of all racial/ethnic backgrounds use the term "integration" when referring to various contemporary social arrangements both in and out of the church. They speak of living in "integrated" communities or of their children attending "integrated" schools. Some even believe they belong to an "integrated" denomination affectionately known as the Christian Church (Disciples of Christ). I've addressed my understanding of the meaning of the term "integration" previously, but there is a need to return to this issue.

The concept of "integration" is beautiful when understood within the context of the correct meaning of the word. According to Webster's Dictionary, the word "integrate" is defined as, "The bringing together of people from different racial or ethnic groups into unrestricted and equal association."[2] Integration understood in this manner is a powerful and attractive moral concept. Achieving "unrestricted and equal association" is a social arrangement African people on the continent and in the diaspora, as well as persons from other racial/ethnic groups, have been striving to attain for millennia.

Blacks within and beyond the Christian Church have struggled to achieve integration within the context of the global market economy and within the socioeconomic and political structures of Western (or Northern) countries. The problem is that as a group, African-American people in general, and Blacks in the Christian Church (Disciples of Christ) in particular, have *never* experienced integration, at least not as this term is properly understood. Neither in my critical reading of history nor in my lived experience have I ever been witness to a sustained socioeconomic and political arrangement where all of God's people were living in "equal and unrestricted association." Contrary to the belief of many who suffer from an "illusion of inclusion," at no time in this country or in the Christian Church have black people, or other

---

[2] David Guralnik, ed., *Webster's New World Dictionary of the American Language* (New York: The World Publishing Co., 1970) 733.

people of color, secured or enjoyed "unrestricted and equal association" with white people. Ironically, both the erroneous belief that Blacks have achieved integration, and their preoccupation to attain it, has resulted in the deterioration and in some cases elimination of the sociopolitical space needed to be exclusively among themselves to address common challenges, needs, and concerns. The declining existence of this critical space is an issue addressed by Manning Marable, who writes,

> Tragically, with the disappearance of legal segregation, the space that permitted the existence of numerous black institutions of civic society—fraternal organizations, historically black colleges, neighborhood associations, faith-based institutions, and many others—began to collapse. These race-based structures embodied a sense of shared sacrifice and collective struggle, and imposed on their participants notions of obligation and responsibility to other African Americans. In this way, the collective lessons of the black historical experience were disseminated and preserved through informal processes of socialization. With the coming of integration, all of that changed. Millions of middle-class African Americans relocated to suburbia, and the vast majority of black college students by 1970 became enrolled in predominantly white universities and colleges. The informal networks for transmitting collective history began to break down.[3]

Making the argument for the need for black Disciples to create space *exclusively* for Blacks in national settings for the purpose of fostering and sustaining empowerment is the focus of this chapter.

As I assess the contemporary landscape within the Christian Church and beyond, discrimination based on race, class, gender, national origin, ability, sexual orientation, and other forms of human expression continues to be a pervasive and destructive reality. One can certainly make the argument that we have made progress in the area of

---

[3] Manning Marable, *Living Black History* (New York: Basic Civitas Books, 2006) 58–59.

race relations in the past three decades. There have been individuals who have clearly benefited from the struggles of our foreparents to secure equity and access in education and employment. Countless examples of individual achievement can be cited, but for the masses of our people the underclass continues to expand at an unprecedented pace. When taking into consideration the proliferation of drugs; infant mortality; the pervasiveness of HIV/AIDS in Sub-Saharan Africa, and especially among black women in the U.S.; rapidly increasing levels of homelessness and persons without healthcare; high school dropout rates; the disproportionate number of black men trapped in the prison industrial complex; and the senseless black-on-black violence (including inter-ethnic genocide in Sub-Saharan Africa), in many ways we are far worse off today than we were on the eve of the Civil Rights Movement and the genesis of the African independence movement.

What will it take to reverse this? I'm convinced that unless we empower ourselves as people of African descent in this country and within the Disciples of Christ, we will not ever realize a socioeconomic and political situation where we are experiencing unrestricted and equal association with those who currently seek only to protect their position of power and privilege. In terms of altering or dismantling oppressive power relations in the United States and in other parts of the world, what history teaches us is clear and consistent. Those who perpetuate oppressive and dehumanizing policies and practice, and view such policies and practices as necessary in order to maintain their position of power, will never concede their power to anyone or any group that operates from a position of weakness.

As African Americans within the Disciples of Christ, we do not wield any significant power. An example of this truth can be seen in a recent development in the national setting of the church. Meeting in 1971 at Louisville, Kentucky, the General Assembly of the Christian Church passed Resolutions 7147 and 7148. These resolutions established a Department of Black Ministry and a Reconciliation Program, respectively. Both initiatives were taken in response to demands made by black clergy and laypersons to rid the church and society of racism. Today, in spite of the expressed opposition of black Disciples leaders, the Department of Black Ministries has been eliminated. In a public letter to the church, L. Wayne Stewart, the last person to serve as director for the Department of Black Ministries, wrote these words of lament just weeks before the office officially closed on 18 October 2007: "Finally, the primary source of most of our historical and current suffering, pain, and problems in the Christian Church (Disciples of Christ) has been and still is racism. An interim remedy for that problem has been the Department of Black Ministries. It is only if we are satisfied that racism in the United States has been eliminated that the Department of Black Ministries should be ended. Otherwise we still need the Department staffed by the most qualified of Black Ministries."[4] Clearly the internalization of racism and other forms of oppression play a role in the "current suffering, pain, and problems" for African Americans and others in the Christian Church and beyond. Stewart's point, however, is that at a time when the proliferation of institutionalized forms of racism in the U.S. persists, the Disciples of Christ power structure's decision to roll back its efforts to combat racism is largely unaffected by black opposition to these decisions.

African Americans within the Christian Church, and in the broader society, are not an empowered people. A statement distributed at the Seventh Assembly of the All Africa Conference of Churches (AACC) in Addis Ababa, Ethiopia, which I attended in 1998, informs my understanding of what it means to be an "empowered people." An empowered people are

1. Rooted in and guided by the living God and committed to seeking, discerning, and doing God's will.

2. A people who prayerfully, critically, and systematically reflect on their historical experience and defines and names themselves and their reality. A people always in dialogue with others, but in final analysis it's "our story" and not "his story."

3. A people who interpret their own history and transmits the story of their people to their children.

---

[4] Dr. L. Wayne Stewart, "Some Reflections on GAR 7147," open letter dated 25 September 2007.

4. A people who develops and controls a system of education for their children that encourages and nurtures their ability to grow spiritually, think critically and to use their gifts and skills for the healthy maintenance and growth of their communities and then for others.

5. A people who love themselves.[5]

By this definition, generally speaking, black people within our communion and beyond are not a healthy people. Resulting from oppressive pedagogy in public and private schools at every level of education, and the ongoing proliferation of dehumanizing racist images in mainstream media, we don't even know who we are and we hate who we think we are. As a people we have been systematically taught to hate Africa, anything African, and the very color black.

This point was graphically demonstrated in the famous experiment by psychologists Kenneth and Mamie Clark. The Clarks set out to illustrate the reality of low self-esteem and self-hatred that plagued black children in the 1940s. The results were presented as evidence in *Brown v. the Board of Education.*

In the "doll test," psychologists Kenneth and Mamie Clark used four plastic, diaper-clad dolls, identical except for color. They showed the dolls to black children between the ages of three and seven and asked them questions to determine racial perception and preference. Almost all of the children readily identified the race of the dolls. However, when asked which they preferred, the majority selected the white doll and attributed positive characteristics to it. The Clarks also gave the children outline drawings of a boy and girl and asked them to color the figures the same color as themselves. Many of the children with dark complexions colored the figures with a white or yellow crayon. The Clarks concluded that "prejudice, discrimination,

---

[5] Program document distributed at the Seventh Assembly of the All Africa Conference of Churches, Addis Ababa, Ethiopia, October 1998.

and segregation" caused black children to develop a sense of inferiority and self-hatred.[6]

The insignificance of the Clarks' finding for our contemporary situation is a point made by a number of persons. Advances in African-American Studies, increased attention given to Black History Month in public schools, and the celebration of Kwanza are cited as achievements that have resulted in a dramatic shift in the self-esteem of black children since the Clark experiment. Countering this position is that in 2005, an eighteen-year-old high school student and filmmaker, Kiri Davis, recreated the Clarks' experiment with twenty-one black children with virtually the same results.[7] This should come as no surprise when children of all races and ethnicities continue to be bombarded with messages and images associating blackness with negativity and evil, and whiteness with purity and goodness. Even today references to the black cat, black lie, black sheep, black Friday, and devil's food cake (chocolate) are used without questioning the impact on how children make sense of their world and themselves. In such a world, the Wicked Witch of West naturally wears black, as do the bad guys in Hollywood westerns. The dominant images of Sub-Saharan Africa and its people and landscape in our textbooks, newspapers, and films are primarily those of starving children, animals, and jungles, coupled with reports of ethnic conflict, as if nothing else exists. We still live in a time when actor Will Smith, upon returning from filming the movie *Ali* in Zimbabwe, commented, "I didn't know there were cities in Africa."

El Hajj Malik El-Shabazz (Malcolm X) was right when he said that any black person who dislikes Africa or things African inevitably hates himself or herself. "If you don't like the root you can't like the tree." Africa represents our sociohistorical, political, and spiritual roots, and black people in the diaspora are the tree. Many black Christian adults have such disdain for Africa, consciously or subconsciously, that they

---

[6] Clark's experiment summary in *Brown vs. The Board of Education*, Library of Congress website, http://www.loc.gov/exhibits/brown/brown-brown.html.

[7] Kiri Laurelle Davis's film, *A Girl Like Me* (2005), documents her experiment. The film won the Diversity Award at the 6th Annual Media That Matters film festival in New York City.

outright reject any attempt to take the Eurocentric image of Jesus out of the church and replace it with a black African image, an image that is consistent with the biblical text and is historically correct. Rejection of the notion of a black Messiah is symptomatic of our disdain for Africa, which is symptomatic of our hatred of ourselves. I'm afraid Kwame Ture (Stokely Carmichael) was right when he said to me, "Black Christians who reject Africa are an example of ignorance at its highest level."[8] Defining ourselves and our reality will lead to self-love. Self-love is imperative if we are to be an empowered people. Without becoming an empowered people, reconciliation and real integration within the Disciples of Christ and the wider society is simply unachievable for black people.

From the time when enslaved African people were associated with the earliest Disciples congregations at Cane Ridge to the present day, Blacks in the Disciples of Christ have never achieved empowerment as defined by the AACC. In spite of the courageous efforts of Preston Taylor and others since 1917, black Disciples leaders' struggles to achieve Christian unity—a unity that encompasses racial equality—have been largely unsuccessful. A disempowered people seeking to integrate with a group who have historically and consistently oppressed them will continue to be treated as second-class citizens by those who are in the dominant position. Before we can integrate, and I believe there is a time for that, we must separate and, with God's help, facilitate self-healing, cleansing, awakening, and empowerment. For the sake of unity, African Americans, to be effective in their effort to realize unity with Whites and others, must first achieve a different kind of unity—unity with themselves.

By "separation," I'm not advocating a mass exodus from the United States or even the Christian Church (Disciples of Christ). Ongoing engagement with persons of goodwill in an effort to realize and sustain the "beloved community" is critical. Jesus' command to "love your

---

[8] The late Kwame Ture spoke these words to me in February 1996, during a conversation in my office when I served as director of the Albert Greenfield Intercultural Center at the University of Pennsylvania. Dr. Ture was our guest lecturer for African American History Month and a guest in my home.

neighbor as you love yourself" is clear. Equally clear, however, is that I cannot love my neighbor if I don't love myself. Without self-love, which is critical for a people to be empowered, reconciliation and Christian unity are impossible. By calling for "separation," I am suggesting it is time for black people within this communion to have intentional and structured time with and among themselves *exclusively*. I emphasize the word "exclusively" here because in my twenty-five years of association with the Disciples of Christ as a minister, I have never been in a national gathering of black Disciples leaders without at least one, and usually more, Whites present. I am convinced that conversation, dialogue, analysis, debate, candor, and expressions of vision, opinion, and critique among black professional adult leaders are all affected—altered, diluted, and toned down—when Whites are present. I stress "professional *adult* leaders" here because I have experienced a sincere, raw, and refreshing honesty when engaging children, youth, and to a lesser extent young adults, no matter who's in the room. A robust, honest, and often difficult debate to heal, plan, and strategize in a national setting among black leaders can never fully occur while Whites are present. Some black Disciples are fearful of "offending" Whites by creating a "black-only" space in a national gathering. Others are protective of the image of the black community and are careful not to expose "dirty laundry" in the presence of "others" in an effort to avoid tarnishing the community's image. Both of these concerns function to impede the occurrence of much-needed honest debate, self-critique, analysis, and strategic planning among black Disciples in *national settings*.

It's important to note that just ten days prior to his death, Martin Luther King, Jr., in a conversation with Jewish rabbis, expressed the need for Blacks to create space to be among themselves. This "weigh station" period was viewed by King as necessary to cultivate healing and empowerment within and among black people. King was clear that he did not advocate the separation of the races as did some within black nationalists and white supremist groups; however, he came to believe that creating strategic space of separation would strengthen Blacks as a group to be more effective in building an inclusive "beloved community."[9] In addition, womanist theologian Jacquelyn Grant, during a conversation in my office at the University of Pennsylvania during the 1992–1993 academic year, made reference to developing a "caucus theology," a concept that affirmed the need for self-identified groups to create exclusive space for themselves. The purpose of this "caucusing" would be to engage in dialogue and strategic planning in an effort to transform the destructive conditions that were uniquely or disproportionately affecting them.

I do not mean to suggest that smaller groups exclusively comprised of black Disciples to plan and strategize ways of responding to the perceived needs of black people and the "whole church" never convene. To be sure, these sessions occur all the time. These smaller gatherings are usually made up of likeminded men and women (mostly men) who are either appointed or self-appointed gatekeepers of the dominant socioeconomic and political arrangements within the church. Decisions and initiatives emerging from these smaller groups of black leaders rarely challenge the status quo or the distribution of resources within the church. As a result, these black Disciples are deemed nonthreatening by those who wield significant power within the church. The need is for black Disciples to create space in national settings where persons, clergy and lay, with diverse theological and political perspectives can engage in a process of critical self- reflection, examination, visioning, and strategizing in a manner that is unencumbered by the presence of white men and women.

Whites who attend predominantly black gatherings generally fall into two categories. Some are well-intended Whites who want to be present at black gatherings because of a sincere desire to fellowship, learn, and offer support. Other Whites are present to carry out the function of the "overseer," motivated by suspicion, fear, and the need to control. These are the protectors of the status quo. The presence of both types function, intentionally or unintentionally, to undermine the

---

[9] For a reference to King's conversation, see James M. Washington, ed., *A Testament of Hope: The Essential Writings of Martin Luther King, Jr.* (San Francisco: Harper Publishing Co., 1991) 666. The conversation with Jacquelyn Grant occurred during her visit as guest lecturer for the Liberation Lecture Series at the Christian Association at the University of Pennsylvania.

development of any serious threat to disrupting dominant power relations within the church or Disciples-led efforts to dismantle the nihilistic threat in the broader society.

When considering black Disciples' attention to ministry in a global context, rarely has there been a time of sustained engagement and interaction between national delegations of African-American leaders within the Christian Church and leaders from among our African global partner churches. Without question there are solid and strategic relationships between individual local congregations and communities in Sub-Saharan Africa and other parts of the African diaspora that have developed through the visionary leadership of individual pastors. However, significant, organized, and sustainable initiatives that are national in scope by African-American Disciples with a goal of mutual empowerment with Africans on the continent are nonexistent.

On many occasions during my travels in Ghana, Zimbabwe, and especially South Africa, many Africans embraced me, saying, "Welcome home." I'm reminded of one pastor from the United Congregational Church of Southern Africa who said to me with penetrating candor, "Where have you been? I didn't think there were African Americans in your church." I was the first African American representing the Christian Church this pastor had met. I don't mean to suggest that I was the first black Disciples minister to connect with our partners on the continent of Africa—there have been many before me. This experience, however, is demonstrative of the need of a sustained and intentional national effort for African Americans to connect. On a consistent basis, African church leaders expressed to me their interest in engaging African-American churches and church leaders directly. Too often, they say, they come to the U.S. and are unable to connect with black churches. They seem to understand, perhaps better than black Disciples as a whole, that the same market and political forces that create the dehumanizing conditions of poverty, violence, disease, homelessness, and the reality of the nihilistic threat in Los Angeles and Detroit are the same forces creating these conditions in Lagos and Durban.

The irony here is that the desire many black Disciples leaders have for achieving "unity" with our white brothers and sisters appears to take priority over achieving "unity" with our brothers and sisters on the continent of Africa and other parts of diaspora. It would be convenient to dismiss this state of relations as yet another consequence of racist missiological practice. There is truth in this analysis; however, the absence of a national agenda and strategy to "unite" with black Africans to combat the common forces that perpetuate pain and suffering among black people globally is a result of choices made by black Disciples leaders. Such choices dictate how, where, when, and with whom we focus and expend our collective intellectual, spiritual, material, and financial resources. Standing in the legacy of black Disciples of Christ who have demonstrated a commitment to achieve equity and unity with Whites within the Christian Church and the wider society—without succeeding in doing so—I argue that there is a need for an ideological and theological shift that causes black Disciples to attain a different kind of unity.

The theme of the AACC Assembly previously mentioned was "Troubled But Not Destroyed." The gathered church leaders envisioned an empowered and unified African church that would take a lead role in reconstructing the African socioeconomic and political reality. In no uncertain terms, they spoke of their desire to develop strategic partnerships with the African-American church. In a real sense, this African agenda represented Ethiopia "stretching out her hands," not to God, but God through Ethiopia to black people in the U.S. These leaders did not deny the importance of being in partnership with others who make up the Body of Christ; they did, however, demonstrate an understanding of our common heritage and the uniqueness and interconnectedness of our historical and contemporary global socioeconomic and political situation. These African leaders spoke of sitting at a common table to enable the breaking down of the walls of ignorance that stand painfully between us—walls built by Western colonialism and sustained by a neo-imperialistic thrust that is fueled by a destructive capitalist global market economy. This of course is a process in which the Western (or Northern) church, including the Christian Church, has played and continues to play a significant role.

The thought of Africans and African Americans sitting at a common table to strategize prayerfully about how they can address their common problems makes some of our brothers and sisters in Christ and others very uncomfortable. Returning to a theme I've already treated is necessary here because it cannot be overstated when calling for a different kind of unity. In North America, any time black people separate and meet among themselves, many of our Caucasian friends get concerned. Fear sets in—the kind of "Great Fear" of which Du Bois spoke—because they don't know what we're doing. Whites are accustomed to controlling what Blacks do—a point clearly demonstrated in the approach to managing Disciples-supported schools for Blacks. When African Americans demand to be among themselves, they are often called racist, separatist, or unchristian. Dr. William W. Hannah, former Associate General Minister and President of the Christian Church and Administrative Secretary of the NCCC(DC), was without question the most progressive black Disciples leader I've known, and one under whom I had the distinct honor to serve for four years while attending seminary. It was not unusual for Hannah to be verbally attacked and accused of undermining the Disciples commitment to church union when he called for excluding Whites from national meetings of black Disciples leaders.

It must be said that many black leaders within the Disciples of Christ—the gatekeepers—also have demonstrated great discomfort at the thought of black Disciples meeting among themselves in national settings without the presence of Whites. The concern here is that such a gathering could upset the white leadership and potentially disrupt various arrangements aimed at maintaining their perceived integrative state of relations. History has shown that any time African Americans want to get together by themselves in an effort to achieve substantive transformation of the conditions in which they find themselves, they come under attack. The experience of Benjamin Chavis-Muhammed (formerly Benjamin Chavis) serves as a classical example of this.

While serving as executive director of the NAACP, Chavis-Muhammed attempted to establish an unprecedented dialogue among black leadership. The purpose of this historic initiative was to create dialogue "between the NAACP and African Americans who carry leadership in the Pan African Community, Progressive Community and the Nationalist Community."[10] Facilitating and sustaining a dialogue among black leadership and their organizations who prior to this time were not involved in any collaborative effort to overcome the challenges facing the black community presented a significant threat to those interested in sustaining traditional structures of power—many of whom were strengthened and protected by the splintering, division, and disunity among the leadership within the African-American community. Chavis-Muhammed's attempt at achieving a different type of unity caused an immediate and decisive response to unseat him from his position of leadership in the NAACP. Some will argue, perhaps rightly so, that Chavis-Muhammed's political downfall was a result of improprieties on his part. Nevertheless, there is no question in my mind that the timing of his attempt to establish this historic dialogue and the level of public scrutiny that ensued and resulted in his removal was no coincidence.

Before integration, reconciliation, or Christian unity can occur within the Disciples of Christ movement, black Disciples must create for themselves intentional and structured forums of separation so that they can be empowered to facilitate dismantling the nihilistic reality in our communities and ultimately reconciliation with others. I believe Jesus Himself understood this process clearly, a process that is biblical and necessary if the Christian Church is to achieve the unity and union it has sought but has yet to achieve. The process of which I refer here is found in the tenth chapter of the book of Matthew.

At the age of thirty, Jesus entered into his earthly ministry, proclaiming, "The Spirit of the Lord is upon me,...[God] has anointed me to bring good news to the poor. [The Lord] has sent me to proclaim release to the captives and recovery of sight to the blind, to let the oppressed go free..." (Luke 4:18).[11] The community of people into which he was born, the Hebrew or Jewish people, was oppressed under

---

[10] Quoted in Conrad W. Worrill, "The NAACP and Ben Chavis," *The Michigan Chronicle*, 24 May 1994.

[11] New Revised Standard *Holy Bible* (Grand Rapids: Zondervan Bible Publishers, 1990) 1163.

Roman domination. There was corruption within the Jewish community by those who decided to co-opt their loyalty and side with the Roman imperialists. The Jewish people had lost a great deal of their heritage through the process of acculturation under Roman domination. As a result of being acculturated into a Greco-Roman worldview, many Jews changed their names and many spoke a new language and developed new customs and values. But then this man named Jesus (Joshua) came on the scene. He taught and trained a cadre of disciples in the ways of God and sent them on a revolutionary mission to "...proclaim the good news. The kingdom of heaven has come near" (v. 7). The disciples were instructed to "Cure the sick, raise the dead, cleanse the lepers, cast out demons" (v. 8a). Jesus, however, gave the disciples a peculiar set of instructions as he sent them on their mission. In verses 5 and 6, he tells them to "Go nowhere among the Gentiles, and enter no town of the Samaritans, but go rather to the lost sheep of the house of Israel."[12]

Was Jesus a separatist or racist? Was he not concerned with unity within a church that he knew would transcend the rather exclusive nature of the Hebrew community to become a radically inclusive church? No! Jesus understood the process of healing and the need to give attention to self in order to realize liberation and reconciliation with others. Strengthen your people first! Heal your people first! Empower your people first! This was Jesus' message. Once empowered, we can then sit at the table of reconciliation not asking for equality, not asking for justice, but demanding it from a position of strength. Where does love of charity begin? It begins at home, and for African Americans and Blacks throughout the disapora, Africa is our home even though many have been trained to believe otherwise. We must strengthen and heal ourselves, our families, and our people first. Then we can develop the ability to love and nurture ourselves. For then and only then can we love our neighbor in a way that pleases God. When we are empowered, when we have reconstructed our stories and learned to define our reality and ourselves, we will love our beautiful redefined selves so much that we will no longer tolerate the

---

[12] Ibid., 1101.

dehumanizing treatment, policies, and institutionally entrenched forms of oppression by those currently in power or anyone else. Black Disciples must commit to achieve a different kind of unity—one that pools together the genius of Mother Africa and her children.

We know that Jesus was no bigot or separatist for instructing his disciples to "Go nowhere among the Gentiles" (Acts 1:8).[13] We know there is a time for everything and there would come a time when Jesus would prophesy that the disciples would be his "witnesses in Jerusalem, in all Judea and Samaria, and to the ends of the earth." But first, "go among the lost sheep of Israel," says Jesus. Fostering internal healing is a necessary step in the process of healing, empowerment, and liberation, which is something black Disciples seem to overlook in their effort to foster Christian unity. Internal healing is a prerequisite if we are ever to realize the vision of being a united church where race, gender, ability, age, sexual orientation, class, theological perspective, nationality, and other human constructions and expressions are no longer used to discriminate, exclude, and destroy. Achieving a different type of unity—an internal healing and empowerment—is a necessary prerequisite if the Disciples of Christ are ever to realize what Blacks like Peter Lowery, Mary Alphin, Sarah Lue Bostic, Rosa Page Welch, Preston Taylor, Emmit Dickson, William Fox, William Hannah, and a host of others have sought to achieve but have not—racial equality in church and society. First black Disciples must create for themselves space to dialogue and to be among themselves, an oasis in the desert of hostility and oppression where black people can be affirmed, loved, and feel safe to challenge and disagree. Black Disciples must create and sustain that space where they can eradicate the consequences of miseducation and rediscover those life-giving values held sacred by our Ancestors—values of family, community, collective responsibility for our children, and respect for our elders and of the earth. Black Disciples must create that space where we can be among ourselves to figure out how we moved from being a people who valued education so much that no sacrifice was too great to build schools or walk 10 miles to attend them, to a place where too many of our children won't walk 10

---

[13] Ibid., 1229.

minutes to a school in their own community. Black Disciples must create the space where the cultural, technological, political, economic, and spiritual exchange between Africans and African Americans in the diaspora will plant the seeds of healing, empowerment, and liberation. Such an exchange and collaborative effort would result in Jarvis Christian College becoming a preeminent institution of higher education and enjoying the presence of a critical mass of students from Sub-Saharan Africa and the Caribbean.

Like any family, there are times when as black Disciples we need to be among ourselves—*exclusively*. This is especially true when the family is not healthy. Recognizing and responding to this need does not mean Blacks don't love brothers and sisters from other racial/ethnic groups, but there are times when you need to be with your immediate family exclusively. Parents, brothers and sisters, aunts, uncles, cousins, and even grandparents are not allowed in. The need to give attention to internal unity, to internal healing, doesn't mean you don't love members of the extended family. It does mean that an opportunity to nurture the core family now exists, thereby enabling that core to love more fully and interact with the extended family and even preventing members of the extended family from exerting intentional or unintentional destructive forms of power.

Total separation is not possible, practical, or even moral. Creating space for periodic opportunities of exclusive periods of dialogue and engagement is functional and necessary. A time for separation is appropriate, it is biblical, and it is Christian. It is right for a threatened and sick person, family, or group to withdraw for the purpose of internal healing and empowerment. An abused spouse who continues to seek "unity" with the one who is consistently being abusive is unwise in doing so; such behavior is self-defeating. It is right for women to create venues to be exclusively among themselves to share their stories and develop strategies to dismantle the violence of oppressive patriarchy. To women, I affirm that it's okay to put up the sign that says, "This gathering is for women only." It is right and it is intelligent for black Disciples to create venues in national settings to share their stories and strategize how to dismantle the nihilism and the pervasive reality of racism in the church and society that threatens our very existence. To black people, I affirm that it's okay to put up the sign that says clearly to our white brothers and sisters (and others) within this restoration movement, "This gathering is for black people only."

It was right for Jesus to tell his disciples, "Go nowhere among the Gentiles, and enter no town of the Samaritans, but go rather to the lost sheep of the house of Israel." In effect, Jesus was saying, "Go heal your people first. Love, like charity, begins at home. There is a time to integrate and a time to separate." Without question, God calls us to integrate, transcending the false social constructions that we've created out of fear and greed and that we use to exploit. God calls the Body of Christ into unrestricted and equal association. So true and so critical is this point that through the Scriptures themselves, God reveals the socioeconomic and political arrangement of the unified New Testament church: "All who believed were together and had all things in common; they would sell their possessions and goods and distribute the proceeds to all, as any had need" (Acts 2:44–45).[14] This method of distributing available goods and resources, one that is antithetical to capitalist methods embraced by our church and our world, is a principle of the Bible that Stone and Campbell, as well as the rest of us, have apparently determined not to be an "essential" component of the "primitive church."

The Need to Tell "Our Story"

The research presented here merely scratches the surface of the agency of black people in education reform within the Christian Church (Disciples of Christ). In the spirit of the Akan tradition of Sankofa, this book is an attempt at a critical "looking back" to enable a more accurate analysis of our current situation, thereby creating the possibility of plotting a life-giving course for our future. I have engaged the research of this topic with a sense of humility and thanksgiving, and with a commitment to honesty without attempting to be completely objective, which quite frankly I believe is impossible. Again, I stand in solidarity with Vincent Harding in "Affirming objectivity and subjectivity as equally necessary to any compassionate rendering of our

---

[14] Ibid., 1232.

flawed and splendid human strivings…. "[15] In doing so, I've been careful to make sure that rigorous analysis was not compromised. It is my prayer that somewhere in the ethereal plane of reality, there are those among my Ancestors who are resting just a bit better because through the publication of this book a portion of their story has been told with integrity. I am aware, however, that untold numbers of African-American voices, and those of others who sacrificed all to provide schooling for their communities, have yet to be heard.

The importance of a people telling their "own story" cannot be overstated—not a romanticized story created in isolation for the purpose of dominating another group or groups, but a story that is informed by critical reflection, analysis, and honesty, and takes into consideration the feedback of how those outside their group experience them. The realization of self-love and empowerment that is crucial to overcoming the nihilistic threat confronting Africans on the continent and in the diaspora cannot be achieved if we do not name ourselves and interpret our historical and contemporary reality for ourselves. For integration and unity within the church and beyond to become a reality, black people must be cured of "historical amnesia" and rediscover who we really are. Our liberation, and perhaps the liberation of others, depends on black people becoming healthy once again. Manning Marable puts it this way: "Historical amnesia blocks the construction of potentially successful social movements. As the gap between the past, present, and future diminishes, individuals can acquire a greater sense of becoming the 'makers' of their own history. Thus, for the oppressed, the act of reconstructing history is inextricably linked to the political practices, or *praxis*, of transforming the present and future."[16]

A component of what it means to be an empowered people as defined by the All Africa Conference of Churches is worth repeating here. An empowered people are "[a] people who interpret their own history and transmits the story of their people to their children." Herein lies the very core of a truly "higher education."

---

[15] Vincent Harding, *There Is a River: The Black Struggle for Freedom in America* (New York: Harcourt Brace Jovanovich, 1992 [1982]) xi.

[16] Marable, *Living Black History*, 37.

BIBLIOGRAPHY

Books

Adair, Douglas. *The Intellectual Origins of Jeffersonian Democracy: Republicanism, the Class Struggle, and the Virtuous Farmer*. Landam MD: Lexington Books, 2000.

Anderson, Eric, and Alfred A. Moss, Jr. *Dangerous Donations: Northern Philanthropy and Southern Black Education, 1902–1930*. Columbia: University of Missouri Press, 1999.

Anderson, James D. *The Education of Blacks in the South: 1860–1935*. Chapel Hill: University of North Carolina, 1988.

Aptheker, Herbert. *American Negro Slave Revolts*. 1943. Reprint, New York: International Publishers, 1964.

Aptheker, Herbert, editor. *The Education of Black People: Ten Critiques, 1906–1960*. New York: Monthly Review Press, 1973.

Barber, William J. *Disciples Assemblies of Eastern North Carolina*. St. Louis: Bethany Press, 1966.

Barnstone, Aliki, and others, editors. *Calvinist Roots of the Modern Era*. Hanover: University Press of New England, 1997.

Bays, Daniel H., and Grant Wacker, editors. *The Foreign Missionary Enterprise at Home: Exploration in North American Cultural History*. Tuscaloosa: University of Alabama Press, 2003.

Beecher, Catherine. *A Treatise of Domestic Economy*. New York: Harper and Brothers, 1841.

Bennett, Rolla James. "History of the Founding of Educational Institutions by the Disciples of Christ in Virginia and West Virginia." Ph.D. dissertation, University of Pittsburgh, 1946.

Berlin, Ira. *Slaves without Masters: The Free Negro in the South*. New York: The New Press, 1974.

Blassingame, John W. "Status and Social Structure in the Slave Community." In *Perspectives and Irony in American Slavery*, edited by Harry P. Owens, 2–5. Cambridge: Harvard University Press, 1967.

———. *The Slave community: Plantation Life in the Antebellum South*. 1972. Reprint, Oxford: Oxford University press, 1979.

Bond, Horace Mann. *The Education of the Negro in the American Social Order*. New York: Ogden Press, 1970.

Boring, Eugene M. *Disciples and the Bible: A History of Disciples Biblical Interpretation in North America*. St. Louis: Chalice Press, 1997.

Bowles, Samuel, and Herbert Gintis. *Schooling in Capitalist America: Educational Reform and the Contradictions of Economic Life*. New York: Basic Books, 1977.

Boylan, Anne M. *Sunday School: The Formation of an American Institution, 1790–1880*. New Haven: Yale University Press, 1988.

Bradley, Harold. *The United States from 1865*. New York: Charles Scribner's Sons, 1973.

Brown, Duncan, editor. *Oral Literature & Performance in Southern Africa*. Athens: Ohio University Press, 1999.

Brugger, Bill. *Republican Theory in Political Thought: Virtuous or Virtual?* New York: MacMillan Press, 1999.

Bullock, Henry A. *A History of Negro Education in the South from 1619 to the Present*. Cambridge: Harvard University Press, 1967.

Burnley, Lawrence. *Pearls of Wisdom: Reflections of [a] Senior Black Disciple Leader*. Volume 1. Indianapolis: National Convocation of the Christian Church (Disciples of Christ), 1996.

Butchart, Ronald. *Northern Schools, Southern Blacks, and Reconstruction: Freedmen's Education, 1862–1875*. New York: Greenwood Press, 1980.

Caldwell, Brenda M., and William K. Fox, Sr. *Journey Towards Wholeness: A History of Black Disciples of Christ in the Mission of the Christian Church*. Volume 1. Indianapolis: National Convocation of the Christian Church (Disciples of Christ), 1990.

———. *Objects of to Partners in the Mission: From Convention to Convocation*. Indianapolis: National Convocation of the Christian Church (Disciples of Christ), 1988.

Campbell, Alexander. *The Christian System: In Reference to the Union of Christians and a Restoration of Primitive Christianity as Plead in the Current Reformation*. Salem: Ayer Company Publishers, 1988 [1866].

Campbell, Thomas. "Declaration and Address of the Christian Association of Washington." In *Historical Documents Advocating Christian Union*, edited by Charles A. Young, 79. Chicago: The Christian Century Co., 1904.

Chesebrough, David B., editor. *"God Ordained this War": Sermons on the Sectional Crisis, 1830–1865*. Columbia: University of South Carolina Press, 1991.

Collier-Thomas, Bettye. *Daughters of Thunder: Black Women Preachers and Their Sermons, 1850–1979*. San Francisco: Jossey-Bass Publishers, 1998.

Council on Interracial Books for Children Racism and Sexism Resource Center for Educators. *Stereotypes, Distortions and Omissions in U. S. History Textbooks: A Content Analysis Instrument for Detecting Racism and Sexism*. New York: Council on Interracial Books for Children, 1977.

Craddock, Frances. *In the Fullness of Time: A History of Women in the Christian Church (Disciples of Christ)*. St. Louis: Chalice Press, 1999.

Creel, Margaret Washington. *"A Peculiar People": Slave Community-Culture among the Gullahs*. New York: New York University Press, 1988.

Cremin, Lawrence. *American Education: The National Experience, 1783–1876.* New York: Harper & Row, 1980.

Cross, F. L. and E. A. Livingstone, editors. *The Oxford Dictionary of the Christian Church.* Oxford: Oxford University Press.

Cruden, Robert. *The Negro in Reconstruction.* Englewood Cliffs: Prince Hall, Inc., 1969.

Cummins, Duane D. *Disciples Colleges.* St. Louis: Christian Board of Publications, 1976.

Cunningham, Effie. *Work of Disciples of Christ with Negro Americans.* St. Louis: United Christian Missionary Society, circa 1922.

Dawson, Martha E. *Hampton University: A National Treasure: A Documentary from 1878 to 1992.* Silver Spring: Beckham House Publishers, 1994.

DeBoer, Clara. *His Truth Is Marching On: African Americans who Taught the Freedmen for the American Missionary Association, 1861–1877.* New York: Garland, 1995.

Du Bois, W. E. B. *Black Reconstruction in America, 1860–1880.* 1935. Reprint, New York: Antheneum, 1992.

Dupre, Louis K. *The Enlightenment and the Intellectual Foundations of Modern Culture.* New Haven: Yale University Press, 2004.

Elias, John L. *A History of Christian Education: Protestant, Catholic, and Orthodox Perspectives.* Malabar FL: Krieger Publishing Co., 2002.

Falola, Toyin, and Steven J. Salm. *Culture and Customs of Ghana.* Westport: Greenwood Press, 2002.

Farhman, Henry. *The Enlightenment in America.* New York: Oxford University Press, 1976.

Felder, Cain Hope. *Race, Racism, and the Biblical Narratives.* Minneapolis: Fortress Press, 2002.

Foner, Eric. *Reconstruction: America's Unfinished Revolution, 1863–1877.* New York: Harper & Row, 1988.

Foster, A. Kristen. *Moral Vision and Material Ambitions: Philadelphia Struggles to Define the Republic.* Landham MD: Lexington Books, 2004.

Foster, Douglas A., Paul M. Blowers, Anthony L. Dunnavant, and D. Newell Williams, editors. *The Encyclopedia of the Stone-Campbell Movement.* Grand Rapids: William Eerdmans Publishing Co., 2004.

Foster, Greg. *John Locke's Politics of Moral Consciousness.* New York: Cambridge University Press, 2005.

Frankel, Noralee. "Breaking the Chains: 1860–1880." In *To Make Our World Anew: A History of African Americans*, edited by Robin Kelley and Earl Lewis, 279–80. New York: Oxford University Press, 2000.

Franklin, John Hope. *From Slavery to Freedom: A History of Negroes in America.* 1947. Reprint, New York: Alfred A. Knopf, 1974.

Franklin, John Hope, and Loren Schweninger. *Runaway Slaves: Rebels on the Plantation*. Oxford: Oxford University Press, 1999.

Fuller, Bertha M. *Sarah Lou Bostick: Minister and Missionary*. 1949. Private printing on file at the Disciples of Christ Historical Society, Nashville TN.

Garrison, Winfred E., and Alfred T. DeGroot. *The Disciples of Christ: A History*. St. Louis: Christian Board of Publications, 1948.

Genovese, Eugene D. *Roll, Jordan, Roll: The World the Slaves Made*. 1972. Reprint, New York: Vintage, 1976.

Goldenberg, David M. *The Curse of Ham: Race and Slavery in Early Judaism*. Princeton: Princeton University Press, 2003.

Green, Andy. *Education and State Formation: The Rise of Education Systems in England, France and the USA*. New York: St. Martin's Press, 1990.

Hahn, Steven. *A Nation Under Our Feet: Black Political Struggles in the Rural South from Slavery to the Great Migration*. Cambridge: Harvard University Press, 2003.

Hall, Colby. *Texas Disciples*. Ft. Worth: Texas Christian University Press, 1953.

Hansot, Elisabeth, and David Tyack. *Learning Together: A History of Coeducation in American Schools*. New Haven: Yale University Press, 1990.

Harding, Vincent. *There Is a River: The Black Struggle for Freedom in America*. 1982. Reprint, New York: Harcourt Brace Jovanovich, 1992.

Harlan, Louis R. *Booker T. Washington: The Making of a Black Leader, 1865–1901*. New York: Oxford University Press, 1972.

———. *Booker T. Washington: The Wizard of Tuskegee, 1901–1915*. New York: Oxford University Press, 1983.

Harrell, Jr., David E. *Quest for a Christian America, 1800–1865: A Social History of the Disciples of Christ*. Volume 1. 1966. Reprint, Tuscaloosa: University of Alabama Press, 2003.

———. *Quest for a Christian America: The Disciples of Christ and American Society to 1866*. Nashville: Disciples of Christ Historical Society, 1966.

———. *The Social Sources of Division in the Disciples of Christ, 1865–1900*. Atlanta: Publishing Systems, Inc., 1973.

———. "Restoration and the Stone-Campbell Tradition." Volume 2 of *Encyclopedia of the American Religious Experience*, edited by Charles H. Lipp and Peter W. Williams. New York: Charles Scribner and Sons, 1988.

Harrison, Peter. *Religion, and the Religions in the English Enlightenment*. New York: Cambridge University Press, 1990.

Harvey, Van A. *A Handbook of Theological Terms*. New York: Collier Books, 1964.

Hawkins, Denise. "A Rich History." *Diverse Issues in Higher Education* 24/13 (9 August 2007): 28–31.

Haynes, Stephen R. *Noah's Curse: The Biblical Justification of American Slavery*. New York: Oxford University Press, 2002.

Higginbotham, Evelyn Brooks. *Righteous Discontent: The Women's Movement in the Black Baptist Church, 1880–1920*. Cambridge: Harvard University Press, 1993.

Higginson, Thomas W. *Black Rebellion*. New York: Arno Press and the New York Times, 1969.

Hillstrom, Kevin, and Laurie Collier Hillstrom, editors. *The Industrial Revolution in America*. Santa Barbara: ABC-CLIO Publishers, 2005.

Hines, Darlene Clark, Elsa Barkley Brown, and Rosalyn Terborg-Penn, editors. *Black Women in America: An Historical Encyclopedia*. Brooklyn: Carlson Publishing, 1993.

Howard, Victor B. *Conscience and Slavery: The Evangelistic Calvinist Domestic Missions, 1837–1861*. Kent: Kent State University Press, 1990.

Hughes, Richard T. *Reviving the Ancient Faith: The Story of Churches of Christ in America*. Grand Rapids: William B. Eerdmans Publishing Co., 1996.

Hurmence, Belinda, editor. *Before Freedom, When I Just Can Remember: Twenty-Seven Oral Histories of Former South Carolina Slaves*. Winston-Salem: John F. Blair Publishers, 1989.

Hutchinson, William. *Errand to the World: American Protestant Thought and Foreign Missions*. Chicago: University of Chicago Press, 1987.

Jackson, Jr., John P. and Nadine M. Weidman. *Race, Racism, and Science: Social Impact and Interaction*. Santa Barbara: ABC-CLIO Publishers, 2004.

Jacoway, Elizabeth. *Yankee Missionaries in the South: The Penn School Experiment*. Baton Rouge: Louis State University Press, 1980.

Jefferson, Thomas. *Notes on the State of Virginia*. Edited by William Peden. New York: W. W. Norton, 1982.

Johnson, Josie R. "An Historical Review of the Role Black Parents and the Black Community Played in Providing Schooling for Black Children in the South, 1865–1954 (Autobiographies, Involvement, Support)." Ed.D. dissertation, University of Massachusetts, 1986.

Johnson, Sylvester A. *The Myth of Ham in Nineteenth-Century American Christianity: Race, Heathens, and the People of God*. New York: Palgrave MacMillan, 2004.

Jones, Edward. *A Candle in the Dark: A History of Morehouse College*. Valley Forge: Judson Press, 1967.

Jones, Jacqueline. *Labor of Love, Labor of Sorrow: Black Women, Work, and the Family from Slavery to the Present*. New York: Basic Books, 1985.

———. *Soldiers of Light and Love: Northern Teachers and Georgia Blacks, 1865–1873*. Chapel Hill: University of North Carolina Press, 1984.

Jones, Maxine D., and Joe M. Richardson. *Talladega College: The First Century*. Tuscaloosa: University of Alabama Press, 1990.

Jordan, Robert. *Two Races in One Fellowship*. Detroit: United Christian Church, 1944.

Kaestle, Carl. *Pillars of the Republic: Common Schools and American Society, 1780–1860*. New York: Hill and Wang, 1983.

Katz, Michael. *Restructuring American Education*. Cambridge: Harvard University Press, 1987.

Kelley, Robin D. G., and Earl Lewis, editors. *To Make Our World Anew: A History of African Americans*. London: Oxford University Press, 2000.

Kelley, Shawn. *Racializing Jesus: Race, Ideology and the Formation of Modern Biblical Scholarship*. New York: Routledge, 2002.

Kendrick, Stephen, and Kendrick Paul. *Sarah's Long Walk: The Free Blacks of Boston and How Their Struggle for Equality Changed America*. Boston: Beacon Press, 2004.

King, Wilma. *The Essence of Liberty: Free Black Women during the Slave Era*. Columbia: University of Missouri Press, 2006

Lewis, David L. *W. E. B. Du Bois: Biography of a Race, 1868–1919*. New York: Henry Holt and Co., 1993.

Lewis, Elmer C. "A History of Secondary and Higher Education in Negro Schools Related to the Disciples of Christ." Ph.D. dissertation, University of Pittsburgh, 1957.

Lincoln, C. Eric, and Lawrence H. Mamiya. *The Black Church in the African American Experience*. Durham: Duke University Press, 1990.

Litwack, Leon F. *North of Slavery: The Negro in the Free States, 1790–1860*. Chicago: University of Chicago Press, 1961.

Liverett, Alice. *Biographical Sketches of Leaders of Negro Work of the Disciples of Christ*. Indianapolis: Department of Missionary Education, United Christian Missionary Society, 1936.

Lloyd, Christopher. *Explanation in Social History*. New York: Basil Blackwell, 1986.

Loewen, James W. *Lies My Teacher Told Me: Everything Your American History Textbook Got Wrong*. New York: Simon & Schuster, 2007 [1995].

Logan, Rayford W. *Howard University: The First One Hundred Years, 1867–1967*. New York: New York University Press, 1969.

Long, John C. "The Disciples of Christ and Negro Education." Ph.D. dissertation, University of Southern California, 1960.

Lyda, Hap. "A History of Black Christian Churches (Disciples of Christ) in the United States Through 1899." Ph.D. dissertation, Vanderbilt University, 1972.

MacCann, Donnarae, and Gloria Woodward, editors. *The Black American in Books for Children: Readings in Racism*. Metuchen NJ: Scarecrow Press, Inc., 1972.

Malcomson, Scott L. *One Drop of Blood: The American Misadventure of Race*. New York: Farrar, Straus and Giroux, 2000.

Marable, Manning. *Living Black History*. New York: Basic Civitas Books, 2006.

Marshall, John. *John Locke: Resistance, Religion, and Responsibility*. New York: Cambridge University Press, 1994.

McAllister, Lester G., and William E. Tucker. *Journey of Faith: A History of the Christian Church (Disciples of Christ)*. St. Louis: Bethany Press, 1975.

McCluskey, Neil G. *Catholic Education in America: A Documentary History*. New York: Bureau of Publications Teachers College, Columbia University, 1964.

McCormick, Richard L. "Public Life in Industrial America, 1877–1917." In *The New American History*, edited by Eric Foner, 93. Philadelphia: Temple University Press, 1997.

McGerr, Michael E. *A Fierce Discontent: The Rise and Fall of the Progressive Movement in America*. New York: Free Press, 2003.

McMillen, Sally G. *To Raise Up the South: Sunday Schools in Black and White Churches, 1865–1915*. Baton Rouge: Louisiana State U. Press, 2001.

Miruka, Okumba. *Encounter with Oral Literature*. Nairobi: East African Educational Publishers, 1994.

Mohorter, J. H. *Survey of Piedmont Christian Institute*. Indianapolis: Department of Religious Education, United Christian Missionary Society, 1930.

Morris, Robert. *Reading, Riting, and Reconstruction: The Education of Freedmen in the South, 1861–1870*. 1971. Reprint, Chicago: University of Chicago Press, 1981.

Morrow, Diane Batts. *Persons of Color and Religious at the Same Time: The Oblate Sisters of Providence, 1828–1860*. Chapel Hill: University of North Carolina Press, 2002.

Nieves, Angel D. "We Gave Our Heart and Lives to It: African-American Women Reformers, Industrial Education, and the Monuments of Nation-Building in the Post-Reconstruction South, 1877–1938." Ph.D dissertation, Cornell University, 2001.

Norton, Herman A. *A History of the Christian Church (Disciples of Chris) in Tennessee*. Nashville: Reed & Co., 1971.

Nuovo, Victor. *John Locke and Christianity: Contemporary Responses to the Reasonable of Christianity*. Dulles: Thommes Press, 1997.

Painter, Nell. *Standing at Armageddon: The United States, 1877–1919*. New York: W. W. Norton, 1987.

Perdue, Jr., Charles, and others, editors. *Weevils in the Wheat: Interviews with Virginia Ex-Slaves*. Bloomington: Indiana University Press, 1976.

Power, Edward J. *Religion and the Public Schools in 19th Century America: the Contribution of Orestes A. Brownson*. New York: Paulist Press, 1996.

Raboteau, Albert. *Slave Religion: The "Invisible Institution" in the Antebellum South*. Oxford: Oxford University Press, 1978.

Rawick, George P., editor. *The American Slave: A Composite Autobiography*. 19 volumes. 1972. Reprint, Westport CT: Greenwood Press, 1977.

Read, Florence M. *The Story of Spelman College*. Atlanta: Atlanta University Press, 1961.

Richardson, Joe M. *A History of Fisk University, 1865–1946*. Tuscaloosa: University of Alabama Press, 1980.

―――. *Christian Reconstruction: The American Missionary Association and Southern Blacks, 1861–1890*. Tuscaloosa: University of Alabama Press, 1980.

Rodger, John. *The Biography of Elder Barton Warren Stone, Written by Himself with Additions and Reflections*. Cincinnati: J. A. and U. P. James Publishers, 1947.

Rudolph, Frederick. *The American College & University: A History*. 1962. Reprint, Athens: University of Georgia Press, 1990.

Rush, Benjamin. *Essays, Literary, Moral and Philosophical*. 2nd edition. Philadelphia: Thomas and William Bradford, 1806.

Schaff, Philip. *Slavery and the Bible: A Tract for the Times*. Chambersburg PA: M. Kieffer and Co.'s Caloric Printing Press, 1861.

Shackleford, Jr., John. *Life, Letters and Addresses of Dr. L. L. Pinkerto*. Cincinnati: Chase and Hall, 1876.

Sherer, Robert G. *Black Education in Alabama, 1865–1901*. Tuscaloosa: University of Alabama Press, 1997.

Sherman, Charles. "*J. N. Ervin in Action*," in The *J. N. Jarvis Lectures: a Trilogy, 1977–1978–1979*. Hawkins TX: Jarvis Christian College Publishers, 1979.

Silber, Nina. "A Compound of Wonderful Potency: Women Teachers of the North in the Civil War South." In *The War Was You and Me: Civilians in the American Civil War*, edited by Joan E. Cashin, 47. Princeton: Princeton University Press, 2002.

Smiley, Tavis, et al. *The Covenant with Black America*. Chicago: Third World Press, 2006.

Smith, C. C. *Negro Education and Evangelism*. Indianapolis: Christian Women's Board of Missions, circa 1901.

———. *The Lum Alabama Graded School*. Indianapolis: Christian Women's Board of Missions, circa 1905.

———. *Jacob Kenoly and His Work in Africa*. Indianapolis: Christian Women's Board of Missions, 1911.

Sobel, Machel. *Trablin' On: The Slave Journey to an Afro-Baptist Faith*. 1977. Reprint, Princeton: Princeton University Press, 1988.

Solomon, Barbara Miller. *In the Company of Educated Women: A History of Women and Higher Education in America*. New Haven: Yale University Press, 1985.

Southern, David W. *The Progressive Era and Race: Reaction and Reform, 1900–1917*. Wheeling IL: Harlan Davidson Pub., 2005.

Spencer, Justin. *Century of Disciples' Progress in the Piedmont District: A Synoptic History*. Roanoke: Roanoke Tribune, 1959.

Sprinkle, Stephen. *Disciples & Theology: Understanding the Faith of a People in Covenant*. St. Louis: Chalice Press, 1999.

Stuckey, Sterling. *Slave Culture: Nationalist Theory and the Foundations of Black America*. New York: Oxford University Press, 1987.

Swint, Henry L. *The Northern Teacher in the South, 1862–1870*. Nashville: Vanderbilt University Press, 1941.

Takaki, Ronald T. *Iron Cages: Race and Culture in Nineteenth Century America*. London: Athlone Press, 1980.

Thiong'o, Ngugi Wa. *Penpoints, Gunpoints, and Dreams: Towards a Critical Theory of the Arts and the State in Africa*. Oxford: Clarendon Press, 1998.

Toulouse, Mark G. *Joined in Discipleship: The Maturing of an American Religious Movement*. St. Louis: Chalice Press, 1992.

Tyack, David B. *The One Best System: A History of American Urban Education*. Cambridge: Harvard University Press, 1974.

Van Ausdale, Debra. *The First R: How Children Learn Race and Racism*. New York: Rowman & Littlefield Publishers, 2001.

Washington, James M., editor. *A Testament of Hope: The Essential Writings of Martin Luther King, Jr*. San Francisco: Harper Publishing Co., 1991.

Washington, James M. *Frustrated Fellowship: The Black Quest for Social Power*. Macon GA: Mercer University Press, 1986.

Washington, Jr., Joseph R. *Anti-Blackness in English Religion, 1500–1800*. New York: Edwin Mellen Press, 1985.

———. *Race and Religion in Mid-Nineteenth Century America, 1800–1850: Constitution, Conscience, and Calvinist Compromise*. Lewiston, NY: E. Mellon Press, 1988.

Watkins, William H. *The White Architects of Black Education: Ideology and Power in America, 1865–1954*. New York: Teachers College Press, 2001.

Webber, Thomas L. *Deep Like the River: Education in the Slave Quarter Community, 1831–1865*. New York: W. W. Norton & Co., 1978.

West, Cornel. *Race Matters*. Boston: Beacon Press, 1993.

Williams, D. Newell. *Barton Stone: A Spiritual Biography*. St. Louis: Chalice Press, 2000.

Williams, Heather A. D. "Self-Taught: The Role of African Americans in Educating the Freedpeople, 1861–1871." Ph.D. dissertation, Yale University, 2002.

———. *Self Taught: African American Education in Slavery and Freedom*. Chapel Hill: University of North Carolina Press, 2005.

Williams, Walter L. *Black Americans and the Evangelization of Africa, 1877–1900*. Madison: University of Wisconsin Press, 1982.

Wilmore, Gayraud S. *Black Religion and Black Radicalism: An Interpretation of the Religious History of African Americans*. Maryknoll NY: Orbis Books, 1998.

Woodson, Carter G. *The Education of the Negro Prior to 1861*. 1919. Reprint, New York: A & B Books, 1989.

Wright, C. T. "The Development of Education for Blacks in Georgia, 1865–1900." Ph.D. dissertation, Boston University, 1977.

Articles

"Alabama Christian Institute Closing." *World Call* 5/12 (December 1923): 37.

Alphin, Mary. "Report to the Board." *Gospel Plea* 28/2 (June 1910): 35.

———. "The Opening of Jarvis Christian Institute." *Missionary Tidings* 31/1 (May 1913): 13.

Alphin, William. "Shall We Do It?" *Gospel Plea* 10/34 (28 June 1905): 3.

Bullan, C. "The Great Want of the Colored People." *Millennial Harbinger* 40/3 (March 1869): 170.

Burgess, T. M. "Head, Hand, and Hear." *Missionary Tidings* 27/3 (July 1909): 99.

Butler, James. "A Voice from the South." *Christian Standard* 1/5 (5 May 1866): 34.

Campbell, Alexander. "Our Position to American Slavery." *Millennial Harbinger* 2/5 (1845): 234.

"Center City College." *Baptist Truth* (26 October 1899): 1.

Colbert, A. E. "The Work in Texas." *Gospel Pleas* 7/10 (5 March 1902): 2.

Cole, W. A. *American Home Missionary* 6 (November 1900): 79.

Council, W. H. "Wise Black Leader." *Gospel Plea* 8/35 (16 September 1903): 1.

"CWBM Report." *Missionary Tidings* 26/6 (October 1908): 237.

David, M. M. "Texas Letter." *The Christian Standard* 31/32 (28 November 1895): 760.

Dickson, Dana. "Jarvis Christian College Celebrated." *The Gladewater Times* 28 (February 1991).

Frost, Thomas B. "Twentieth Annual Report of Negro Work." *Missionary Tidings* 31/7 (November 1913): 269.

"Goldsboro Christian Institute." *The North Carolina Christian* 37/11 (December 1956): 11.

Hearne, Virginia. *Missionary Tidings* 27/11 (March 1910): 457.

Henry, Kenneth. "Unknown Prophets: Black Disciples Ministry in Historical Perspective." *Disciplania* 46/1 (1986).

Hurdle, A. J. "The Work in Texas." *Gospel Plea* 12/7 (12 February 1902).

"Indianapolis Convention." *Christian-Evangelist* 34 (28 October 1897): 674.

"Jarvis Christian Institute." *Missionary Tidings* 31/1 (May 1913).

Jenkins, B. A. "The Way Out of Egypt." Address by B. A. Jenkins. *The Christian Standard* 35/42 (28 October 1899): 1376.

"Jonesboro, Tennessee School." *Missionary Tidings* 26/8 (December 1908): 368.

Lehman, Joel B. "The Work Among the Negroes." *Missionary Tidings* 27/8 (December 1909): 365.

———. "Is It Worth While?" *Missionary Tidings* 28/1 (May 1910): 9.

———. "The Work of the CWMB Among the Negroes." *Missionary Tidings* 28/7 (November 1910): 232.

Lipscomb, David. "Our Relation to the Negro." *Gospel Advocate* 25 (12 September 1883): 580.

Loos, Charles L. "The Catholic Scheme for Freedmen." *Millennial Harbinger* 37/10 (October 1866): 473.

———. "The Catholic Church and the Freedmen." *Millennial Harbinger* 40/9 (October 1869): 573.

Love, Emmanual K. "Center City College." *Baptist Truth* (26 October 1899): 1.

"Lum Alabama Graded School." *Missionary Tidings* 30/3 (July 1912): 94.

"Lum Graded School." *Missionary Tidings* 25/7 (November 1907): 273.

McGarvey, John W. "What Shall We Do for the Freedmen." *Apostolic Guide* 19 (11 November 1887): 584.

Manire, B. F. "Mississippi State Meeting." *Millennial Harbinger* 39/10 (October 1868): 583.

"National Colored Christian College." *Christian Standard* 23/2 (14 January 1888): 29.

"The Negro as I See Him." *Gospel Plea* 11 (22 March 1905): 3.

"Negro Work." *Missionary Tidings* 32/7 (November 1914): 306.

Norton, Mary Beth. "The Evolution of White Women's Experience in Early America." *The American Historical Review* 89/3 (June 1984): 593–619.

Pendleton, William K. "Tennessee Manual Labor University." *Millennial Harbinger* 39/4 (April 1868): 227–28.

———. "The Great Want of the Colored People." *Millennial Harbinger* 40/3 (March 1869): 172.

"The Piedmont School of Industry." *Missionary Tidings* 18 (February 1901): 249.

Pinkerton, Lewis. "Kentucky." *Christian Standard* 1/7 (19 May 1866): 53.

———. "Miscellaneous." *Independent Monthly* 1/10 (October 1869): 343–44.

Powell, Frederick D. "Ethiopia's Hands." *Christian-Evangelist* 30/43 (26 October 1893): 675.

Power, J. C. No title. *Christian Standard* 5/44 (27 October 1870).

Schell, Clara. "A Sketch of the Colored People of Washington, D.C." *Christian Messenger* 21 (October 1882): 471.

Schwager, Sally. "Educating Women in America." *Reconstructing the Academy* 12/2 (Winter 1987): 336.

Sears, O. B. "The Piedmont School of Industry." *Missionary Tidings* 20/3 (July 1902): 80.

Seller, Maxine Swartz. "Boundaries, Bridges, and the History of Education." *History of Education Quarterly* 31/2 (Summer 1991): 197–98.

Small, Sandra E. "The Yankee Schoolmarm in Freedmen's Schools: An Analysis of Attitudes." *The Journal of Southern History* 45/3 (August 1979).

Smith, C. C. "History of Our Mission Work Among the Negroes." *American Home Missionary* 6/3 (March 1900): 17, 22.

———. "Secretary's Report." *Missionary Tidings* 27/2 (June 1909): 62.

———. "The Principle Underlying Training of the Negro." *Christian Standard* 40/44 (29 October 1904): 1519.

"State Report for Illinois." *Christian-Evangelist* 30/43 (26 October 1893): 45.

"They Went to Africa: Biographies of Missionaries of the Disciples of Christ." Indianapolis: United Christian Missionary Society, 1945.

Thomas, James H. "The Martinsville Christian Institute." *Missionary Tidings* 22/7 (November 1904): 261.

———. "The Piedmont School of Industry." *Gospel Plea* 6/42 (30 October 1901): 7.

Thornberry, James L. "A Suggestion to Colored Christians of the South." *Apostolic Times* 4 (21 January 1875): 1.

Washington, Booker T. "Industrial Education." *Gospel Plea* 8/42 (28 October 1903): 6.

Williams, D. Newell. "The Pursuit of Justice: The Anti-Slavery Pilgrimage of Barton W. Stone." *Encounter* 62/1 (Winter 2001): 2.

Woodward, C. Vann. "History from Slave Sources." *American Historical Review* (April 1974) 79.

"The Work in Georgia." *Baptist Truth* (16 November 1899): 2.

INDEX